CLOWN WORLD

JAMIE TAHSIN is an award-winning documentary director, producer and journalist from South-East London. Jamie is best known for the Emmy-nominated Vice documentaries *The Teenage Mafia Academy* and *The Dangerous Rise of Andrew Tate*, as well as *Andrew Tate: The Man Who Groomed the World?* (BBC). Jamie has been investigating Andrew Tate for a longer period than any other journalist in the world, from 2019 to the present day.

MATT SHEA is an award-winning documentary director, producer and presenter who has worked on films including the Emmy-nominated *Gaycation* and the Grierson-nominated *Chemsex*. Matt produces and presents *High Society* on Vice, about drug use in the UK, and directed the award-winning film *Time To Die* about the global underground euthanasia movement. Matt presented the Vice/BBC documentaries *The Dangerous Rise of Andrew Tate* and *Andrew Tate: The Man Who Groomed the World?* and has written for Vice, the *Sunday Telegraph*, and others about the phenomenon.

CLOWN WORLD

FOUR YEARS INSIDE ANDREW TATE'S MANOSPHERE

JAMIE TAHSIN AND **MATT SHEA**

QUERCUS

First published in Great Britain in 2024 by

QUERCUS

Quercus Editions Ltd
Carmelite House
50 Victoria Embankment
London EC4Y 0DZ

An Hachette UK company

A CIP catalogue record for this book is available
from the British Library

Errors in quotations from transcripts and interviews
are consistent with original material.

HB ISBN 978 1 52943 782 9
TPB ISBN 978 1 52943 783 6
EBOOK ISBN 978 1 52943 785 0

1

Typeset in Arno Pro by CC Book Production

Printed and bound in Great Britain by Clays Ltd, Elcograf S.p.A.

Papers used by Quercus are from well-managed forests and other responsible sources.

CLOWN WORLD

Contents

PART THREE:
THE MEN BEHIND THE MEN

Prologue

'Are you bleeding? Is it because I called you the wrong pronoun?'
Andrew Tate jeered to the assembled leaders of his War Room. A
6 foot 2 kick-boxing champion, he had just punched Matt in the
face. They were both wearing boxing gloves, and Matt was a willing
participant. But he had been lured here under false pretences.

We were inside a fight gym in Bucharest where Tate had told
us we could film him sparring. When we arrived, he said, 'Put
some gloves on'. Matt was about to be taught a lesson which, after
four years of investigating Tate, we still believe to be the central
tenet of Tate's philosophy: that violence underpins absolutely
everything.

Tate's inner circle was also sparring. The sound of fists pummel-
ling flesh was periodically interrupted by a boxing timer. Nearby,
the most physically intimidating man we had ever seen was sub-
jecting a young War Room neophyte to a 'ground-and-pound
finish', pressing him to the floor with his body while striking him
repeatedly. The other men laughed at the display. The lumbering
giant was professional UFC (Ultimate Fighting Championship)
fighter Luke Barnatt, aka 'Bigslow'. He was 6 foot 5, had two giant

cauliflower ears and a grim, expressionless face as impenetrable as a medieval helmet. Later, when Matt would ask him about the philosophy of the War Room, he would say, 'If you have the capability to kill someone physically in the street – which I have, and I don't – then that's much better than someone who doesn't have the capability and doesn't, because he can't anyway. I believe every man on the planet should be able to go to war. Me and you, we go to a bar, trust me, I'm the more confident guy. Because I know I can handle every situation that's thrown at me. You can't.'

Another man, though not participating in the violence around him, had a look of spiritual rapture as he drank it in. He sported a wizard-like beard and a velour tracksuit emblazoned with a rhinestone chess piece, the insignia of the War Room.

Tate told Matt he had ten more rounds to endure. Tate's last punch had drawn blood, but leaving then would have attracted ridicule and cut short our mission to infiltrate Tate's inner circle. The timer went.

'Let's go,' Tate said.

'Can I at least fight someone closer to my weight size?'

'Sure.'

This turned out to be a mistake, because though 'Tig', the man Tate beckoned over, may have been shorter than Tate, each of his biceps was wider than Matt's head. His punches built with power each time, until a final right hook caused Matt to lose consciousness for a moment, and Jamie was forced to jump in, while Matt asked Tig to stop.

'You asked me to stop,' Tig said, 'but if this were a street fight, could you ask the other person to stop?'

Matt was beginning to learn. In promotional videos for the War Room, over shots of men training in combat sports, smoking cigars and eating steaks, a pseudo-sensei voiceover declared: 'Life is competition. Competition is violence. In many modern forms of competition, we have attempted to water down the violent aspects. To replicate violence in the most sanitised way. We have full-grown men growing as large and strong as possible to put a ball in a net,' the voice continued, dripping with disdain, 'as opposed to hurting each other.' Was he saying that sport was a bad thing?

'But the sentiment is the same. It's a group of men at war with another, with one team being victors and the other being losers. The largest, strongest, most beautiful tree violently crushed the surrounding saplings in a quest for resources. Every time I see beauty, I see the struggle required to create it . . . The more sophisticated my understanding of the universe's state of constant war, the happier and more content and peaceful I feel. You are meant to struggle. You are here to suffer. If you do neither of these things, you are either dead or invisible. If you want people to care who you are, become familiar with pain. If you do not struggle to become an exceptional man, you are nobody, and every female will prove to you: you may as well not exist.'

If you want to understand the itch that Andrew Tate and the War Room have been scratching in young men, then this is it. Men desire conquest. The longing to go through some kind of hardship – whether it's waging a war or unclogging a drain – and emerge on the other side victorious, is crucial to many men's sense of self. This can be healthy, but in men who suffer from insecurity, it's dangerous.

Tate's appeal preys on male insecurity and the need to compete with other men, especially for women. We feel this when, for example, another man flirts with our partner in front of us. We feel some internal engine flutter into life; the same engine that powers sexual desire and jealousy is powered by fear of other men. This is what having your masculinity challenged feels like.

Tate prises open those insecurities and targets them with his marketing, telling men they need to experience more hardship to make themselves better. The first step in this conquest is to buy his courses, with membership to the War Room costing £3,000 a year at the time of our reporting in August 2022.

But to describe Tate simply as an opportunist exploiting young men for money doesn't fully explain his rise to prominence. Many men shirk from the contemporary dialogue around mental health. Therapy and emotional vulnerability do not work for everyone. 'Depression isn't real,' is Tate's common refrain. Some men would rather see themselves as Genghis Khan, charging across the plains of their depression, instead of accepting the inevitable hardship of existence and seeking help.

Tate says that modern life is too comfortable, that to become a real man you must go through suffering, and that this will lead to successful conquests. Tate could use this notion to motivate men to achieve good in their lives and their communities. But in his world, combat and violence are the purest form of conquest, while women and money are the most important.

This is where things get dangerous. The anthropologist Margaret Mead wrote: 'Every known human society rests firmly on the learned nurturing behaviour of men ... This behaviour, being learned, is fragile, and can disappear rather easily under social conditions that no longer teach it effectively.'*

When men are made to feel weak, we double down on traditional masculine traits to feel stronger. We judge ourselves according to

---

* Margaret Mead, *Male and Female*, William Morrow & Co., 1970, p. 189, 192.

the apparent conquests of men we idolise – on social media, in video games and in films. Many young men judge themselves against Andrew Tate. This is all part of his plan. When you consider that in 2023, 47 per cent of twenty-five-year-old men in the UK were still living with their parents, compared to just 29 per cent of women of the same age, there is a vast ocean of inadequacy and low self-worth to be plumbed by Tate's exploitation.[*]

Matt getting his face pounded in the War Room was an unpleasant experience designed to make him feel his own inadequacy in the realm of physical combat, but strangely – as he would later be told by many of Tate's fans – millions of young men would do absolutely anything to be in Matt's position.

Over the next week, we would see first-hand how Tate's empire is built on making men feel deficient, and then offering solutions that require buying further into the group's ideology. We would also see how this conditioning can make men dangerous.

For Matt in particular, Tate and his brother, Tristan, putting him through the psychological and physical trials of the War Room would lead him to grapple with his own masculinity. But this inner journey would happen alongside an investigation into the Tates and their War Room that ultimately uncovered more than just a movement shifting young men towards chauvinistic attitudes.

In the years that we've been investigating Andrew Tate, he has become a household name that to many, defines a new era in misogyny. In August 2022, few people know about the War Room, though. They instead know the thirty-six-year-old Anglo–American kick-boxer-turned-influencer as a viral misogynist,

---

[*] https://www.statista.com/statistics/285330/young-adults-living-with-parents-uk-by-age-and-gender/

whose motivational videos, flashy lifestyle and controversial views have made him the most googled man in the world. Tate's videos have been viewed 13 billion times on TikTok alone. He became incredibly famous, incredibly quickly.

At the peak of this rise to fame, we happened to be with Andrew Tate, inside his compound and secretive network. Throughout this period and for a further two years, we would investigate Tate and his inner circle, eventually uncovering the dark truth behind the War Room.

Our story begins during Tate's good years, when the followers were flooding in, and the allegations were still to come.

PART ONE

The Tate Machine

CHAPTER ONE

Paging Andrew Tate

In November 2019, Jamie received an email about 'two webcam millionaires' who were beginning to build a devoted following in 'the manosphere'. As a mid-90s millennial Vice journalist who spent his time trawling the internet for cults and conspiracies, it piqued his interest. The email was sent by his colleague Lexi Rose, whose friend's younger brother had apparently been 'lured into the manosphere' by one of these webcam millionaires: Andrew Tate.

The manosphere is an umbrella term given to different online groups, websites and blogs, all of which deal with different topics 'for men', primarily sex and relationships. These groups are distinct and propagate different views, but underpinning all of them appears to be a shared foundational belief that the world is being manipulated in 'unnatural ways' to make life easier for women, at the expense of men. The manosphere includes involuntary celibate men, known as 'incels', who lambast the perceived unfairness of the modern 'sexual marketplace' that has left them sexless. While incel groups vary in the staunchness of their beliefs and their propensity for violence, they are considered by many to be the most dangerous group in the manosphere, with some appearing to support the idea of legalising rape, or even the ownership of female 'slaves' for sex.[*]

Men Going Their Own Way, or MGTOW, are a separate group in the manosphere who, like some second-wave radical feminists, support the complete separation of the two genders. MGTOW believe that society has been so corrupted by the influence of feminism that it is no longer salvageable. As such, followers support men forming their own distinct societies, separate from their female counterparts.

Tate didn't fit into either of these two groups, but instead was a combination of two further categories: a PUA and a red-pill influencer. PUAs (pickup artists) are men who claim to be able to teach their followers the science and skills of seduction – essentially how to meet and approach more women, and eventually have sex with them. Prior to the explosion of incels, PUAs were the figures in the manosphere who were most successful in breaking through to mainstream culture, with Tom Cruise even playing a character inspired by PUA Ross Jeffries in the Paul Thomas Anderson film *Magnolia,* and celebrity figures like Derren Brown demonstrating PUA techniques on mainstream British TV shows. As Jamie soon discovered, Tate was constantly flaunting the beautiful women he was with on social media, including his numerous webcam workers, many of whom he claimed were also his girlfriends. Tate believed his own triumphs with women explained why his webcam business was also so successful, and he had begun to create courses teaching other men how to attract women using his own 'methods'.

Red-pill influencers in the manosphere are a subgroup of the

---

[*] In March 2021, new data suggested between forty and fifty people in the US had been killed by people who held the ideology.

MRA, or Men's Rights Activists, who borrow much of their language from the film *The Matrix*. In the 1999 sci-fi hit, the protagonist Neo is given two options: the red pill or the blue pill. If Neo chooses the blue pill, he will return to the simulation that is his life, living in ignorance, albeit relatively happy ignorance. If he chooses the red pill, he will see life as it truly is. As Morpheus, a fictional leader in the resistance movement against 'the machines', tells him, 'I show you how deep the rabbit hole goes'. Red-pill influencers offer to 'red pill' their followers by showing them the 'truth' of the world. This truth, or red pill, is used as an explanation for all the woes that men may experience, usually focusing on concepts like marriage and divorce, fidelity or the general 'degeneracy' of liberalism. Tate was fundamentally a red piller, in that he claimed to be able to identify men's problems and solve them with his unique brand of misogyny. Those who have been red-pilled by a particular influencer will tend to denigrate others outside of the group, calling them 'sheep', 'normies' or, one of Tate's favourite terms, residents of 'Clown World'.

Lexi's email to Jamie included a link to the Instagram account of her friend's brother, who Lexi claimed had paid thousands of dollars to join something called the War Room. Visiting Tate's website, Jamie could see that the War Room was Tate's latest product – a private network of men who would be trained by Tate to achieve the pinnacle of masculinity and wealth, using Tate's supposedly tried-and-tested techniques. The website claimed that membership to Tate's War Room would give you direct access to Tate, as well as the ability to 'network with millionaires', attending private War Room events around the world. From looking at the Instagram account that Lexi shared, it was clear that the men who were joining Tate's War Room admired him. In one photo, the young man leaned over a chessboard opposite a friend. The way the photo was framed, and their rigid poses, were identical to a post on Tate's own Instagram, where he sits opposite his brother, Tristan. The young man had captioned his own post, 'The king moves one square at a time and the queen can just zip across the board' – a direct quote from Tate himself, referring to how much easier life is for women. As Tate would explain in one of his YouTube videos, to get on a superyacht in Miami a man would have to work his whole life and make millions of dollars, but for a girl, 'it's just one DM to a guy with a yacht'.

Statements like this were at the softer end of Tate's views about women. Looking at his burgeoning YouTube channel 'Tate Speech', it wasn't difficult to find extreme misogyny and sexism being spouted with the abrasive and, to some, comedic tone that Tate would become famous for. In his videos, Tate would propose his 'solutions' to the problem of modern liberalism, arguing that women should take some responsibility for their own sexual assaults, and that the world would be a better place if women had their 'body count' (a pejorative term for their number of sexual partners) tattooed on their heads. Tate's views were so extreme, and his delivery so bombastic, that people debated in the comments whether he was genuine or a Sacha Baron Cohen-style comedian who was embodying a fictional character.

In late 2019, Tate was by no means a celebrity figure. He wasn't even the biggest 'manosphere' influencer. In fact, Tate was relatively fringe, with fewer than 50,000 followers on Instagram. But something about him seemed completely different. Tate was perhaps the first 'manosphere' or 'masculinity' influencer who actually possessed some of the superficial 'attributes of masculinity' that followers would be told they needed to cultivate. He was tall and strong, an ex-world-champion kick-boxer and was considered conventionally attractive by some. If Tate was to be believed, he was also incredibly wealthy and had numerous girlfriends. Manosphere influencers preceding him were older men, often out of shape, with seemingly unenviable lives. They sat in front of webcams lecturing their audiences, but beyond that appeared to do little else. Tate, on the other hand, flaunted a life that was attractive to many men. And he promised he could teach his followers how to have the same life – his primary marketing tool being the cultivation of envy.

What's more, most followers of manosphere influencers prior to Tate had chosen to remain anonymous, hiding behind user-names and avatars, suggesting either a level of shame or at least an awareness of the social unacceptability of the views they were engaging with. Tate's followers, by contrast, proudly associated themselves with him. They would repost his videos on their social media accounts, many using their real names and faces. Tate's fans appeared to feel no shame, or that there was no risk in their public support of him.

And finally, it was Tate's War Room that truly set him apart. Such was the level of devotion he was able to elicit from his followers that they were willing to pay thousands of pounds to join his network and be taught by him at events around the world, behind closed doors, away from the prying eyes of the public.

All told, this was beginning to look like a story worth following, and a world worth sending a documentary reporter into.

That month, in November 2019, Tate's website, Cobratate.com (Tate has since claimed that this website never belonged to him) was advertising 'The Test': the biggest event in the War Room calendar. A members-only event that would take place in Romania, this would be a test of the attendees' manhood, devised by Tate himself. Beyond that, little information was given, but it seemed like a chance for our reporter to immerse himself in

Tate's community while also finding out what these men were talking about behind closed doors. But without Tate on board, this wouldn't work as a documentary, so it was time to see if he was interested.

Jamie – 26 November 2019

I start writing an email as though it is aimed at a member of Tate's staff, rather than Tate himself, lending him the grandiosity it seems he would want, despite my assumption that he is managing the address himself. I decide to keep it brief and say that I've recently come across the War Room and am interested in covering it in a documentary for Vice. I press send and click back onto one of my other tabs at random. It's a video of Tate describing why men should never be friends with their sisters, referring to his own sister, Janine, as a 'dumb Bernie supporter'. 'When I see a brother and sister who are really close, it's just weird.' I get less than a minute into the video when a notification pops up at the top right of my screen: a response from Tate's personal email.

Hello.

It's Andrew Tate here.

Please msg me on Instagram *@cobratate* to validate you work for vice.

I am interested in speaking on the phone.

I quickly pull up my phone, go to his account, and type a message: 'Hi Andrew, it's Jamie from Vice.' Tate immediately

*responds, 'call me', followed by his phone number. I look
around at my colleagues who are all either chatting quietly
or staring intently at their laptops. I don't feel like having my
first call with Andrew Tate with them listening in. Meeting
rooms in the Vice office are impossible to get hold of, so I head
towards a row of tiny edit suites. Inside, I mentally prepare
for the call. Normally, I would just go over my pitch and think
through the questions that could arise, but I realise this call
might be very different. When I make films about controversial
and unpredictable characters, I behave as though every phone
call is being recorded, knowing that it likely is. But having
watched Tate's videos it dawns on me that there is a good
chance this could just be Tate trying to bait me for content,
given his propensity for public trolling. Would he spend his
time trying to pull me into saying something weaponisable,
only to post it on his social media pages with the caption 'Tate
destroys liberal Vice journalist'? I take a deep breath, remind
myself that if I'm aware it's a possibility, then I won't say
anything he can use, and I type in Tate's number.*

*The phone rings only once before I hear Tate – that
uniquely identifiable accent, a grating mix of Luton and
Chicago: 'Hello! Is that Jamie?' The next forty minutes pass in
a moment. Tate seems excited, but in no way nervous. I start
off by giving my pitch, and I begin to tell him what Vice is. 'I
know who Vice are,' Tate laughs. 'You guys used to make cool
films about gangs and war zones, and then you went full lib
and everyone hates you.' Despite this, I can tell he's keen on
the idea of a Vice film about him, and he begins to give me a
pitch of his own. I should be making a film about him and his
brother, Tristan, the webcam millionaires who have moved to*

Eastern Europe. He is 'very well connected' in Romania, and if we came to make a film about him, he could show us some 'real mafia shit'. He assures me of his connections by pointing out that the next War Room event will be held inside the Romanian parliament in Bucharest.

I feel like I'm being played – a classic case of a narcissistic character overselling their personal story in the hope of attracting some media attention and fame. I try to pull Tate back to what I'm really interested in: his War Room, and the message he teaches to a group of paying men behind closed doors. Tate seems wary. 'See, the thing is the War Room is a private network, and to be honest with you, I think most of the guys won't want you there, because they hate Vice, and know it will be a hit-piece.' He then follows up, 'Don't get me wrong. I have no problem with you trying to do a hit-piece on me, but not the War Room.' I assure him that we're also interested in him and his brother as individuals, and that we would cover their story in the documentary as well. Tate seems to perk up but can't refrain from taking shots at Vice, maligning me for working for such an organisation. His tone suggests he could be joking, but as is often the case with Tate, it can be hard to differentiate his act from his reality. At one point he calls me 'cucked', and I can't help but smile at hearing an insult I've read so many times in strange parts of the internet, finally uttered in real life. Even funnier, it's directed at me, and is coming out of the mouth of Andrew Tate.

Tate seems happy with my various responses to his barrages, and I don't think I've said anything that I would mind him posting on his Twitter, so it's a good time to wrap things up. Tate must be happy as well, because we end the call

*with him confirming we can come and film him in Romania
for a documentary. He'll be in touch about the War Room, but
no promises. I hang up and exhale slowly, breathing properly
for the first time since his voice initially boomed through my
phone. Back at my desk, I tell Cosmo that Tate's up for it in
theory, and he asks me how he was on the call. I think for a
second. 'Weird. He could be sort of charming at times, but also
called me a cuck, so I'm not really sure.'*

*I open up his Twitter and find he's posted about our call.
His tweet contains a screenshot of my first email to him,
accompanied by the message:*

Vice news have heard about THE TEST and want to attend.
This email came 2 days after I secured the ROMANIAN
PARLIAMENT to launch the first stage of THE TEST.
THE TEST will be the greatest thing in modern history.
Imagine a game show – TATE STYLE.
ARE YOU READY?

*Despite not wanting us to film his War Room, Tate is
happy to use our request as an advertisement to sell more
spaces. I message him asking him to delete the tweet – a test
of how this relationship might go. He replies, 'No problem
brother,' followed by a love-heart emoji, and seconds later the
tweet disappears.*

In 2019, Tate was trying to achieve internet virality and fame, and
agreeing to participate in our documentary wasn't the only route
he was taking. He wasn't going to wait around for TV producers
to give him a break; he was taking matters into his own hands, and

social media was his weapon of choice. Tate had always been active in that arena, becoming a prolific user of Facebook in the 2010s. His most successful posts weren't his pictures or videos, but his controversial statuses. In posts that made racially charged jokes or in which he referred to himself as a pimp, Tate would get levels of engagement that his other content wouldn't attract. These statuses would incite such strong emotions in Tate's Facebook friends that reels of comments would appear under each post as people debated back and forth.

When Tate got on Twitter, it appeared that he had been drawn in by the possibility of doing the same thing on there, with the added ability to break out of his own social circle. Compared to Facebook, your reach on Twitter was not as limited. When he first joined, he used the same shock tactics that he had developed on Facebook, making racially charged jokes about footballer Ashley Cole and his then wife, Cheryl, and homophobic jokes about the rapper Drake. But these tweets didn't take off; there were enough people on Twitter making dissenting statements. It was becoming a crowded market. But Tate persevered, gradually building his follower count, which would then disappear when his accounts were banned for violating community guidelines. Over the years, Tate would hone his skills, creating content that was so shocking, it was guaranteed to be shared. In 2017, he managed to have one of his first viral 'breakthrough' moments.

Jon Rosenberg is an award-winning US-based comic-book artist who took to Twitter in 2017 to ask the public for help. One of his sons had cerebral palsy and had been accepted for a surgery that could relieve his condition, but being the US, the surgery was expensive, and so Rosenberg shared a link to a GoFundMe page asking for help. Spotting an opportunity to cause some outrage,

Andrew Tate chimed in on Rosenberg's Twitter thread, writing: *'Do you feel like a failure that the amount you need to help your own son is less than a quarter of what I spend on one of my 5 cars?'* Tate followed up with, *'I will help you if you ask'*. Finally, he concluded, *'It's nothing to me, youre comic books have failed but i'm a success. Ask nicely and I'll save your son.'*

You can be the judge of whether this was a genuine offer of help from Tate, but his mocking tone towards a man seeking help for his disabled son caught the attention of Twitter. The post gained traction as people commented and reposted it, variously deriding Tate for his lack of humanity and laughing at what they thought must be a joke from an account that wasn't intended to be taken seriously. Either way, Tate's comments were being shared. These shock tactics would become the core of his approach to social media. He wouldn't just be offensive and objectionable – he would be so offensive that the internet couldn't help noticing it. Ironically, the added attention that Tate brought to Rosenberg's post meant that the donations received exceeded the amount required for his son's surgery.

The same year that Jamie began his interactions with Tate (2019), was the year Tate would begin to see some real 'success' on Twitter. When journalist Mike Stuchbery wrote an article criticising Stephen Yaxley-Lennon, aka Tommy Robinson (fellow Lutonian and an acquaintance of Tate), Yaxley-Lennon posted Stuchbery's address online (a form of internet intimidation known as doxing), at which point Tate began trolling Stuchbery, eventually turning up outside his house and banging the door, threatening him and going through his bins. Tate shared the whole interaction with his growing audience on Twitter, posting a picture of himself outside Stuchbery's home, further exciting his and Yaxley-Lennon's audience who subsequently began piling on Stuchbery. They thought it was hilarious. They loved the idea of a journalist engaging with Tate in a 'Twitter argument', only for that same journalist to be confronted in real life. The posts went viral.

Also in 2019, Tate would have arguably his most viral Twitter moment prior to his ascension to global fame. On 5 May (one day after Star Wars Day), Tate lambasted fans of the Star Wars franchise, opening his tweet with the claim: *'Never seen Star Wars. None of them. Never will. Omg you're missing out. Maybe. You're missing out on being a multi millionaire. Keep your movie.'* He went on to say:

> Everyone who's ever watched star wars in human history is absolutely dirt poor. No exceptions. Only I can save you. Even watching a star wars trailer may leave you homeless, on the street, with aids. Only I have the path to absolute financial freedom. Do not follow the Jedi. Follow the Jesus [Tate] . . . Sorry for flexin on you broke boys. I know you're upset. But you're about to get real mad 🤭 I'm at the hotel. Bout to take your momma to the dark side. Ima use the force . . . nice and slow . . . That's right. I am your father.

Tate's post blew up, climbing to the top of the already trending *Star Wars* topic on Twitter. His thread encapsulated all he had learned about creating shock content on social media. He had taken a subject loved by a particular subgroup on the internet (*Star Wars*) and derided it (using inflammatory and offensive language), prodding an audience who would be quick to defend their beloved film franchise. Even those sharing Tate's post alongside captions calling him an 'idiot' or 'beyond parody' were helping Tate achieve his aim of going viral.

By exaggerating his trolling to such an extreme extent, Tate had found a way to break through the noise of social media. Not only had he learned how to generate engagement, but he had worked out that he could turn that engagement into money, by using it to direct people towards his courses. The above thread contained an advert for Tate's 'PhD Course' (full name: Pimping Hoes Degree): *'Has a girl ever tattooed her name on you? No? It's because you've watched star wars. Luckily I teach you the secrets to the female mind – not only how to get them – but how to make them do anything you say. Change your life today. Here: https://www.cobratate.com/product/how-to-get-girls/ . . .'*

The thread even contained a link to the War Room, which he'd created that same year, *'Do you have cool pictures of you with cigars? With piles of money? On tropical islands? No? You spent too much time watching dorkwars. Luckily you can join my war room and supercharge online money making. TODAY. Read the reviews yourself. https://www. cobratate.com/product/war-room/'*

Knowing that Tate was desperate to achieve fame, and that he knew how to get it, Jamie was wary of giving him what he wanted – a large platform on which to generate engagement. The documentary project needed to be fronted by a reporter who could hold their own with Tate, who had the nous to dig below the surface and who would work with Jamie to investigate what was really going on. To gain access to the War Room they needed to be a man, capable of charming Tate, or allowing themselves to appear to be charmed by him in order to get deeper into his world. Matt Shea stood out as the right candidate. He had hosted some of Vice's most popular and challenging films, and being both British and American, like Tate, he also spoke with an unusual fusion of accents that would at least give them something to relate over. Jamie called Matt, who, without hesitation, joined the project.

Tate's excitement for the upcoming documentary didn't seem

to wane. Two weeks after their first phone call, he sent Jamie an email which read, '*What we waiting for? The worlds mind needs blowing.*' Despite this, he still seemed wary of guaranteeing us access to his War Room: '*I think before we do the war room piece we do a general piece on us both. Meaning you can come Romania anytime.*' Jamie continued to push for access to the War Room, and Tate told him he would be in London in December, and they should meet for a drink to discuss it. Concerned that this could still be an ambush or just an elaborate troll, Jamie asked Cosmo to come with him.

Jamie – 16 December 2019

I grab Cosmo and head down the road to The Book Club in Shoreditch, a faux hipster hybrid of café and bar, two minutes' walk from the Vice offices. Nervous about meeting Tate face to face, I make sure we get to the café five minutes early in a bid to gain some semblance of control over the situation. At least I can choose where we sit. I want to be far away from the ears of any other customers, given the rants I've seen Tate go on via his YouTube channel. Tate had wanted to have our meeting in the office itself, but I didn't fancy bringing him in. I still don't trust him at all.

We arrive only to find that Tate has had the same idea and is early himself. I've got a message from him, 'we're pulling up'. Cosmo holds the table and I head outside to meet Tate, spotting a McLaren that has mounted the pavement a few metres from The Book Club's front door. Out steps Andrew Tate, flanked by his brother, Tristan, whose hulking size makes even his 6 foot 2 brother look small. Tate flashes me a startlingly white grin as he walks towards me, then shakes my hand with surprising softness. Tristan, on the other hand, keeps his face blank and emotionless, always following a metre behind his brother.

Inside, I introduce them to Cosmo who rises to shake their hands. Tristan extends his hand for a shake this time, but that feels like the extent of the niceties we'll get from him. Cosmo and I order mint tea, Andrew Tate a sparkling water and Tristan a pint of beer. For a 3pm meeting in a café with the media, this feels like a power move. I can feel the eyes of a few tables on us, but I'm sure the curiosity stems from the size of the two brothers and their McLaren out front, rather than from recognising them as fringe internet celebrities.

Tate's eye contact is intense. He has a way of looking at you as though he's completely engaged, incapable of being distracted by whatever else is going on in the room. He's on a charm offensive, smiling and laughing where possible, but isn't holding back all the same. 'I know this is going to be a hit-piece,' Tate says, 'but the question is whether I want to do it anyway.' I talk to him about what we can do to combat his concerns, which are primarily around the privacy of the members of his War Room. 'We could look at ways to keep them anonymous? They could wear masks or something . . .' I suggest. Tate seems interested for a moment (he would later shoot this idea down, fearful that the group would look like a 'right-wing militia'), before embarking on another rant about the liberal decline of Vice.

The rest of the meeting proceeds in a similar manner to my first call with Tate, only I feel much more nervous throughout, and he's more obviously excited. Perhaps he feels that this, a

Vice documentary with the potential to go viral, is his next chance at breakthrough fame.

Tate, Cosmo and I go back and forth, with Tate rapidly firing his best lines at us while Tristan watches in almost complete silence. At the end of the meeting Tristan addresses me directly for the first time, stating, 'I don't think it's a good idea, and I don't want to do it. But if Andrew wants to do it, I'll do it.' I don't really know how to respond, so I just smile and say, 'Great'.

Forty-five minutes pass, and I'm mentally exhausted. The adrenaline I started the meeting with has gone, and I just want to wrap things up now that the access seems secured. Finally, the Tates indicate they have to leave. We shake hands one last time and they climb into their McLaren, pulling away with that distinctive supercar roar, unblocking the Shoreditch pavement once again. I look at Cosmo. Cosmo looks back at me and says, 'Well, he's definitely a character'.

Jamie spent the next few months putting things in place for the shoot, which was due to take place in Romania in June 2020, when the War Room members would be undertaking Andrew Tate's test. He stayed in regular contact with Tate, speaking every other week on the phone. Tate frequently sent Jamie updates in the form of voice notes and pictures of him in glamorous locations around the world.

As we were making the final preparations, the world was thrown into uncertainty with the arrival of the Covid-19 pandemic. In a matter of weeks, international travel between numerous countries was banned, with lockdowns coming into force across the world, preventing people from leaving their homes or gathering in groups.

Jamie checked in with Tate, receiving an email in response: *'We might have a delay here. Full lockdown. And no idea when it's ending.'* Tate seemed hopeful that the hold-up would only be temporary and set a new date for The Test, in August that same year.

Tate was one of the early adopters of Covid-19 conspiracy theories, decrying the global lockdowns as a globalist mission to control us. Covid-19 allowed him to break out of the manosphere, enter the broader public conversation and bleed into the wider world of conspiracy theorists. He used his platform to criticise those he saw as cowering to government policies about Covid. Not long into the pandemic, Tate began making videos of himself continuing to travel around the world and refusing to wear a mask in public places, getting into arguments with restaurant owners and petrol-station attendants. He quickly began to feel that Covid-19 was not sufficient reason to put the documentary on hold, and in August began pestering Jamie for a further meeting in London. Jamie explained that both Vice's internal policy and the government's guidance meant this wouldn't be possible. The majority of War Room members at this point were from the US and UK, and with travel bans in place between these countries and Romania, The Test was delayed again, and again.

Despite this, Tate was becoming more and more determined to get some sort of coverage in Vice, and frustrated that a pandemic in which he did not appear to believe was preventing it from happening. The pandemic was also having a momentous impact on the film and TV industry, with restrictions regulating how shoots could go ahead, social distancing remaining in place and regular testing a requirement for all crew and contributors. Tate continued to insist that we begin filming, messaging and calling Jamie regularly to demand it. By the spring of 2021, Tate was becoming inexorable. In a bid to quell his anger, and maintain access, Jamie and Matt agreed to film a socially distanced scene that we could use somewhere in the film. Tate was due to collect a new Lamborghini he'd purchased from a showroom in London, and Jamie decided this would make for a good first meeting for Matt and Tate, so he planned to film Tate collecting the car followed by a 'walk and talk'. The Tate brothers would be flying in from a War Room event in Miami, and judging by their social media posts, they'd been using the relaxed rules in the city not only to host War Room events, but to attend nightclubs and bars around the place. The executives at Vice noticed this in the lead-up to the shoot, and asked Jamie to check with Tate that they would be following quarantine rules and getting PCR tests upon arrival.

Tate replied via WhatsApp: *'I don't obey covid rules and never have this entire time. They're not enforceable. Only sheep obey. I'll lie through the border and ignore all quarantines and testing . . .'* Shortly after, he followed up: *'oh I understand. Are you worried I might have covid?* 😂 *I'll provide a negative test when we meet don't worry. Covid ain't killing you G I believe you're strong.'* When Jamie replied that it was now a standard part of the process for Vice's risk assessments and insurance, Tate responded immediately: *'I'll bring covid tests. Negative. I'll get one when I leave Miami today. If it helps. But from a moral perspective I want to make it clear anyone afraid of the common cold with a 99.9% survival rate is a fucking moron. Legitimately a moron. With a low IQ. It's been a year and a half. It's never going away. Get the fuck over it. So tell your insurance company that.'*

Jamie reported back to Vice, who insisted that if Tate and his brother were refusing to quarantine in accordance with government guidelines, they couldn't let filming go ahead. Twenty minutes later, Tate came back: *'Covid pussies. I have a negative test. Grow some balls.'* Given that Tate regularly bragged about being able to get fake vaccine documentation and PCR test results, his negative test was meaningless. Tate continued: '*As long as companies like vice act like total cowards and capitate o all freedoms being removed over a disease with a 99.99% survival rate, it'll never end. This current situation is built on the backs of the deep cowardice companies like vice display. You should feel deep shame being associated with such a weak minded organisation. And quit. I'm leaving then. Driving to Romania. I'll be back here 25th of this month with ANOTHER negative test and I'll have ANOTHER super car. If vice stops being babies.*

Covid was frustrating Tate, but it was also in part responsible for his growing audience. There was such a rapid proliferation of conspiracy theories that it was almost impossible for the average person to avoid them. Conspiracy theorists had often spoken of a 'new world order' or a global agenda that sought to enslave the common person to benefit an indeterminate group of world elites. Now that governments around the world were telling their citizens to stay at home, and threatening to prosecute them if they disobeyed, these same people jumped on board to claim that their predictions were coming true. In the UK, from April to May, trust in the 'news media' when it came to Covid-19 fell by 11 per cent, and trust in the government fell even more dramatically, by 19 per cent.[*]

Tate was one of the many influencers who joined this movement. What's more, growing levels of anxiety and depression from a lack of social interaction made each of us more susceptible to these very conspiracy theories. Covid also led to a dramatic increase in the average person's screen time, with young people in particular

---

[*] https://reutersinstitute.politics.ox.ac.uk/trust-uk-government-and-news-media-covid-19-information-down-concerns-over-misinformation

spending more time online. By some estimates, children's screen time increased by an average of 1.3 hours per day during the pandemic.* Seeking social interaction, community or information they felt they could trust, people looked to the internet. What many of the young men who sought refuge there found was Andrew Tate and his War Room.

Beginning 17 May 2021, the British government allowed socialising outdoors in groups of up to thirty, so long as social distancing was maintained. It was our chance to appease Tate, get something in the can for our documentary and give him the chance to meet Matt for the first time on camera. On 27 May we met Andrew at The Mandrake, a boutique hotel in London's Fitzrovia, where he was staying. Jamie went into the lobby to meet Tate, who rose with his signature smile. He was accompanied by a British woman in her twenties. Tate left her to accompany Jamie out to the front of the hotel, only to have her catch up with them as they were approaching the front door. 'I need a room key to get back into the room to get some stuff,' she said, holding out her hand to Tate. 'So ask someone behind the desk,' Tate replied curtly, in a tone we'd yet to witness outside of his YouTube videos. 'Dumb bitches, am I right?' he turned to ask Jamie, as they headed out to meet Matt.

'I hear you just bought a Lambo,' said Matt.

'I've got a few cars. I think it's my seventeenth car. So . . . I wish I could be rich, but I'm stupid, and I spend it all on cars.'

'Well, you're doing better than me. I don't own a single car.'

'In London you don't need one, my friend. In London you don't need one. But in Romania, I mean, there's plenty of nice roads and stuff.'

---

* https://www.ncbi.nlm.nih.gov/pmc/articles/PMC10087086/

(It would seem bizarre to recall this over a year later, after Tate had repeatedly called Matt a 'brokie' for flying on Wizz Air).

'I saw this morning you wrote "rules are for poor people" on Instagram. What does that mean?' Matt asked.

It was at this point that Tate launched into his first diatribe in our presence. He had the gift of the gab and was able to weave everything – the Covid pandemic, tax laws, the justice system – into a unified conspiracy against young men. This wasn't equivalent to the kind of nonsense you'd hear from, say, Alex Jones, the notorious conspiracy theorist who once claimed that a 'gay bomb' created by the Pentagon was turning the 'frogs gay'. Amid Tate's ramblings, there were a few kernels of truth. Some of it resonated.

'So society has a set of rules, and those rules are designed to keep people in perpetual slavery. Those rules are not designed to allow people to be free and sovereign individuals.

The system is deliberately designed to oppress and keep people working jobs which barely pay their rent and everyone is semi-depressed. But it doesn't matter because the elites get to do whatever they want. So, the rules are for poor people. And when you understand how to break the rules, then you can find a very easy way to become rich.'

He was rebranding hyper-capitalism as a rebellion against the elites, in the same way Trump did. It brought to mind the Steinbeck quote, when he says America would never have a communist revolution because instead of 'self-admitted proletarians' they just had 'temporarily embarrassed capitalists'.*

But how did this all connect to masculinity?

'Masculinity is rebellion and always has been rebellion. How

---

* 'A Primer on the '30s,' *Esquire* (1 Jun 1960).

can you rebel if you have a boss? Finance is a huge part of masculinity because masculinity is rebellion and freedom. If you have absolutely no money, you're a slave to the system.

'Buying a Lambo for me? It's not even an expensive purchase anymore. But I think another part of being a man – a large part of being a man – is signalling status. Why do you think billionaires buy yachts? They don't need yachts. They don't want yachts. Why do they want one two feet bigger than the one next to it? It's just a status symbol, isn't it? I already have seventeen cars. I didn't need another one. But it's just one of those things.'

Tate then brought it all together against the cornerstone of his philosophy: violence. 'I want to do what I want. I don't want anyone to tell me I'm not allowed to leave my house because I might get a cold. I think that's absolutely insane. And the fact that everyone else out here was ok with that was just mind boggling to me. You know, like didn't men used to charge on horseback across the plains, underneath the sun, at the pikes?

'And I'm not even a violent person. I can fight on the street. That's not what I do. But violence has always been the underpinning of masculine interaction since the dawn of human time. Might makes right.'

Matt asked, 'Do you find that when you make violence such a major underpinning of your life that it has any negative consequences in how you feel? I'm just thinking about those pikemen – a lot of them probably had PTSD.'

Tate replied, 'When I'm talking about violence, I'm talking about an underpinning life philosophy. I'm trying to explain that the world always has been and always will be violent. Right now, there's Chinese hackers trying to hack American servers. It's a never-ending conflict all around the world. It's a war for resources, a war for states. It's a war for females. When you walk in the club and there's another man in the club, he wants a woman. This is all war, this is all the men have ever done – is compete. We've removed the competitive element from masculinity and we're trying to pretend it's not true. But it's absolutely true. It's always forever been true.

'Everyone believes in violence, but most people believe in violence by proxy, right? They believe in violence, but they don't want to do it. They want the police to do it, right? Even though the basic bottom-line punishment for all of Western civilisation is violence, at some point. I get a parking ticket. I don't pay the parking ticket. They add fines. I don't pay the fine. They give me a court date. I don't go to court. They send police to arrest me. I resist arrest. The police become violent. And the words and the letters and the talking all ends at some point with every single law, all the societal structures, the tax man, the parking wardens, all of it. At some point it comes down to violence.'

'Ok, I'm with you,' Matt responded.

'Violence is the underpinning of society and it's the underpinning of masculinity.'

CHAPTER TWO

Webcam Dreams

Journalists are always looking for red flags. Andrew Tate's were incredibly large and red, but rather than hiding them, he would wave them in our faces, like a matador trying to provoke a bull.

By late 2019, Tate had had very little press coverage, apart from a few kick-boxing interviews and articles about his tumultuous appearance on *Big Brother*. There were, however, a couple of digital-only pieces from British tabloids profiling Andrew and Tristan: 'Two young British men raking in millions from webcam sites where men hand over a fortune as they fall for models' fake sob stories'. The interviews gave the impression that it was the Tates who approached the journalists, eager for coverage of their webcam empire. In one interview with the *Sunday Mirror*, Tristan and Andrew Tate bragged about tricking men into thinking they had a genuine chance at a relationship with the webcam models, in order to elicit more money from them: 'It's all a big scam . . . it's their problem not mine'.

Running a webcam business that aimed to exploit vulnerable men was ethically dodgy, but not necessarily illegal. Webcam is a large and growing part of the online sex industry, and many women are employed by legitimate companies and managers. Romania alone has around 5,000 registered webcam companies. Tate made no secret of his involvement in the industry, and if you were to look at the 'Who Am I?' section on his website at the time, you would find this (since-deleted) description: 'My name is Andrew Tate. I'm a retired 4x World Champion kickboxer who is now a multi-millionaire, and I'm the most competent person on the planet to teach you about male-female interactions. How did I become rich? Webcam.' The real red flag, though, was the content of the courses that Tate was selling, promising to teach men how to start similar companies of their own, and giving an insight into how he claimed to have built his empire.

Two of Tate's most notorious courses were his 'PhD' ('Pimping Hoes Degree') and a supplementary course, 'Webcam Dreams'. The PhD appeared to be Tate's number-one product, the one he spent most time promoting online. Its name was crude, and in true Tate fashion, designed to shock and engage. If you purchased the course, you'd receive an almost two-hour-long video in which Tate himself, wearing a Storm Gym t-shirt and a tight white leather jacket, laid out his diagnosis and cure for the state of male and female sexual dynamics. At least, this is how Tate would sell it to you, but what the course really seemed to do was teach those who bought it how to apply the tactics of a pimp, but in a digital age. Think of it as a masterclass course, but instead of Martin Scorsese teaching you filmmaking, you have Andrew Tate teaching you 'pimping hoes'. Our impression was that it explained how to attract unsuspecting women, and then gradually make them more submissive, until you have complete dominance over them. Once an unsuspecting subject is perceived to have passed Tate's PhD test, she is ready to be converted from dating prospect to webcam worker. The men who make it this far in Tate's course are encouraged to use the teachings in the 'Webcam Dreams' course to get these women working for them in the online sex industry, passing over their earnings to their 'boyfriends'.

Tate's logic seemed to be that certain women were more susceptible than others to doing sex work and giving the money to their 'pimp', and that it was easier than ever to find and exploit them in the online world. All you had to do was make these women fall in love with you and sell them a dream.

We found a copy of his video course online. Tate begins his course by telling you that what you're about to learn is comparable to the skills used by 'street pimps.' He then appeals to incels and PUAs by describing the supposed imbalance of power in the 'sexual marketplace' that makes such skills necessary. Whereas incels lament the unfairness of it all, often lashing out in anger, pickup artists believe there are tricks that can be used to manipulate the situation in your favour. Tate claims that largely, all women think the same way, and in the PhD course says, *'if you know the rules to the game, if you can bend the rules, or you can put yourself in the right position so that the rules of the game favour you, you should be very happy women think a [that] particular way.'* Tate invokes the use of deception when meeting a woman and putting her through his PhD test, telling his students to lie about their jobs, and to make up more interesting and enticing backstories. As he states, *'We live in a world where you cannot play fair anymore'*. This isn't about sex; this is about money. In his Webcam Dreams course, Tate makes it clear: *'If you saw the PhD course you saw [that] your goal is to inspire a girl to make money and give you the money'*.

For Tate, sex plays a key part in knowing when a person is ready to be converted to a webcam worker, claiming: *'You have to fuck* them. *And they have to love you. It's essential to the business because otherwise, women have no loyalty.'* Later in his course, Tate states: *'I don't mention webcam until after I've had sex with the girl. If you're on dates, and you're trying to mention it and shit, it just doesn't work. It puts them off . . . You continue as normal, no mention of webcam. You fuck the girl. After you fucked the girl you do the PhD test. If she passes the PhD test, and she wants to be with you. Then you start mentioning things like, Yeah, but you know, you're always busy. You're always at work, you can come work for me. So as I said, you cannot try and approach girls [directly] to do webcam.'*

According to Tate, a woman cannot know that you are approaching her for webcam from the outset, and thus the whole process begins with an information imbalance and deception. Passing the PhD test requires a woman to be so submissive to a man that they will do anything he says. Tate uses himself as living proof to his students that this is possible: *'I've never met a woman who will not do the basics of what I say. Bring me coffee. Turn up where I tell her to. Listen to me. Not talk to other men. Basic things. But some are better blueprints than others.'*

Tate seems to imply his students control these women through emotional manipulation and the weaponisation of sex. In his PhD course he tells them: *'Your girl should want sex more than you get it . . . That's a healthy relationship. It shouldn't be the other way around, because that puts her in a position of power. You can not let these women ever be in a position of power.'* Once the girl has been converted to a webcam worker, Tate says the power and control are maintained by preventing her from seeing other people, particularly men, and controlling the passwords to their webcam accounts. It is crucial to not let them have access to their accounts, or even speak directly with their customers, as both scenarios would allow the woman to cash out her own money and leave or start a relationship with one of her online admirers.

Tate borrows language from the street pimping community, referring to the first girl you successfully recruit as your 'bottom bitch' (a term used among street pimps, meaning the prostitute who sits at the top of their hierarchy, often recruiting and managing future prostitutes). She is generally considered to be the most loyal of a pimp's prostitutes, and the one who has been with him the longest. Tate, with apparent seriousness, tells his students that your bottom bitch is the one you need most control and influence over. This is because she will do the selling to future recruits, not you. When dating a new girl who you think could be a potential recruit, you introduce her to your bottom bitch, who plays along as an ex-girlfriend who now works for your webcam company. Tate creates a hypothetical scenario in which you go out with your new girl but invite your bottom bitch along: *'Your bottom bitch is the one who does the selling. You don't do the selling. The girl has to hear from a girl. And this is where your bottom bitch has to be trained. So as I said it's so important to have a good first girl. My first girl was so good. It was easy.'* Tate then gives examples of what your bottom bitch can say to your new girlfriend to make webcamming seem more attractive: *'I get so much money, it's a lot of fun. And we stay at home and then we're gonna go to Thailand. I'm soon to be working in Thailand and we [can] stay there for as long as you want. You should come with us. It's gonna be so much fun . . .'*

If the pair hit it off, Tate suggests trying to get them on webcam together that first night, introducing alcohol into the situation: *'So the new girl can sit there, and just sit with the other girl and get drunk. Give them a bottle of vodka.'*

The method that Tate teaches in his PhD course bears a striking resemblance to something called the 'Loverboy Method', typically associated with human trafficking and coerced prostitution, in which a man weaponises affection to lure potential victims and puts them to work in the sex industry. They often seduce their targets with compliments, gifts and promises of family or a lavish lifestyle, but with the sole purpose of ensnaring that person into a position where the loverboy can exploit them in the sex industry. On Tate's website he claimed that more than half of the seventy-five girls he had working for him were his girlfriends at the time, and none of them were in the adult industry before meeting him. All it took was a simple Google search for Jamie to discover this, but it indicated that the Andrew Tate story may be much bigger than people realised. He began to develop a theory that Tate was not just a fringe manosphere influencer, but potentially also guilty of exploitation, human trafficking and making money by teaching other men to do the same. The documentary had become an investigation.

What Tate was doing here wasn't completely novel, but it placed him within a corner of the manosphere occupied by PUAs. Figures like Roosh V and Ross Jeffries had amassed large followings in this arena, but Tate's teachings placed him both within and outside of the classification of a pickup artist (he liked to distance himself from the term, as he claimed they were all 'dorks'). Whereas figures like Roosh and Jeffries were teaching their audience how to get more women to have sex with them, Tate promised to teach his students how to get more women to have sex with them, and have those same women make them money.

When Jamie first called Tate to broach the topic of making a documentary about him, he tentatively asked about his webcam business, not wanting Tate to know quite how aware we were of it for fear of spooking him and losing access. Tate, however, boasted to Jamie that his business was still running in Romania, and that if Vice came there, he would show us round one of his webcam houses-turned-studio, and introduce us to one of his 'girlfriends' who worked for him on webcam. It was a promising start, although we could hardly trust a carefully selected associate of Tate's to tell us about how she came to work for him in the digital sex industry. But then Jamie came across something else that began to solidify our suspicions.

Jamie – 5 January 2020

I've been trawling through Andrew Tate's Twitter for weeks, and while there are some interesting leads to follow, they all come from Tate himself and so it's hard to know what's real and what's bullshit. At this point, I'm more interested in what other people might be saying about him, so I turn to one of my favourite websites for initial research – Reddit. I can't find a subreddit for Tate, and when I search for his name I mostly find links to people selling his courses at reduced prices, or the occasional reference to Tate on Big Brother. *I opt for a different approach, and open up the subreddit r/Romania, typing Tate's name into the search bar. It's a bit more fruitful, but most posts are just gossip: links to Tate appearing on Romanian 'Starz News', surrounded by women, or headlines about him and his brother arriving in supercars at a Bucharest nightclub. I dutifully plug each post into Google Translate, hoping for something interesting, only to find more celebrity chat, mentions of TikTok star girlfriends, and huge bar tabs in Bucharest nightclubs. As I scroll further through the search results a post stands out. Unlike the others, it has no article or video attached to it, just a short paragraph in Romanian.*

*I go again, plugging it into Google Translate, and begin
to read. A swelling feeling builds in my stomach as I make
my way through the post, which claims that Andrew Tate
(referred to as 'this webcam money guy from England who's on
Romanian TV . . .') was messaging girls on Instagram whom
the post's author knew, asking them out on dates and offering
to pick them up in one of his supercars. The issue with this, the
poster pointed out, was that his friends were all sixteen and
seventeen, currently attending various high schools around
Brasov, about three hours from Bucharest, where Andrew's
brother, Tristan, owns various properties and businesses. 'I'm
worried he might be trying to recruit Romanian girls for his
webcam studio . . .' the post concluded.*

*I think back to Andrew Tate's courses, and pull up my
folder of transcripts, typing in the word 'Instagram'. A
reference pops up in Tate's PhD course, and I pull up the time
code, finding its place in the video and pressing play: 'We
live in the world of the internet. So the first thing you need to
start getting laid today is, your number one tool to get laid,
Instagram. Instagram is the new dating fucking app . . .'*

*Tate goes on to tell men how they can curate their
Instagram pages to be more attractive to women, which
messages to send to get their attention (providing screenshots
of his own examples of those supposedly 'working') and how
to use Instagram's search feature to find women all over the
world, to begin building up a selection of 'prospects' in all the
cities you frequently travel to. Tate's advice was to type 'find a
nightclub' in the city of your choosing, look at pictures taken in
the tagged location on Instagram and start messaging.*

I pull up Tate's Instagram and look for myself. He follows just over 3,000 accounts. This isn't going to be a quick process. I open a new spreadsheet and begin to go through each account, cross referencing each identifiable person with their other social media accounts, and any public records about them available online. Lots of the accounts are private or use pseudonyms, but I'm able to track down details on about 500 of the accounts Tate's following. It's a pretty wide variety, but one trend is clear: there are lots of young women. Some are influencers or successful models, but many have relatively low follower counts, often under 500, and are predominantly posting from across Eastern Europe, particularly Romania. There are seven university students, all nineteen years old. Too young for Tate in some people's eyes, but nothing legally wrong with that. There are at least three eighteen-year-olds who are still in high school in Romania and have their schools listed in their page bios. Again, nothing illegal, but not a great look.

Then I find something else. Seven accounts belonging to younger teenage girls, ranging from fifteen to seventeen. One is in the US, one is in Moldova and the other five are near Bucharest and Brasov, Tate's two main bases in Romania. Four of the girls have their ages or high schools listed in their bios. I take screenshots of all the accounts, and of Tate following them, and log them in the spreadsheet.

Two weeks later, I check in on Tate's Instagram. He's stopped following most of the teenagers' accounts, and in their place is a host of different young women. I immediately call Matt to update him on the results of my search. 'I think this guy could be grooming women.'

CHAPTER THREE

Set Your Blood on Fire

Ten months after Matt first met Tate in London in May 2021, we were beginning to get anxious. Covid restrictions had prevented us from filming, but Tate's popularity had continued to grow. It was only a matter of time before other journalists began looking into the story, leading to a race of the worst kind. Or, from the heights of his newfound fame, Tate might rescind his interest in being involved in any kind of documentary.

On 27 April 2022, Jamie woke up to a Google alert: 'Police Raid MAGA "King of Toxic Masculinity" in Human-Trafficking Investigation', reported the *Daily Beast*. 'The raid was prompted by reports that an American woman had been abducted.' A Romanian news website released a video, filmed through the gaps in the gate to Tate's compound on the outskirts of Bucharest, in which heavily armed police officers in balaclavas, 'Politia' written on their backs, paced up and down in front of a collection of supercars.

Jamie immediately messaged Tate, who he'd been in regular contact with for almost two and half years at this point, asking him what was going on. Fifteen minutes later, Tate replied, *'Pure lies. Nothing happened,'* before sending a series of voice notes in which he claimed the police were searching for a missing girl in the area and had searched his house along with '*four other houses on the street*', before taking him and Tristan to the police station and releasing them an hour later without arrest. Tate admitted they had to give a statement but claimed '*so did like 20 other people*'. He ended his message with a defence that he would come to use frequently against our own reporting, '*The Daily Beast hates me from old stuff, so just make things up . . . If I wasn't rich and famous it wouldn't be a story, it's just standard operating procedure.*'

Two weeks later, when Jamie spoke to Tate again, it appeared he had forgotten about his original explanation. This time, he said, Tristan had been seeing an American woman who had come to visit him in Romania. Unbeknown to Tristan, the woman had a boyfriend back in the US, who was asking why she was staying with these guys in Romania. According to Tate, the woman lied to her boyfriend, claiming the Tates were holding her against her will, at which point the boyfriend called the US Embassy, who contacted the Romanian police. He claimed that the woman had already been kicked out of his house, and far from holding her captive, he and Tristan were refusing to let her back in. This telling of the events does not match up with the evidence later submitted in Tate's indictment, including WhatsApp conversations between the alleged victim and her family.

On various podcasts and interviews, Tate would give a third account of why he and his brother were raided, claiming that he had been 'swatted'. Swatting is the act of calling the police or emergency services to a person's address, claiming a serious crime is taking place, such as a murder, or someone being held hostage, in order to harass and intimidate the person being swatted. This was a growing trend online, with members of the viewing public 'swatting' online streamers, and watching them being raided by armed police units, often while still streaming live to their audience. Dramatic scenes unfurled with streamers speaking to their audience as military-style police units broke down their doors in real time, armed with assault rifles, forcing them to the floor while their audience watched. Despite not being on a livestream at the time of the raid, this is what Tate claimed had happened to him and his brother, including in a viral interview with Tucker Carlson, by many metrics the most successful current right-wing political commentator in the US, where Tate's claim went unchallenged.

In the months that followed, Tate skyrocketed to new levels of fame, becoming the most googled person in the world and one of the most-seen faces on TikTok. Any young man who opened the app would likely be fed videos of him by the algorithm, within hours, if not minutes.

'Private jets are like Ubers,' he boasted in one TikTok video: 'This is what you guys don't understand: you're brokies, you don't get it. I can have lunch in Geneva. And then around four o'clock I can get bored, fly home, and be home by six. When you can Uber around earth in real time, it's very hard to not do anything. "Tate, it's Cannes film festival." "I don't wanna go to Cannes film festival." "Yeah, but Leonardo DiCaprio is on this boat." "Don't like him." "Yeah, but he's gonna be jealous of your girls." "That's true." Quickly: boom, jet, bang, flex on Leonardo, boom, back on the jet, bang. Yes, I'm filthy rich.'

On 9 May, Tate set a date for us to arrive. We were to fly with him in August, via private jet. Vice just needed Tate to send over details on the insurance for what we assumed was his own private jet, and the film shoot could finally be booked in. But Tate didn't want to send those details, and he got more and more angry when we kept asking for them. Jamie, it turned out, wasn't a 'real man' for needing the insurance details of the private jet. He was beholden to his bosses at Vice and to 'the system', unable to act according to his own will; an effete slave, whining about insurance details, while real men flew unencumbered across the world as they pleased, answering only to themselves. So, the shoot was at a standstill.

This was puzzling, because – even if we were 'cucks' for needing to see an insurance document – it should have been a simple issue to solve. After weeks of back and forth, Jamie realised Tate didn't actually own a private jet. He had planned to rent one, and that's why he didn't want to provide the insurance. And he didn't want to let the company he rented from know he was filming on board with journalists, without their permission. Had Tate repeatedly berated us about masculinity and slavery to avoid admitting to something that made him seem marginally less rich?

Jamie tried one last time to get the insurance details, but Tate was over it. 'For fuck's sake G, this is a headache. Take Wizz Air, then.'

Our journey to Romania was tense. Matt was not looking forward to the shoot. Over the next week, he would be more than just a fly on the wall. He would be participating in The Test (which Tate charged his followers $5,000 for the privilege of participating in. We were lucky to be getting free entry). *'If you're going to build better men, the only way to do that is to go through something,'* Tate said on his podcast, Tate Speech: *'They used to throw a twelve or thirteen-year-old boy into the wild and see if they came back alive. The problem with the world today is that it's too easy* [. . .] *True happiness as a man comes from strength* [. . .] *you go through things which do not completely destroy you, but they test you and they damage you to the point that you know you're going to be a different person afterwards* [. . .] *So, for this reason, I put together The Test.'*

Matt – 5 August 2022

Tate never said what The Test was, only that it would be terrifying and difficult, and that I probably would not be able to handle it. I have done dangerous assignments before. I have interviewed the Albanian mafia in Montenegro and been forced to take a medley of twelve different drugs at gunpoint by a Colombian cartel in the slums of Medellín. But whereas in those situations any potential risk involved would be because things didn't go to plan, in this one, the idea is to scare me. Who knows what he has in store?

Jamie – and our bosses at Vice – have been clear that I don't have to do anything I don't want to do. In fact, my employers have forbidden me from doing anything too dangerous. But I've told Jamie that I plan to do The Test no matter what. This is simply because I do not want to come across as weak and afraid. I'm being filmed not just by Jamie but by Tate's crew as well. I have to give Tate credit for knowing how to prey on men's insecurities. I'm making a documentary – I am meant to be in his head – but he is getting in mine.

To help with the fear, I've been desperate to find out anything I can about The Test. I've watched a video the Tate brothers released – a kind of advertisement for the event. In it, a man can be seen sprinting for his life through a post-apocalyptic landscape of abandoned buildings, intercut with close-ups of chess pieces being taken, then falling. Running round the corner of a barbed-wire fence, he comes face to face with a huge man in a black leather trench coat and demonic monkey mask. It fades out. I don't feel any better.

*But it's not just The Test that makes me apprehensive.
This will be a very difficult line to toe as a presenter. Go in too
critically of his views and we will lose our access quickly. Go in
too softly and I'll (rightfully) be accused of giving a misogynist
a free ride. Normally, the solution in these situations is to feign
a kind of benign curiosity and let them hang themselves with
their own rope – but that won't work either because Tate is too
smart.*

*I have been lazy with some past documentaries, where
I could afford to wing questions and pieces to camera. Not
this one. Tate has gone unchallenged for far too long, free to
speak to millions of young boys on social media. Now we have
the privilege of being the only journalists with access to the
person who is influencing half an entire generation of young
men (a survey by Hope Not Hate has found that 52 per cent of
sixteen-and seventeen-year-old boys in the UK have a positive
view of Andrew Tate, and are more likely to have heard of
him than of Rishi Sunak, UK Prime Minister at the time of
writing).* I felt the weight of the job properly for the first time.
If I fuck this one up it might actually have an effect on society.*

Jamie – 6 August 2022

*The satnav counts down the minutes to our arrival as I drive
further and further into the suburbs of Bucharest, with Matt
in the passenger seat and our two cameramen, Charlie and
Joe, in the back. I narrowly avoided two accidents on the*

* https://hopenothate.org.uk/wp-content/uploads/2023/02/state-of-hate-
2023-v7-1.pdf

way here – one with a car driving the wrong way round the roundabout, and another when we were overtaken by a car doing double the speed limit. Joe googles traffic accidents in Romania and tells us that they had the highest number of road fatalities in Europe in 2020. I try to calm my nerves by telling myself I'm already doing the most dangerous part of this shoot, driving a car in Bucharest, but it doesn't seem to stop my foot trembling slightly every time I release the clutch to change gear.

After almost three years of constant phone calls with Tate, we are finally going to enter his compound. 'In 100 yards take the next right, then in 300 yards you will have arrived at your destination.' Looking around, I'm beginning to wonder if I've put the address in wrong, and I feel a slight panic building, worrying about being late. Tate has been constantly bragging about his wealth, sending me pictures of his numerous supercars in various exotic locations, and calling me from yachts in Croatia and skyrises in Dubai. With this in mind, looking around, we can't be in the right neighbourhood. Approaching the final right turn, on our left is empty scrubland, and on our right what looks like a large factory that has been abandoned early in its construction, with thick weeds covering piles of unused cinder blocks. Following the directions, I make the right turn and pull up next to a cemetery at the furthest end of the street from where Tate's compound is supposed to be. A woman with a scarf around her head walks through the cemetery gates, holding a large bunch of plastic flowers.

Turning to Matt, I give the team my plan for filming his entrance. I can tell that he is rehearsing his questions in his head, but from the outside he looks remarkably calm. I try

*to channel some of that energy, feeling my anxiety building.
Matt and Joe get out of the car and I pull away again slowly,
heading down the road as the loose gravel and dirt kick up,
hitting the wheel arches of our car. Then I see it, right at the
end of the road, opposite a block of modest flats: a large brick
warehouse with dark black cladding and a red trim. It seems
a far cry from the luxurious mansion that Tate flaunts on his
Instagram. If it wasn't for the separate security entrance and
two armed Romanian men out front, wearing matching 007
t-shirts, I probably wouldn't have noticed it.*

*I pull up next to the security guards as they walk towards
my window, craning their heads to get a good look at my face.
'Hi, I'm Jamie from Vice, I'm here to see Andrew Tate.' They
nod, and one of them mutters something in Romanian into
their radio. The metal gates open with a loud clunking sound,
revealing two large LED signs bearing the name 'Tate' and
a red-tiled swimming pool. A woman in her early thirties
beams at me. Two women in bikinis sit by the pool, deep in
conversation with the hulking figure of a man I recognise
as Tristan Tate. And there he is, walking towards me in his
signature skin-tight trousers, with his shirt open to his navel.
Andrew Tate. His smile is the biggest I've ever seen it, and it
feels impossible to break his gaze, except when the sun glints
off his diamond-encrusted watch.*

*'You're driving in Romania? You're a brave man!' Tate
leaned through the window and shook my hand. 'Park down
there and then come on in.' He points to a small space on the
side of the road.*

*'Will we be ok to leave our camera bags in the car here?' I
ask.*

'We have two guys with guns, they'll be watching your car,' he replies, gesturing to his security guards. 'Anyway, Romania is really safe, that kind of stuff doesn't happen here. This isn't London.'

I let out a nervous laugh and pull into the indicated space. Camera and microphone in hand, Charlie, one of our cameramen, and I walk through Tate's gates, coming face to face (or more like face to chest) with the 6 foot 2 Tate for the third time since I first spoke to him, almost three years ago.

'How are you?' I ask, with a tone that implies I'm very aware of the sudden change in Tate's celebrity status.

'I'm the most famous person in the world!' Tate says, his smile breaking into a laugh, clearly enjoying the fact that he now has statistics to back up this statement.

'Where's Matt?' he asks.

'He's just waiting down the road,' I reply. 'I wanted to come and check everything was all good and put a microphone on you so we can film you meeting.'

Tristan is now up, and walking across the compound towards the front door. I turn to him, 'Hi, Tristan'. He looks at me with an emotionless stare and continues into the house without breaking his stride.

'Yeah, he's not so up for this, but don't worry, he'll be fine,' Tate reassures me.

Normally, I have to ask contributors to unbutton their shirts to attach the concealed microphone to their chests, but Tate's style choices mean he is already primed and ready, the Cobra tattoo on his left pec uncovered and glistening in the sun. Charlie and I repeatedly move the microphone around, struggling to find a place to put it so that it's not visible on camera. Finding a

portion of unexposed chest on Andrew Tate is no mean feat, but
eventually we hit on a suitable spot under his right pec where the
sound seemed usable, and we're ready to go.

'Ok,' I say, looking up at Tate. 'I'll go and get Matt, we'll
come and ring the front gate again and he'll take it from there.'

'Great,' he shoots back, exuding confidence.

I walk back through Tate's front gate to retrieve Matt and
Joe. 'Right,' I tell myself. 'No going back now.'

Like last time, Tate, was all smiles as he shook Matt's hand.
'Good to see you!'

Tristan, who Matt hadn't yet met, sat by the pool, speaking to
the two young women in Romanian. Matt walked over to shake his
hand and received only a glare.

'I don't think they really want to say hello,' Tate told him. He
joked about throwing Matt in the pool, 'for cinematic effect'. 'How
good is it going to be if I just grab you and fling you in?'

He showed us his Ferrari, Lamborghini and Rolls Royce. Matt
asked whether he always had this level of security.

'It's better to be paranoid. Isn't it better to be prepared? You knew
you were coming to see me. So, as a professional, intelligent adult,
you've decided to be paranoid and be prepared. So, I know you've
been, like, running marathons, you've been training every day in
the gym, you've been working out. You're trying to, you know,
expand your mind playing chess. You're about to be tested to War
Room standards. I'm sure you weren't just sitting around smoking
weed, being a jackass, right?'

'Oh, no,' Matt half-joked. 'That's exactly what I was doing.'

'Vice. What can you do?'

Whereas the outside of the house looked like a run-down

warehouse in a poorly maintained car park, the inside appeared more like a Harrods catalogue. Expensive-looking speakers flanked what must be the largest TV screen money could buy.

A muscular man in his twenties sat behind a series of computer monitors, instructing students of Tate's 'Hustlers University', an online community and course subscription that promised to teach students Tate's secrets of wealth creation. His name, we were told, was Cousin Luc.

Women in stilettos cleaned surfaces as soon as our cameras started rolling, then disappeared when the cameras were off. One of these women, Tate said, was Georgiana Naghel, who the Romanian press had once referred to as his girlfriend (though Tate also referred to her as his 'personal assistant'). 'She's a witch,' Tate warned us – a literal one, he stressed. We were told not to speak to her.

An American man with a grey, wizard-like beard and embroidered silk kimono leered over a computer, barking orders at another woman. We were told not to speak to him either.

'I've never seen a television that big,' Matt said.

'Yeah,' Tate explained, 'I've never watched a movie, ever. It just feels a bit . . . I don't know. I think with the internet and the modern world we've all developed, to some degree, a form of ADHD. We're all, like, scrolling and that and I can't just sit and watch a movie anymore. I try, but it just gets boring. End up on my phone . . . So, I just leave the screensaver playing,' he said, looking up wistfully. 'It's a nice screensaver.'

Tate offered Matt two coffees within an hour. When Matt refused the second cup, he taunted, 'You think it's poison or something? You're scared of my coffee?'

Matt explained that too much caffeine would make him feel anxious.

'Anxiety is good,' Tate retorted.

We hadn't heard this take before. 'Is it?'

'Drink coffee,' he went on. 'Set your blood on fire. That's how you conquer the world, my friend. Don't be weak.'

We noticed a painting of Tristan on the wall, looking menacing. It suddenly struck us how strange it was that these two brothers in their mid-thirties lived together in this compound that felt like a reality-TV set.

'Do you ever plan to move in with your girlfriend or wife or something?' Matt asked.

'I'll always live with my brother,' Tate answered. 'I think that men are empowered when they live with other competitive men,' he went on. 'My girlfriends, my women, whatever, can come round the house. Sure, they can stay here for extended periods of time. But I will never live alone exclusively just with a woman, because I think that's where men go soft.'

He proudly showed Matt a photo from a newspaper clipping in which he, as a five-year-old Illinois state chess champion, beat a team of three nine-year-olds. But this verging-on-endearing moment came to a swift end as the thought of chess set him off on a diatribe about the TV show *The Queen's Gambit*, whose protagonist is a female chess prodigy. It was, he said, 'propaganda' designed to make us believe women were smarter than they actually are. The rant extended to other films and TV shows. Everywhere, fathers were portrayed as 'bumbling idiots', whereas women were portrayed as physically and mentally superior. All of Hollywood was in on it. He had a particular gripe with action movies that showed heroines successfully taking on multiple male adversaries. 'That would never happen!'

'I was on track to be a chess grandmaster, but I diverted to fighting instead,' he beamed, pointing to his four framed kick-boxing world-champion belts.

Tate continued to opine about women's brains, and about how the coronavirus pandemic wasn't real. He spoke, as always, with the authority of an expert – and no doubt his millions of followers saw him that way. This annoyed Matt. It's one thing, he thought, to gain an audience by giving life advice on masculinity, fighting or making money. But why should millions of people believe a totally unqualified man's views on something like a pandemic or neuroscience?

'I have a question for you,' Matt interjected. 'If, say, you had a serious engineering problem, like your car was broken, and you needed someone to repair it. Would you trust me to repair it?'

'Fuck, no,' Tate answered.

'Why not?'

'Because you're not qualified.'

'Ok. So, are you an expert in epidemiology or biology?'

'Oh, we're talking about experts?' Tate bristled.

'Are you, though?'

'I don't need to be.'

'Because if you aren't, then why would I trust your opinion on whether we should wear a mask? Or your views on coronavirus?'

'Very good,' interjected Tate.

'Why would I also trust your opinion on women's brains or any of these other issues? Because I don't think that you have done the same level of studying these things as the professors and academics you disagree with.'

'Do you think that the professors and the academics and the studies which are used to support the enslavement of man are completely accurate?'

'Well, I don't think that the enslavement of man is a thing that's going on.'

'Locking people in their houses, taking their businesses away, preventing them from leaving their house?' Tate fumed. 'And forcing them to cover their face is not enslavement?'

Like his rant on *The Queen's Gambit*, this revealed something about Tate's opinions, based as they were in rebellion against some perceived agenda to enslave men, rather than in any rational deduction. In this respect, they resembled leftist revolutionary discourse. One could imagine similar claims being made on the opposite end of the spectrum: TV shows as patriarchal propaganda or public-health decrees being used to prop up racial hegemony. Maybe the appeal of Tate's 'movement' to men was not its rebellion against anything real, but rather the adolescent act of rebellion itself. A new kind of punk.

And, like punk, it was an appealing escape for young people who felt depressed, alone or left behind by the world. But there was one major difference: whereas rebellious youth movements of the past could trace many of their issues to a system of oppression that needed to be torn down, this was a rebellion of the unoppressed looking for an enemy to blame. So, where did that rebellious anger and energy all go? What was it directed towards? Covid lockdowns, gender politics and making money, it seemed.

Worried he had threatened continued access to the War Room with this challenge, Matt defused the conversation. 'Can you show me what's behind there?' he asked, pointing at a large metal door.

Tate used a thumbprint scanner to gain us entry into a cigar lounge. Inside was a safe which he opened, revealing several passports, millions of dollars' worth of watches and gold bars. Tate continued to explain his theory of gender, detailing how men suffered from inequality because they were expected to fight on the front lines of wars, whereas women got to 'choose husbands from the winning side'.

Tate's points were wrong on too many levels to dispute in real time. Like entire Rubik's Cubes, his falsehoods would take too long to unscramble, and where would you start? He spoke of men having 'higher societal pressure' than women, because whereas women were just 'expected to be pretty', men were expected to be 'tall, rich, smart, interesting, funny, well connected and charismatic'. Had he considered that being defined by prettiness rather than other traits like intelligence was itself oppressive, or that handsome, stupid men also succeed in society, or that women had fewer avenues to wealth, or even that most people did expect women to be intelligent, charismatic and a million other things all at once? But to ask these questions would be to forget that his was a discourse designed for TikTok, where the intention was to draw fans in with a kernel of truth, and hope that they wouldn't question the rest. Matt turned to a topic we had been curious about: Hustlers University.

'I can't say too much about it, but I run Hustlers University, which is currently the biggest online educational platform in the world. I teach people how to make money with modern wealth-creation methods. We've grown extremely fast: 110,000 students now inside of a year. So, we are literally the largest online university on the planet, and the only one that's actually of value because we teach people how to make money for real, not bullshit garbage. Do you have a degree?'

'Yes,' said Matt.

'How many cars do you have?'

'None.'

'Do I have a degree?'

'I don't know. Do you?'

'No. How many cars do I have?'

'Quite a few.'

'So, that just proves that higher education is a fucking scam. It's a lie. I've been telling people for a long time. It's a lie and it's a scam. And they agreed with me, they said, "but what else am I supposed to do?" With me being the man I am – a man of action – I created my own school. How much money do you think I make a year?'

'I would guess that you make about one to two million dollars a year.'

'You're in trouble because you're about to do the War Room Test and you're already proving an absolute lack of perspicacity. I said to you earlier that there were 110,000 students inside of my school. If you were any kind of serious journalist, you'd know how much my school costs – $49 a month; 110,000 times 49. It's about $5.5 million. A month.'

Later that night, back at the hotel, we delved into Hustlers University to find out what 'secrets of wealth creation' it taught. It was an online platform that contained a chatroom and different courses in things like e-commerce, copywriting and trading crypto-currencies.

Moderators encouraged 'students' to share videos of Tate saying controversial things. If someone signed up using your link, you got 48 per cent of their fee. That was one way that Tate became famous and rich so quickly – by incentivising the internet to do it for him. This goes some way to explaining why there are so many videos of Tate on social media. It isn't him posting these – it's his army.

This ingenious method, combining affiliate marketing, social media and shock content appeared to be central to Tate's agenda.

But there was another component to Tate's marketing. He was able to directly address depressed young men, make them feel heard and then offer himself as the solution.

'"It's ok to be sad because I'm a fucking loser and you don't understand because it's ok",' Tate mocks, in one video, imitating the millions of depressed young men who stumble upon him. 'Bro, I don't give a fuck how depressed you are. And the world doesn't give a fuck. If depression is crippling you so badly, why are you defending it? Why are you so desperate for depression to be real? You fucking dumbass. You motherfuckers who aren't happy need to learn to be grateful. Even though you're a little fucking worm, sitting in his mother's basement with his hand covered in his own jizz, there's still someone out there who would swap lives with you, believe it or not.' Would it be less depressing if his hand was covered in someone else's jizz? Perhaps, actually.

A common refrain of Tate's was, 'You can either keep on smoking weed and playing video games and be a loser forever, or you can join Hustlers University'. And this shaming continued once inside the chatrooms. One thirteen-year-old said, 'Literally my whole day is fucked, I feel like shit, disgusted with myself, everything. I not only didn't go to the gym like I was supposed to this morning, but I relapsed and jacked off like an idiot.'

A senior War Room member responded: 'Cherish your experience of shame and embarrassment.'

Another student said in the chatroom: 'Guys this thing about "Everything is a war" perspective . . . Man it makes everything so much easier, so much more meaningful. It's so much more easier with time to get over your downs and wake up from your downhills, it's a war, that's what it is. War war war. You give up in war, you die.'

Hustlers University doesn't just target young boys. It has also helped create a new global subculture of young and middle-aged men who are now ubiquitous on social media. They post pictures with captions like 'wealth is a mindset'. They live in places like Dubai and Miami, pose next to supercars (which they often don't own), post videos of themselves buying Rolexes (or pretending to buy Rolexes) and frequently recommend signing up to particular financial schemes or purchasing certain cryptocurrencies. They talk constantly about working hard to become rich, but strangely the only two methods of making wealth that seem to exist in their worlds are trading cryptocurrencies and forms of e-commerce like drop shipping (selling stuff directly from manufacturers to customers so you never have to spend money acquiring stock). Almost all of them do combat sports.

'Make the year your own bitch,' says one video by Luke Belmar, a crypto-trading, Rolex-wearing internet personality who frequently references Tate on social media. 'Take the year and own it once and for all. Every single year you get shit on, dude, every single year you get smacked left and right. You wake up – you're anxious. You go to sleep – you're depressed, and you're tired. You wake up – you got nobody in your corner. You go to sleep, you're lonely. Like, dude, what the fuck is going in your life? What kind of year are you trying to live?'

There will be some men who feel unaccomplished, and whose happiness may be improved by tough-love encouragement to 'stop smoking weed and playing video games' and instead work at something productive. But too often it seems the work that young men are being encouraged to do involves purchasing courses from Tate himself, rather than going after their individual aspirations. This has made Tate millions of dollars.

While we tried to figure out whether anyone had used the method of manipulating people into buying aspirational 'self-help' courses to get rich before, we stumbled upon the 'fake guru' technique, developed in the 1980s by a man named Tom Vu, a Vietnamese immigrant based in Florida who became famous for a series of late-night infomercials. These involved a supposedly wealthy figurehead who promises to reveal the secret to gaining a fortune like his – if you buy his seminars and courses. To pull it off convincingly, the figurehead must fully commit to playing the role of a successful businessman, hiring supercars and posing with models to advertise his success to the world.

'The knowledge you will learn in my seminars', he instructs, as the camera zooms out to show two bikini-clad women at his side, 'will make you financially independent for the rest of your life.' Then, in the next shot he is standing on the deck of a yacht. 'You don't have to ask your boss for a raise anymore. You can give yourself the best raise of your life. Come to my seminar.' These seminars can cost up to $16,000.

Vu was later sued by former students and investigated for false advertising, though never formally charged with a crime. He was, however, the forerunner of a technique that has since exploded on social media.

There's YouTube 'venture capitalist' Dan Lok, author of *F.U. Money: Make as Much Money as you Damn Well Want and Live your Life as you Damn Well Please!*, who claims to be an expert marketer and, like Vu, has a rags-to-riches story about his ascent. He posts videos of himself 'closing deals' and always redirects people to buying his courses. Lok has 1.8 million Instagram followers.

Then there's Tai Lopez, an 'aspiring renaissance man, an author, a member of MENSA: the high IQ society, and a self-made millionaire in his 20s'. Lopez's Instagram bio boasts: '1.4 Billion YouTube views. 545,000 paid students.' And, of course, the call to action: 'DM me "money" to get what I think is the best online business in 2023.' Lopez has 2.8 million Instagram followers.

These early influencers have given rise to a whole ecosystem of smaller fake gurus – those who learn the only real lesson in making money from fake-guru courses, which is to start selling your own. Luke Belmar, mentioned above, is the founder of the Capital Club, to which membership costs $369 a year. The Club offers courses like 'Freedom entrepreneur blueprint', 'Social dynamics' and 'Unlock ecom profits'. Like Tate's War Room, it sells itself as exclusive, claiming to be 'invite only' and to have a 14.76 per cent acceptance rate. In his marketing videos, Belmar can be seen doing push-ups in Andrew Tate's car park or addressing groups of teenage boys with tips. In one video he orders a boy to 'name five people you can call right now to wire you a quarter million'. The boy sheepishly responds, 'You?' Belmar then launches into another lecture about how having access to people with capital is how rich people become rich. This access is, of course, what you supposedly get when you join the Capital Club.

On social media – especially if the algorithm knows you're a young man – fake gurus are like ants. Once you notice one, you begin to notice hundreds. These men exploit a truth they've figured out about the Instagram era: the only thing that matters is the image you project of yourself. From that first sleight of hand, you can spin an entire empire of illusion.

Like Tom Vu's, a key component of Tate's marketing is to set himself up as the source of true knowledge and discredit traditional sources, such as psychologists, schools and experts. He says in one video, *'Don't bother with studying; you can either go to university, look at books and study and be a geek or you can learn to*

*make some money, because they don't teach you how to make money.
Have you ever seen a college professor with a McLaren and a Lambo
and an Aston Martin standing next to a Porsche? No. You've never
seen any of this. I know how to make cash. We're gonna cut the garbage, cut the gender studies.'*

We noticed a message in the Hustlers University chatroom in
which a young boy asks for advice on how to convince his parents
to let him quit school. Another asks how he can dump his friends
who aren't 'hustling' at his speed. Another is encouraged to ditch
his medications. 'Psych meds are the worst bro, they're not made
to make you better,' the Hustlers University member says. 'They're
made to nullify you, and to keep you a slave.'

These young men and boys are led to believe that they are lib-
erating their minds from the education system, their parents and
even medical professionals. They think they'll become rich, and
successful with women as a result. Instead, their minds now belong
to Andrew Tate, who claims to make $5.5 million a month from
their subscription fees.

We had come to Romania not just to investigate Tate's message and
growing influence, but also to find out if he was a criminal, actively
and currently exploiting women for his own financial gain. Now
that we had been welcomed by him and been marched around his
compound, it was time for our first sit down-interview of the trip.
We wanted to press Tate but were wary that this was day one, so
decided to give him the illusion of a tactical advantage, by sitting
down to conduct the interview over a game of chess.

Looking down at his pieces, Matt asked Tate about his PhD course.

'The Pimping Hoes Degree,' Tate sighed. 'Ok. Which is a play
on words. Of course. Don't take it all too literally. Don't have a

meltdown. I, at one point in my history, most people who follow me know this, owned a webcam company. It's just me telling the story of me owning a webcam company.'

Jamie interjected, 'I saw on your website that every single webcam worker starts off as your girlfriend . . .'

'Well, that's not true. It's literally not true that I had seventy-five women working for me that all started as my girlfriend. We were a professional business, a professional outfit.'

'*But* some of them . . .?' Matt prodded.

'Did some – some – of my girlfriends, who were my girlfriend, and then they saw the business and were like, "Oh, cool. I'll try." – yeah! But this was many, many years ago.'

'Didn't you at one point say in one of your podcasts that, with the "girls that started as your girlfriend", and then did work for you in the webcam industry, one hundred per cent of the profit went to you?'

'I didn't say that. Ultimately, the profit went to me in that we were a couple. The King and Queen worked together just like [on a] chessboard.'

Trying a different route, Matt asked, 'Have you heard the term "loverboy" before?'

'The Loverboy Method? Yeah, yeah. But these girls were not prostitutes. These girls were girls sitting on a computer most of the time, fully clothed like an office job. You've got the girls who work at Vice HQ, sitting on a computer, just talking and typing. That's what these girls did. Less than 20 per cent of the girls who work for me even took their top off. They'd just sit there and talk on a computer. So, it's not . . . There's no loverboy involved. It's a matter of . . . it's a very professional outfit doing it, very professionally, providing a very professional service. The girls got paid ridiculous sums of money. I've made more women millionaires than you'd possibly believe. I've absolutely done more than any feminist in that regard. So, there's no loverboy involved. There's no forcing girls to do something they don't want to do. There's no sex involved.'

'But I guess one of the concerns that people have about the Loverboy Method—'

'Ok, no, firstly, let me let me correct you, because I'm a professional—'

'Is that people might consider it a form of grooming.'

'Nobody has concerns. Nobody is going to sleep at night giving a fuck. People don't like me, right? That's fine. I'm very aware of the image I give out. I understand why it's going to annoy some people. Especially life's losers. They're trying to find a vector to attack me through. That is very different to concern, right? There's no female who's come out saying, "I worked for Andrew, and it was exploitative". Not one. This is just an attack vector. What they're doing. It's an attack vector!'

Matt tried to interrupt Tate's rant, but Andrew scolded him, repeatedly claiming that 'no women ever complained . . . Please don't interrupt me. Please don't interrupt me. Ok? I'm not going to sit here and discuss a scenario which is completely not true. We can talk about attack vectors. That's fine. But for you to sit here and pretend that genuinely goodhearted people have some serious concerns about the wellbeing, that's all bollocks. That's not true. Because nobody has any concerns. No girls are complaining. It was years ago.'

CHAPTER FOUR

Family Ties

It's difficult to overstate the influence that Andrew and Tristan Tate's father had on them. Emory Andrew Tate II was born in Chicago, Illinois on 27 December 1958. (Andrew's full name is Emory Andrew Tate III.) Emory Sr was an international master in chess and won the Indiana state championship six times. The grandmaster Maurice Ashley called him a 'trailblazer for African–American chess'. On 17 October 2015, Emory Andrew Tate II died at the age of fifty-six, after suffering a heart attack during a chess tournament.

The day we arrived at the Tate compound in Romania, Andrew sheepishly handed us a piece of paper with a story written on it. He said it would be read out to all the War Room attendees when they arrived and he was allowing us an early look. It began:

And so it happens that on this day, exactly 500 years ago, Master Po died.

At 5am, after morning exercises, Master Po addressed the adepts regarding a mission to eradicate the Hyarushi Clan. They were masters in the art of poisons, a cowardly, yet highly effective skill.

Po warned us that the mission was so dangerous as to be deemed impossible with no hope of return.

In the story, most adepts refused, but the main protagonist and a few others then volunteered to accompany Master Po on a 'suicide mission of murder' for which 'total annihilation' was the 'only acceptable outcome', battling with the Hyarushi Clan. He worried, 'My finger techniques to the eye were lethal, but I had yet to make them bloodless, as per Po's command. Blood on my shirt was unacceptable. Even in the heat of battle, I feared Po would spot my stained shirt and later reprimand me . . .' He then watched as Master Po defeated Yiho, the leader of the Hyarushi Clan, in hand-to-hand combat. Master Po was victorious, but one of Yiho's poisoned darts had pierced Master Po's skin.

The next morning, the adept found Master Po frozen, apparently dead, in the lotus position and 'suppressed a deep cry, the effort ripping an important abdominal muscle'.

But then, Master Po unexpectedly awakened. 'In a full voice, if a bit hushed, he asked: "Why is there blood on your shirt?" Upon return to Wudan, he punished me severely,' the story ended.

Tate was coy about who Master Po was meant to be, but it wasn't difficult to figure it out. In a tweet, he captioned a photo of his father playing chess with 'Master Po'. On a podcast, he once mentioned his father's death, saying, 'My father died during a chess tournament, which is the best possible death I could've wished for him; he died in battle as he should [have]. He was a warrior his entire life.'

The anime-inspired tribute to his late father was, if a little juvenile, endearing. The Tate brothers adored their father. Tate fans also revere Emory Andrew Tate II as a kind of John-the-Baptist figure.

To this day, they repost Emory's archived tweets with captions like, 'Honor for us to have the privilege to learn and lean on your teachings' and 'incredible insight from a master himself'.

'Master Po' is revered for his discipline over suffering, a theme that is integral to Tate's conception of masculinity ('suppressing a deep cry, the effort ripping an important abdominal muscle'). Tate's followers frequently refer to the mythical realm of Wudan (perhaps based on the mythical Taoist Wudang sect of martial artists), and the 'white path of Wudan' as a journey of hardship one undertakes to achieve power. Tate's War Room has published comic books set in Wudan, in which stories are 'written by Andrew Tate himself' and focus on the relationship between Master Po and his apprentice as they battle 'the Matrix' (Tate's term for the global conspiracy to shut down his agenda to free young men) and 'resist the slave mind'. Excerpts frequently appear on social media.

Tate told Matt about his father when they played chess at his house in Romania, before the conversation turned to his webcam company.

'I'm awful. In the grand scheme of chess. Yeah, I'm awful. I'll destroy you, of course,' he taunted.

'Yeah, absolutely,' Matt accepted.

'But in the grand scheme of the game, I'm not good.'

Matt, resigned to losing, moved a pawn experimentally. 'Let's get this guy out here. See what he can do. He's not going to come to any harm there, is he now?'

'My father was very good. One of the most respected chess players in history. I grew up around chess tournaments. Obviously, I played chess. I was very young. I think you have to be born with a certain thing. I don't know if I ever would have been as good as he was.'

'Did he influence you a lot? Your dad?'

'Oh, absolutely. Yeah, of course. It was his job, right? A father's job is to imprint on their son. That's the whole point of having the last name. The point of progeny and bloodline. Why would I have a son who doesn't want to think anything like me? That's the reason kings had sons and their sons would go and represent the empire. There's the natural state of man.'

'What kind of father was he?'

'He was authoritarian, but that's not a bad thing. That's a very good thing.'

'Why do you say "but"?'

'Because. Because I know what you're going to say. You're going to say he was authoritarian. "So, you grew up from an authoritarian background. So, you're an authoritarian person, blah, blah, blah." I think there's a lot of negative spin put on authoritarian, upright upbringings. There's a lot of negative connotation associated with having a father who is very, very serious about discipline and respect and basic things that have always existed since the dawn of human time.'

'Did he enforce his views with physical violence?'

'Well, that's a loaded question. Did I get hit if I made a mistake? Yes, of course. I don't think there's anything wrong with that. I think that for most of human history, children were hit when they made mistakes. To sit and say that children cannot grow into functioning adults if they get smacked, if they make a mistake . . . Also, I'm not saying "beat children". Of course not. Don't hit a kid for no reason. Don't beat a child. But if a child makes a serious error, to say there's absolutely zero physical repercussion, I think, is wrong. For the longest period of human history, kids were hit. Would you agree that in the fifties, sixties, seventies you made a mistake, you got smacked? Right. So, what's the big deal?'

'I suppose we now know a lot more about child psychology.'

'Do we?' Tate mocked. 'Of course. We know so much more about everything. That's why men are women, and people are dolphins. All this bullshit. For the longest period of human history, kids got smacked when they made a mistake. We built the pyramids. We went to the moon. We built all of civilised society. Every single thing around you was built on the back of children getting hit when they make a mistake.

'Let me tell you something, my friend,' and his next words would turn out to be his most prophetic, 'the real world does the same thing. If you make too big a mistake, if you run your mouth too much or are too loud and too obnoxious, you're too disrespectful, that's what's going to happen. You're going to get hit. So, I don't think there's anything wrong with a child learning that lesson early – that there's authoritative figures in your life. The bottom line of punishments always comes back to violence.'

'So, if you were to you deal with your own kids, would you do the same thing? And would it be easy for you?'

'*If* I had children? If they made a mistake, which I deemed was a serious error. Depending on the mistake, depending on the situation, depending on the child, depending on a bunch of factors, I would say that there is a possibility of physical punishment. That does not mean I'm going to beat my child at random, does not mean my child will be abused, does not mean I'm an abusive person. It means that in certain scenarios I would deem a physical punishment necessary. That is the standard throughout human history. It's the standard on 99 per cent of the planet still today. It's the standard even in the West, in most places: you fuck with your parents too much, you get a smack. So, don't sit here and pretend that's the worst thing in the world. You would say we've learned more about child psychology, blah, blah, blah. Well, I'm talking about all of human history, right? Perhaps you're right. I'm not even saying you're wrong, because I'm a professional. What I'm saying is that your worldview is untested. My worldview is tested. It built modern society. We'll talk in a couple hundred years. If you don't die and be a pussy.

'Now move. Lose your queen.'

Matt moved his queen to her inevitable death.

'I'm taking your queen. Story of my life. If your father is raising you and you're standing in his face and disrespecting him, you should learn the lesson that if you disrespect a full-grown man, there's a physical repercussion. I was raised perfectly. I could not have hoped for a better father.'

'Do you think that really shaped your worldview?'

'I think what shaped my worldview is that my father was an exceptional individual, so having an exceptional father made me an exceptional man. Exceptionalism was always a subject that was discussed. It was something that was always talked about at the dinner table. Expectations were always ridiculously, ridiculously high. I was moved up many grades in school. I aced every single test. I was not raised with, "I hope you're happy", I was raised with "I hope you're a professional. I hope you conduct yourself in the right way. I hope you're a fantastic man – and being a fantastic man isn't about being happy." You can be a fantastic woman if you focus your life on being happy. If you're a man and you only focus on hedonism, you are not going to be a good man. In fact, I'd argue you'd be a very bad man. You see the people on earth today, the men who are out here doing drugs, being idiots, running around drinking all the time, and their only concern is being happy – they are not good men. The good men of society that do good things for society, do things they don't want to do because they feel a sense of duty and honour. So, being happy as a man really is not so important. I was never raised to be happy. I was raised to be fantastic at different things.'

According to this way of thinking, being happy is frivolous and feminine and therefore if you are a man, you should suffer and accomplish things. Maybe that's why Tate has managed to sell so many courses – he has wedded insecurity about productivity to insecurity about masculinity.

'The feeling of superiority is intrinsic to masculine contentment. You feel happy when you feel BETTER than others. We've evolved to compete,' says one of his Instagram posts.

But was Tate as productive as he claimed to be? Or was this all part of the carefully crafted illusion to make others feel insecure enough to buy his courses? Tate tells people he never had time for fun, because he was always working. But he certainly seemed more hedonistic than he let on, lounging around the pool with a cigar and chatting shit with his brother all day.

One woman who knew him back in Luton in 2015 told us that while Andrew and his brother claimed to be incredibly hard-working, in reality they would just sit in their underwear most days watching reruns of *Come Dine With Me* and *Maury*.

'Great men' of history seem to be obsessed with talking about their work ethic. Napoleon told Méneval, his private secretary from 1802 until 1813, that he worked sixteen hours every day. Elon Musk is another man who harps on about how much he works, claiming to sometimes do 80- to 100-hour weeks – and yet somehow he finds the time to level up his video-game characters (if you know about video games, you know that it's very unlikely he would have reached level 100 in Diablo IV while also working the hours he claimed).

Whereas most of us possess an inner critic that tells us to work harder, but we try to counter this with compassion, Tate basically asks us to scrap the self-love and keep beating ourselves up about our insecurities. We are lazy. We need to work harder. Otherwise, other men will outperform us and women won't love us.

Tate frequently told his followers a story about losing a chess tournament when he was seven years old, and his dad's anger that followed. 'And I said, "But I was tired, Dad," because we drove from Goshen down to Indianapolis which was a six-hour drive. He got furious. He said, "Andrew Tate, you, don't make excuses." And I remember, he kept me up late for the next week and a half. I'd be up at six for school, and he'd keep me up to three, four in the morning playing chess. I'd sleep like two hours, get up, go to school, I'd come home. My mum would go crazy: "Let him sleep, Emory!" And he'd be like, "Quiet, woman. Chess, chess, chess, chess." For about a week, I was running on two hours of sleep, and he was giving me these grandmaster chess puzzles from a book at, like, 2:30 in the morning. I remember him sitting with whiskey. He'd be drunk and his friends would be laughing. I'd be sitting there trying to keep my eyes open, trying to complete the chess puzzle. And after day five, I finally worked one out and he said, "Look, see, you're tired, but you did it because it's easy to come up with excuses when you lose." You have to perform.'

We had heard Tate tell this story to others in person. He did so with a smile and a nostalgic glint in his eye. His audience would give him a knowing chuckle. But to Matt, parts of it sounded abusive. Whether it was true or apocryphal is difficult to say. What's certain is that it served a purpose. It was part of the myth-building – the path of Wudan – whereby Tate achieved superhuman status through the suffering and hardship 'Master Po' put him through.

But who was Tate's father, outside of the myth? To find out, we tried to build a picture of the real Emory Andrew Tate II. Luckily, it turned out, he was an early adopter of Twitter and left behind an intriguing digital footprint.

For one thing, he had his son's tendency to catechise on the virtues of 'Tateism'. On 22 September 2012, he tweeted: 'Life only has 3 categories. Cause and effect. Purpose and intent. Action and reaction. When you master all three realms you begin Tateism.'

His tweets also contained conspiratorial leanings. On 28 February 2013, he posted: 'It appears the insanity of the ruling elite is exposed worldwide now. They will kill you. Keep your mouths shut, behave as sheep. #sadlife'. A comment on this tweet suggests that Tate's followers see his family as spiritual leaders akin to self-help gurus or political thinkers. '10 years later, Salute Prophet Emory Tate,' it says. If you think this is said in jest, think again. Another reply even quotes scripture, 'All those the Father gives me will come to me, and whoever comes to me I will never drive away. John 6:37.'

Emory Tate's tweets also hint at a misogynistic, right-wing worldview. On 13 September 2012 he said of the convicted domestic abuser and NFL player Chad Ochocinco Johnson: 'Ochocinco not NFL? Chad Johnson? Got arrested beating a woman? Now, like or not, we got a real brotha. #bleed.' And in 2015, he posted to Facebook a brutal denouncement of the women who Bill Cosby assaulted: 'I just figured it out!!!!!!!!!!!!!! How many of Cosby's accusers were already young drug using c*** sluts . . . looking for the payday on the biggest black dick in the business??? How many brought their own drugs? Clearly weed was smoked and alcohol imbibed in huge quantity. Now one pill and one poke from Bill, and the whole story is of a damsel in distress? Then who is this whore in dis dress?' We found this post because Tate himself tweeted a screenshot of it.

Another tweet from 28 March 2013 reads: 'Gays (esp men) can't reproduce so they need YOUR children. Men will marry men to get tax break/govt benefits. Gay divorce will clog courts. #NO '

Keen to delve further into the Tate family, Matt managed to track down a cousin of Andrew's. She spoke in a way that was immediately familiar, and claimed she'd led a far more incredible life than Andrew Tate – like Tate she needed little prompting to chat about her own ventures and grand plans.

Asking her about Andrew, she referred to his 'orchestrated fucking press,' calling it 'corny' and telling us she doesn't click on his posts because that's what he wants everyone to do.

She went on to say she couldn't even speak to certain members of her family about Andrew because they think it's all a conspiracy, and that he's being set up. She said one of her family had been bragging about him just a few days before chatting to Matt, saying how successful he was, and that they've 'seen the cars'. She recounted: 'And I'm like, "What the fuck? [. . .] do you know what he's doing to women?"'

We were most interested in what she had to say about Emory Tate Jr II. She explained that he was a 'high-IQ individual', but that he lacked the 'day-to-day tools' it took to live a quality life. 'So, he would always be dressed bummy and, like, not showered'. She went on to say that her mother enjoyed his company because he was so eccentric, and when he came to town she'd listen to 'all the crazy shit this motherfucker had to say, like being electrocuted.'

She laughed at the memory, before continuing. 'Electrocuted on an escalator. While he was spying. For Russia.'

'For Russia?' Matt asked.

'For Russia, yes. And he spoke Russian fluently. He spent a lot of time there. When the escalator he was on electrocuted him, it marked him, and he showed my mother a mark. And he said that that was an attempt on his life.'

'That's crazy.'

Tate once claimed on a podcast* that his father worked in air-force intelligence, translating bugged conversations, and held 'the record for the fastest assimilation of a foreign language for learning Russian fluently in fifteen days, head to toe'. We have no doubt that Emory told his family this was the case, nor that he spoke Russian and worked for the military. But fifteen days? Tate said he knew this to be true because he had been messaged on Facebook by one of his dad's colleagues in airforce intelligence, who claimed that his father learned languages in an 'inhuman' way.

On the podcast, Tate goes on to explain that his father was discharged from the military after he was diagnosed with narcissistic personality disorder (NPD).

According to Tate, Emory claimed that the NPD diagnosis was the result of a disagreement between himself and his commander over the translation of a single Russian word. If Emory had accepted the discharge, he would have gained a military pension. But he refused and quit, stating, 'My sanity is not for sale'. According to Tate, when the family was broke, his mother Eileen would shout, 'You could have had money, Emory!' and Emory would repeat this line in response.

In response to the cousin's story about the botched assassination attempt on Emory, Matt asked her, 'Did you ever get the sense

---

* https://www.youtube.com/watch?t=13141&v=iv-C4CVGk28&feature=youtu.be

that maybe he could have made that shit up, or do you think it's all true?'

She said she thought Emory and Andrew shared a desire to feed off the shock of others. 'So, it could have been sixty per cent real, forty per cent bullshit, you know? [. . .] Who the fuck knows?'

Hearing this story reminded us of one of Andrew Tate's videos, in which he dresses as Neo from *The Matrix*. He claims to hold the key to 'breaking free from the Matrix'.

Maybe the main trait Andrew Tate inherited from his father was not chess prowess or a superhuman work ethic but being a brilliant fabulist. More than this, both Tate and his father appeared to blur the line between reality and fantasy to make themselves more interesting. In Emory's story, he was an action hero battling Russian agents. In Andrew's, he is Neo, battling the Matrix.

One of the biggest questions about Tate is whether his persona is genuine or a performance. Perhaps to a generation that grew up with social media, this distinction is of diminishing relevance. Tate was an early master of this grey space between self and performance, but the next wave of influencers is continuing his work.

A recent example is HStikkytokky, a twenty-two-year-old fitness influencer who, like Tate, is known for outspoken, often misogynistic rants ('The majority of black girls aren't fit', and 'Here is a message to all women in the world: If you are fat, sort it out. You got one job.'). He has around 750,000 followers on Instagram, where he posts videos and photos of his lifestyle in Dubai. Fast cars, Rolexes, women in bikinis, boats . . . He was one of the fastest-rising influencers to come out of the UK in 2022. Early that year, he posted an extraordinary video, in which he addressed his followers: 'Guys, I'm gonna clear this up because it's just fuckin' my mental so bad. I've been living a lie. The biggest lie on social media for a while, I think. That car is not mine. Anyone who believed I've got half a million quid and I bought that outright . . . I didn't even finance it; it was rented. I couldn't afford to rent it anymore; that's why it's gone back, and I lied about it being crashed. And yes, on top of that, the watches . . . They're all my friends' watches. Not even my friends, just people I know who let me wear them for a few weeks for a bit of social promo on the back-end for them. Life as an influencer is so hard nowadays, and I constantly feel like I have to keep levelling up and doing something else to impress you guys. And I've lost who I was.' He later claimed that this, too, was a lie. No one knows the truth, but to his followers it doesn't seem to matter.

When their parents divorced, the Tate brothers left Chicago for Luton, England, with their mother, Eileen, who was English. It was there that Tate got involved with kick-boxing, winning seventy-six of eighty-five fights. He and Tristan also had their first brushes with fame.

Like Donald Trump, it was under the lights of reality TV that the Tate brothers first began to master their performance of self, and how to shape that performance in relation to an audience's desires.

Tristan appeared on Channel 4's *Shipwrecked: The Island* in 2011, where he played the role of a bully. He insulted a contestant called Kitten, telling him, 'The reason you've done nothing in the real world is the same reason you're leaving now. You're really lazy, you're incompetent, you can't handle a free holiday . . . you're never going to get anywhere in life.'

Andrew first appeared on Channel 4's *Ultimate Traveller*, in 2010. His contestant intro clip is the first display of his trademark cockiness: 'I'm very mentally strong, and if I want to achieve something I achieve it. Because I've never been in a situation so far in my life where I've wanted something and didn't get it.' Next, he was on the seventeenth series of Channel 4's *Big Brother*, but was removed reportedly when a video surfaced of him slapping his then-girlfriend, a webcam sex performer who went by the name Kiss of a Cobra. She assured the public the act in the video was consensual via a post on Tate's Facebook page.

Tate's cousin had told us that his number-one desire was to be famous. On reality TV, he and his brother found an arena where loud, controversial personalities thrived. The final piece of the formula would be social media. Creating a character on social media, though, is a dangerous game.

The blogger Gurwinder Bhogal defines the phenomenon of 'audience-capture syndrome' as a process by which influencers become radicalised by their audiences.[*] On his blog, Bhogal discusses the true tale of Nikocado Avocado, a failed vegan influencer whose audience's increasingly destructive demand for him to overeat on camera led him to replace vegan cooking videos with extreme meat *muk-bangs* (videos where a content creator is filmed eating large amounts of food). He amassed several million subscribers, but became a morbidly obese caricature, emphasising his own apparent grotesqueness in his videos.

Bhogal argues that people's identities are always being refined, and therefore rely on constant feedback from others. He mentions several psychological phenomena as proof: the spotlight effect, by which people tend to overestimate how much others notice them; the watching-eye effect, by which people behave more altruistically in the presence of images that depict eyes; the Proteus effect, by which people in virtual spaces act like their avatars in order to fulfil others' expectations; and the Michelangelo phenomenon, by

---

[*] https://gurwinder.substack.com/p/the-perils-of-audience-capture

which lovers become 'sculpted' by their perceptions of each other into ideal versions of themselves.

Bhogal says that the shaping of a content creator's personality is not a mere business decision, but 'the gradual replacement of a person's identity with one custom-made for the audience'. This especially seems to apply to Tate, who typifies Bhogal's claim that influencers 'find that their more outlandish behavior receives the most attention and approval, which leads them to recalibrate their personalities according to more extreme social cues than those they'd receive in real life . . . becoming crude caricatures of themselves'.

In this respect we, the audience, are partially to blame for Tate, who is reflecting externally the internal tantrum that some frustrated men are having.

The other difficulty with this ambiguity around self versus performance is that it can be deployed as a defence. US podcaster Joe Rogan said of Tate: 'A lot of what he does is like satire. He plays the role of this boastful misogynist . . . but then also says very wise things.' Tate's lawyer has also said he plays a 'character'.

Like his father before him, Tate enthrals people with the stories he tells about himself. His rise to fame has been characterised by blending reality and myth. In order to find out what he was really like when there were no cameras, we would have to speak to those who knew him intimately – from his past.

But first, we would have to make it out of the War Room alive.

PART TWO

Into the
Manosphere

CHAPTER FIVE

Sparring Partners

Our first interview with Tate in Romania had been difficult at points, but we had found a balance. We had managed to probe into his misogyny and potential criminality, but when the interview drew to a close, he didn't tell us to fuck off. Instead, he disappeared into one of the many bedrooms labelled 'out of bounds' and re-emerged in his kick-boxing attire: a black vest and green camo shorts so skin-tight that they threatened to cut off the blood supply to his thighs. Tate said he would be sparring a UFC professional at his gym in Bucharest, and we were welcome to come if we thought the shots of him training would be useful. We wanted to get as much from Tate as we could while we had him, so Jamie played the obedient yes man, and Tate gave him the location of the gym. They would meet us there in an hour, he told us; he wanted to eat first, and black plastic boxes filled with steak and chicken began to appear in his kitchen.

We drove down a series of narrow residential streets, searching for a gym hidden among the rows of uniform flats. Outside one of the blocks, we noticed a collection of supercars parked up, including two Ferraris that were being watched over by a group of security guards wearing the same 007 t-shirts we had seen at Tate's home. One of the guards approached us and ushered us inside. In a cramped space on the top floor, we found a small boxing gym, painted with the same distinctive black and red design that we'd seen in Tate's compound. Inside, Tate was joined by a small group of men, divided into pairs and taking it in turns to repeatedly pound each other, sparring with the intensity of a street fight. Three less athletic men were slouched against the wall, watching Tate and the others with deep concentration from the sidelines. These were some of the so called 'generals' of the War Room – its most senior members and Tate's closest associates, invited to spend time with him in Bucharest before the rest of the War Room arrived for The Test the next day.

After being leaned on by Tate to put on the gloves for himself, Matt endured two beatings, one from Tate and then one from Tig, a senior War Room member, the rest of Tate's generals watched on, sniggering and whispering to each other. An attractive man wearing gold Versace boxing shorts kept pausing his training to look over to Tate and Matt, smiling every time Tate landed a jab. Jamie recognised the man from some of the War Room's videos as Jonathan Bowe, 'the Money Pilot,' also known as 'the Right Hand of Wudan'. Sat on the gym floor was Dylan Madden, another War Room general whom Jamie recognised from social media. Dylan was in his twenties when he moved to Romania to live with Tate in 2019. It was at this point that he began to cultivate a new personality online, talking about how his life had 'levelled up' since meeting Andrew, with Dylan now regularly making six-figure deals (manosphere men are always referencing mysterious, indistinct 'deals'), and sleeping with '10s' (women who are considered a 10 out of 10). Dylan was one of the more public members of Tate's War Room, a 'professor' in Tate's Hustlers University, who now claimed to be an expert in copywriting.

But the most intriguing of the generals was sat next to Dylan: the 'spiritual face' of the War Room, and the self-proclaimed 'greatest hypnotist in the world', Iggy Semmelweis. We'd seen Iggy at Andrew's home the day before, and in War Room videos where he stood in the shadows, shooting animated fireballs out of his hands. An older man, he sported a long grey beard and all-black tracksuit, sleeves pulled up to reveal tattoos depicting dragons and mythical battle scenes. When we walked in, Iggy turned to scowl at us. Every time our cameras panned his way, he shot the same look down the barrel of the lens.

After shaking off the near knockout from Tig, Matt sat at on a bench at the side of the gym, trying to catch his breath. A large man approached him with his hand outstretched. This man wasn't dressed for boxing; he was wearing a black polo and cargo shorts, aviator sunglasses perched on his bald head. Despite his attire, though, it was clear from his size that if he wanted to, he'd have a good chance of annihilating almost anyone in the room. With a gentle smile he offered his hand to Matt.

'I'm Joule, by the way, man.'

'Hey, I'm Matt.'

'Yeah, I'm gonna be looking after you guys for the next few days, making sure everything is ok.'

'Ah, amazing, thank you. So, you work for Andrew?'

Joule broke out into a grin, 'I'm one of the friends,' he explained, making quotation marks with his fingers around the word 'friends'.

'Oh, nice. Ok.'

Joule slapped Matt on the shoulder. 'Mate, you stepped up; that takes balls.'

Matt laughed nervously.

'No, it's scary stuff, bro. You did well.'

'Thank you, thank you. I appreciate it.'

'And you hooked in with the second round as well; it was good.'

It was now that Jamie began to suspect that Joule was on a charm offensive. Matt, however, began to smile. 'Really?' he asked. Even Jamie couldn't work out if the smile was genuine.

'Every man noticed it, and everyone respects you more as a result.'

'Really?' Matt asked again.

'It's good shit,' Joule confirmed. 'That's what it's all about. No one expects you to beat a pro.' Joule then laid out the proposition. 'It's: does he have the courage to step up? And you did. You did well. That's what it's about, man.'

Joule exchanged phone numbers with Jamie. 'I'll stick with you guys, just to make sure you're ok. But I wouldn't worry. Everyone will be briefed and I'll make sure they all treat you well.'

They watched as Tate began to spar with UFC champion Luke Barnatt in an impressive show of skill. Jamie racked his brain for insights, thinking back to the boxing classes he'd once taken with a friend, and fights he'd watched with his cousin growing up. His sparse use of technical language seemed enough to convince Joule, who lit up at the knowledge that one of the Vice crew had spent time practising a combat sport.

'You should get in there with Luke!' Joule suggested.

Jamie looked up at Luke, 6 foot 5, currently landing a left hook below Tate's ribcage. 'I'm not sure . . .'

'When else will you get the chance to say you sparred with a UFC professional? It's a great learning experience. He's not going to hurt you, man.'

Jamie searched for the best excuse he could think of. 'I would love to, but I'm working. It's one thing the reporter having a concussion,' Jamie said, gesturing to Matt jokingly, 'but if I have one too, I'll have a lot of explaining to do to my bosses.'

Joule didn't seem convinced but decided to ease up. 'Fair enough, man,' he replied, laughing, 'fair enough.'

We could tell already that, in the War Room generals' eyes, Matt was passing their tests. He had agreed to spar with Tate and Tig, even though he didn't know how to, and it was a scary experience. Jamie, though, was failing. Even having boxed before, he squirmed out of putting on the gloves.

Jamie was reminded of a childhood memory of wanting to back out of a rollercoaster at Thorpe Park but then going for it anyway after his uncle had sternly told him to bottle his fear. When the ride finished, Jamie had felt like a new person, a smile beaming across his face: he'd not only overcome a fear but was also rewarded with a thrilling experience for doing so. It was one of the first times he could recall feeling insecure about his masculinity. Jamie looked at Matt, who at this moment seemed full of adrenaline, sporting a wide grin. Perhaps there was something to this War Room philosophy?

One of the other men in the gym turned to Joule to ask him a question, referring to him as 'Sartorial'. Jamie turned to him, 'Sartorial?'

'Yeah, in these circles I'm known as Sartorial, or Sartorial Shooter.'

It appeared all War Room generals were required to have unusual monikers.

'Don't worry, though, you can just call me Joule.'

As the sparring drew to an end, we said our goodbyes and left the gym. It was time to get some rest before the five-hour drive to

The Test the following morning. Joule was the last to see us off: 'Call me when you get there. I'll come and meet you at your hotel.'

The Test would be held in the Carpathian Mountains of Transylvania, not far from Brasov, Romania's sixth-largest city. The drive was beautiful, weaving through mountain roads, surrounded by forests dotted with ancient wooden houses. Bucharest was a modern city, and its residents seemed well off. Their GDP per capita is more than double that of Romania's second-wealthiest region, Timiş. But the further we drove from Bucharest, the more the poverty became noticeable. According to a 2023 report from the EU Commission on Gender Equality, women in Romania are poorer than their male counterparts, with 36.2 per cent of them at risk of falling into poverty and facing social exclusion. Poverty is also widely considered to be one of the most significant risk factors for becoming a victim of human trafficking.

Our four-and-a-half-hour journey had become six by the time we'd stopped for a questionable 'hotdog pretzel' from a rural petrol station, and Jamie's numerous cigarette breaks. The sun was beginning to set as we pulled up to Hotel Soimul, a no-frills two-star establishment with small box rooms and a large, beige-coloured dining room. The building was built into the slope of the hill, surrounded by miles and miles of beautiful mountain countryside. Most importantly, it was roughly 100 metres down the road from the hotel where the War Room members would be staying, and where The Test would take place. That was the four-star Piatra Mare hotel, which had an indoor swimming pool and a conference hall, but still didn't match up to the levels of luxury that the 'multimillionaire' members of the War Room claimed to enjoy. (Tate had warned us that it wouldn't be the sort of hotel he would usually stay in: this was The Test, after all, not a holiday.)

We checked in and Jamie texted Joule to let him know we had arrived. Two minutes later he replied: 'Greetings, mate. I'm in the lobby of your hotel, ready to head over when you are.' We went down to meet him while Joe and Charlie finished getting the camera equipment ready.

In the lobby, we found Joule wearing a tight-fitting grey and baby-blue suit. The material clung so tightly to his enormous arms that he seemed even bigger than when we'd met him at the gym. Before we left for The Test, Joule had some ground rules for us that had come directly from Tate. The first was that Joule was to escort us everywhere, at all times, whenever we were in the War Room's hotel or at an activity. If he wasn't available, we would be appointed another chaperone by Joule or Tate. The second was that we were not to speak on camera to any members of the War Room without asking Joule first, who, in turn, would then ask Tate. Both rules were non-negotiable and if we tried to break them, the filming would end, and we would be asked to leave.

We couldn't work out if the rules were in place because they didn't trust us, the 'fake-news' media, or because they didn't trust their own members, who might say something to us that Tate and his generals wouldn't want caught on camera. Probably, it was a bit of both. The rules were limiting, and put us in a situation that we typically tried to avoid as journalists, but what choice did we have? We agreed.

Joule led the way to down the road to the Piatra Mare hotel, and we started filming Matt as he approached the front doors. Joule had obviously made Tate aware of our movements, as he appeared at the entrance just as we made it to the top of the steps. He greeted us, telling us we were 'in a beautiful place for a beautiful experience', and then asked us to put our cameras away. The members had arrived and were waiting in the main event hall where the War

Room's opening ceremony would take place, imposingly named 'the NATO room' after a strategic summit held there in 2004. We were welcome to join the ceremony, but first Tate wanted to speak to his War Room alone. We were sent to wait with Joule in his room, until his phone finally buzzed, letting us know that it was time, and we were allowed to meet the War Room members.

We started recording and walked through a set of large doors, Matt leading the way into a vast and sterile conference space with blue carpeting and metal chairs in rows of twenty. Seated on the chairs were roughly a hundred men of varying ages. They turned in unison to look at Matt, before bringing their attention back to the front of the hall where Tate stood, atop a stage with a huge banner behind him bearing the words 'The War Room', accompanied by the distinctive chesspiece logo. Matt looked around for somewhere to sit, keen to begin his immersion, but every seat was taken. There was, however, a stack of chairs at the back of the hall, and Matt looked at them sheepishly. Was this the first part of The Test? Show initiative? It was all starting to get into our heads. Matt grabbed a chair from the pile and added it to the final row, sitting next to a tall man in his mid-twenties who raised his head to look at him, ignoring Matt's nod of hello.

All the while, Tate stood on the centre of the stage, arms folded, as one of his own cameramen walked up and down the aisle, trying to get the perfect slow-motion shot of Tate presiding over his War Room. 'Got it?' Tate asked. The cameraman nodded. We expected Tate to begin his speech, but instead he walked off stage. At the side of the room there was another row of chairs, positioned to watch over the War Room attendees. Sat there were Tristan Tate, Dylan Madden, the Money Pilot, Luke Barnatt, and Iggy Semmelweis – the War Room generals. Tate joined them as Iggy Semmelweis took his place on stage.

Iggy was as intriguing as ever, wearing a dark grey, wide-brimmed trilby and a custom velour tracksuit adorned across the back with a diamante depiction of the War Room's logo. He sat down, taking a moment to look around the room before reaching for his microphone.

'Ok, let's start out with some ground rules. We are guests in this hotel.' Iggy paused to make clear that what he was about to say was deadly serious. 'Our reputation precedes us everywhere that we go now. We've seen the master and commander in the War Room go parabolic in these last few weeks. All eyes are on us, not just him. We are all guilty by association. We're all misogynists, we're all racists. We're all white,' Iggy then pointed towards two black members of the War Room, 'black,' then pointing at an East Asian man, 'yellow, brown, green, purple. Nationalists.' Iggy paused again, for dramatic effect. 'They won't respect our height, our weight, our creed, our cultures, our religions. We'll all be tarred with the same brush. We all knew this when we joined the War Room. Don't make it easy for them. Be kind to everyone that you come in contact with. Let the other people go onto the elevator before. Be kind to everyone that you come in contact with, the same way that we are in our outside world. We are the professionals. The consummate professionals. Quick with a smile. Light with a joke.'

Iggy spoke with an unusual intonation, pausing between words at random. These pauses grew longer as he completed his warning and began to give instructions to the War Room members: 'Take a moment to stretch out a little bit as you're sitting around. For those of you who are in the "new Great Hall" [which we later found out was a private chatroom on Telegram for members], 'you know what you should be doing right now . . .' Iggy cracked his knuckles. 'Squeeze out the old energy!' His eyes lit up as he looked out at the audience. 'Allow the new energy to flow inside . . .' He made a swimming motion with his hands, almost drawing the shape of a heart in the air. 'For all you trance junkies, this is around the time where you go into a deep and relaxing trance . . .' Just as some of the audience, Matt included, began to close their eyes, Iggy snapped, 'Not yet. Let's see. Because I have a spell to weave,' he said, pulling a piece of paper from his pocket and unfolding it, 'a tale to tell.'

Before he embarked on his spell, we were given one final warning: 'Some of you who have not encountered me before . . . This is your very first time in real life meeting. You might want to keep your eyes wide open because the story is, "He's a hypnotist, and if you watch him closely, you can see exactly what he's doing". And that's fine. That's all fine.' Silence permeated the room as Iggy's gaze panned across. 'For the rest of you. This is the moment when you're going to want to put both of your feet, flat on the floor, and ground yourself into your chair. Put your hands relaxed on your knees or in your lap, as you like. Close your eyes. Take a nice deep breath and sit for a spell.' All the men had their eyes closed, apart from Tate and the generals watching.

Iggy began to guide us in a meditation that felt like something you'd find at a wellness retreat. 'Let the stresses of the day slowly fade away, as you listen to the sound of my voice. And let me tell you a tale of old Wudan.' The men surrounding Matt were in deep trance. Matt briefly opened his eyes to look at Jamie and mouthed, 'What the fuck!?' Once we were in a 'trance state', Iggy read to the room the story of Master Po that Tate had shown us back in Bucharest. In a slow, hypnotic tone, he spent fourteen minutes telling the tale of 'the adept' taking on Master Po's impossible challenge, ending with Master Po, previously believed to be dead, admonishing his student for having blood on his uniform. As Iggy read the final words, 'such is the way of Wudan', silence hung across the room, broken only by the occasional murmur from the conference room's air-conditioning system.

But the meditation wasn't stopping here. 'Breathe in. Breathe out. Breathe in. Breathe out. All of you have answered the call. All of you have gathered for The Test.' As Jamie walked around the room, ensuring Charlie and Joe were getting the right shots, he could see men's faces, bursting with intensity, their eyes pressed firmly shut. 'Breathe in. Breathe out. And as you listen to the sound of my voice, know this: that what happens in the days ahead, will alter, change, transform, your life . . . On to the next weeks, months, years and decades ahead . . .'

With a dramatic flair, Iggy finally removed his glasses from his head. Looking out across the War Room, he went on, ' . . .and the men you now embark upon the test with, you will be knowing for the decades . . . coming. Your sons will marry their daughters. Your daughters will marry their sons. You will create legacies. We will create dynasties.'

Matt surreptitiously opened his eyes again; this was getting really weird. But Jamie wasn't there. He was on the other side of the room filming Tate, stern and emotionless, like a general looking over his troops. Tristan smiled, enamoured with Iggy's performance. Iggy promised the men that by participating in the War Room, they would enter into an elite echelon of men – men who enjoyed 'juicy steaks and smoother cigars', raising 'strong sons and beautiful daughters', led by 'our master and commander'.

The men's eyes had been closed for over twenty minutes now, as Iggy pulled the War Room back to the story of Master Po and to Emory Tate Sr, a prophet among Tate's followers. 'More than three decades ago, a great man embarked on the work of a lifetime, to create the perfect man. It cost him his life, it cost him his marriage.

He trained the young boy to be the very best at chess. Imprinted on him an indomitable will of fierceness, of fury to learn, to process the data. To express himself with joy, with fury, with creativity. With an insatiable lust for life. And then, as the international master of chess that he was, Emory Andrew Tate II, put his most valuable pieces, his sons, into the most impossible situation that the world could ever create. Transporting them across an ocean, into an environment and a culture that they didn't know. Half black. Half white. Into a poor, downtrodden council estate, with only one message to really burn inside of their hearts: you're a Tate; show me what you can do.' Iggy let this final line hang in the air, as the men surrounding Matt breathed in the apparent power of the statement. 'And now we're seeing it. Now all of us are embarked upon an adventure . . . An epic. An odyssey which has transformed our lives already and will continue to transform all of us.'

Entering his twenty-second minute, Iggy continued his meditation, before bringing his sermon to an end with a series of instructions that only just about made sense to us, punctuated with numbers ascending from one to four, 'Centre yourself, gentlemen. And as you continue to listen to the sound of my voice . . . One: each of you will have this opportunity.

Two: slowly as you feel more and more comfortable, within the next . . . Three: seconds ahead. Slowly . . . And only as you feel more comfortable . . . Four: to process all of what I've been talking about for the last few minutes. This time, knowing full well that you will take these lessons, as you process them over the next few days, weeks and months, and make your lives a joyful experience, an expression of strength. Purpose. Will. Power. And joy. And only now, as quickly as you can, open your eyes, and look at me.'

As the men followed his final command, Iggy held his gaze on one particular member, who found Iggy staring at him as he 'awoke', rubbing his eyes. Iggy smiled, 'Hey. How you doing?' He winked at the young man, before looking up at the rest of the War Room. 'Gentlemen,' he said, 'welcome to The Test.' And with that, he got up and left the stage, to be replaced by the 'master and commander', Andrew Tate. This was the moment the men in the room had been waiting for, the moment they'd paid for, and many of them seemed to be in a state of almost spiritual rapture. But Jamie and Matt were still trying to process the oddity of what they'd just witnessed.

'I don't need a microphone,' Tate barked as he climbed the steps to the stage. 'I'm just going to shout.' He had the room's attention immediately. 'Before we begin, I want all of you to understand something. It is not my intention to lie to you. Anything I say is going to happen, is going to happen. And in the next ten minutes, as I speak to you, I want absolutely none of you to lie to me or yourselves.' Tate then asked the room to give him examples of his own greatness, and why he was fit to be the leader of the War Room. Their hands shot into the air.

Tate pointed a man, who stated, 'You're the Top G. Mastery across all sigils.'

Tate smiled, 'The Top G . . . thank you. What sigils? Which ones do I have a mastery of?' All three categories given in response received a nod from Tate: the iron mind, fitness and the cherries. This sounded like the nonsensical ramblings of a lunatic, but everyone nodded in agreement. Tate reassured them, 'Yeah, there's the cherries, there's the money and there's the physicality. Right?' Again, nods of agreement. (In Tate's PhD course he suggests including a cherry emoji in messages you send to women online, in order to spike their curiosity.)

Tate picked out other members of the crowd, who, in turn, gave their reasons why Tate was a worthy leader. He wanted to know what he had done with his life that made him deserving of a following.

'The fighting. All the businesses you ran. And your experience with women.'

A nod from Tate. Another man is called on:

'The things your family taught you?' This one draws a murmur of approval.

'Going through painful experiences?' one suggested.

Tate was pleased, 'Exactly'. He let the room hold for a moment. 'Because, as a man, you have to go through things which are painful, you have to go through things which are traumatic, because you're not going to be very good at being a man if your life has been easy. You can take a man, give him every physical attribute, every God-given gift. You give him a whole bunch of money, great parents . . . But if his life has been easy, he's not going to be very good at being a man. I'm not saying I think he's not going to be a good person. I didn't say he's not going to be a good person. He's not going to be very good at being a man, because to be a man, you must be able to do things you don't particularly want to do. That's the whole point. The best men do exactly that.'

It was a telling distinction for Tate to make, between a 'good person' and a 'good man'. For him, the two categories are separate. When Tate talks about a good person, he is using the word in the ethical sense – a 'good' person is good because they act in an ethical way, or at least they have ethical aims or ambitions. But when he talks about a 'good man', he is using the word in another, qualitative sense. A good car, or a good book is good because it performs the specific functions expected of it well. In the same way, for Tate, a good man is one who performs what Tate sees as the required functions of a man: determination and a willingness to sacrifice. A good man is one who is closest to Tate's idealised 'form' of a man. You might be a morally good person without being a good man. It was clear from Tate's speech that for his War Room, being a good man was more important than being a good person. Factors like being strong, determined and willing to do things they don't want to do are more important in the shaping of a man than whether he is morally 'good'.

Tate brought his audience back to the story they had just heard. 'The first key lesson is there is no shame atop Wudan. All of you are about to face a choice. Regardless of whether you choose option one or option two, there is no shame, nobody is going to be scythed. You don't even have to choose publicly. Nobody is going to hold it against you, there is no shame. We only believe in action and inaction; there's no such thing as shame. Right?' Shame was not useful to men, he explained. 'If you're walking down the street and somebody comes up to you and your girl, he's bigger than you, or you're outnumbered or whatever, the concept of shame is a distraction. You're either going to do something about it or you're not. It's action or inaction. That's how the world functions. Right? So, there's no shame atop Wudan, which is the first thing.' Members shot glances at each other, perhaps trying to distinguish who would feel comfortable saying no in the presence of their master and commander.

'The second thing is, the adepts were asked to go on a mission which they could not complete, and most decided not to go . . . A few for some reason thought, I can't win this, but I'm gonna do it anyway. And that was the story.' Some of the men began to slowly nod their heads, as if they were finally understanding the importance of the story Iggy had told them. 'I welcome you all to The Test. I want to make sure that all of you enjoy this experience, which is going to be transformative. And for a transformative experience which is absolutely and utterly rewarding, there has to be a degree of risk . . . It's impossible for me to give you a reward with no risk at all. So, I had to put something together, for all of you, that involved an element of risk, so that you can feel the reward of participation.' The moment we'd been waiting for was finally coming. Tate was about to reveal what The Test would entail. Matt took solace in the fact that many of the young men in the room looked just as nervous as he felt, some even more. Tate allowed the silence to swell, before finally putting us out of our misery.

'In three days from now there is a cage-fighting event, and every single one of you has been paired with a professional fighter. The professional fighter has been training for the last eight weeks, like he would for any other fight, with the intention of destroying whoever turns up and gets in the cage.' A smile broke across Tate's face as he made this final statement. Some audience members emulated his grin, trying to channel Tate's seemingly unshakable confidence. 'We have professional fighters here from Russia and Poland, and each one of you is paired up. You will fight at a public event, on national television, and . . .' At this point, Tate broke out laughing, holding his hands in the air like a criminal trying to profess their innocence, '. . . it's a real fight! You are welcome to do your absolute best to beat this man. This is not a game, this is not a joke, there is not going to be some surprise at the end. You're going to end up in a cage with a man who is trying to hurt you. Because by doing that, you actually might win, and then there's a reward. Perhaps you might lose, and you can learn something about yourself.'

Matt looked up at the camera filming him and mouthed, 'I think that's gonna be a strong "no" from me!' We knew, however, that Matt would have to go along with whatever The Test was in order to retain our access to the War Room and Tate's inner circle. But could we really put Matt, who, prior to doing several rounds with Tate and Tig, had never fought before, in a cage with a professional MMA (Mixed martial arts) fighter? What's more, a fighter that Andrew Tate had specifically chosen for him, flown in from Russia or Poland? Or perhaps Matt could join the men who said no, and see what they would spend the next two days doing. There's no shame atop Wudan, right?

Small pieces of paper were passed around the room. Tate told us we were to write our names on them, and either a 'yes' or 'no'. We would then be separated into two groups for the remainder of our time in at The Test, but Tate reassured us that if we said yes now, there would still be chances to pull out before the fight. 'You have one hour to think. Talk to each other, talk to leadership, talk to anyone in the room, except for me, don't talk to me. Make a decision.' With this final line, Tate clapped his hands together and walked off stage, heading back to the line of generals.

Tate walked over to Tristan and Iggy, and unbeknown to him, we could still hear him on his microphone.

'What are you doing? This is crazy,' Iggy was complaining to Andrew; he didn't appear to be happy with the idea of this test.

'Don't worry, bro, it's professional. We have ambulances. It's gonna be fine,' Tate replied, chuckling.

They were speaking with a performative energy, and some of the men near by started to notice. Iggy stormed away from Tate and the generals, continuing to complain about The Test and that Tate was endangering the members.

Tristan whispered in Tate's ear, 'Iggy is so good'.

Tate responded with a concealed smile, 'That's cos Iggy is fucking Hollywood, bro.'

Something strange was going on, but we didn't have time to worry about it. We needed to make a decision about the fight.

The men began to form circles around the War Room generals,

seeking out advice about which choice they should make. The biggest circle was forming around Luke Barnatt, with the men keen to hear the opinion of a professional UFC fighter. Matt wandered towards the circle.

'Only you can decide what the right move is, but it's important to think about which decision you will regret more,' Luke told them. 'That being said, this is a real fucking fight.'

One man in his early thirties, sporting a large beard and gold chain, clearly felt ready for the challenge. With a puffed chest, he told the other men that there was no chance that he was going to say no. This was a once-in-a-lifetime opportunity.

The other War Room attendees pretended Matt wasn't there, totally avoiding eye contact and ignoring anything he said. Before we had been invited into the conference hall, War Room leadership had spoken to them about something – it seemed clear they had been told not to trust us.

We went to the back of the hall, out of earshot of Tate and his men, and the debate began.

'I'm not sure you can do it, man,' Jamie started. 'You don't know how to fight. We have no idea who you're fighting. We have limited-to-no control over the situation. It would be kind of insane for you to do it.'

Matt protested, 'What do you mean? We have to do it! It's the only way we'll get to keep spending time with Tate, and it might help us ingratiate ourselves with them. These guys clearly respect fighters, so why don't I fight and win their respect?'

Jamie wasn't convinced. 'Dude, if you get knocked out, if you break a bone, I am liable for that. I don't want that on my head!'

We went back and forth for another five minutes. Then Matt suggested, 'What about if I say yes now; we can always pull out later?'

'Ok, we can do that to find out a bit more. But you're going to have to pull out before the fight.'

Matt wasn't pleased.

'Remember, "there's no shame atop Wudan".' Jamie said with a smile.

Matt grinned and wrote his name and the word 'yes', depositing the paper in the box at the back of the room.

'You're going to do it?' Tristan Tate asked Matt. 'Good for you, man,' he said sternly, patting Matt on the shoulder.

As the hour drew to a close, the men took their seats after finally making their decisions. Roughly one third of them would be joining Matt in the cage, while the others chose not to fight. The paths had been decided.

A dinner took place that night, to which we were not invited. The War Room's doors would be closed to us until the following day, when Matt would join the other 'yes' men in the pre-fight preparations.

Joule was waiting for us in the reception of the Piatra Mare hotel the next day. True to our word, we didn't go anywhere without him and had let him know our exact arrival time. We were escorted through the hotel to a smaller conference room with a row of windows overlooking the large hall that we had been in the day before. The room was filled with around thirty men, some clearly confident, shadow-boxing the air, while others stood nervously with their hands behind their backs, maybe questioning the decision they had made in the heat of the moment the day before.

Tate wasn't here yet, and the session was being led by Sebastian Veru, a short, strong-looking man with full-body tattoos. He was a close friend of Tate's and the owner of the Romanian fighting league, the RXF. Veru's teenage son was helping him hand out War Room t-shirts and boxing shorts to the men in the room.

'Ok,' Veru began, 'you have chosen to fight, so there are some things we must do first.'

Matt and the other men were told that they would need to line up and give their weights, before choosing the songs that they would walk out to at their fight. After this, they would need to have blood tests to confirm that none of them had blood diseases or infections that could be passed on to their opponents.

'Why am I more nervous about having my blood taken than getting in the cage with a professional fighter?' Matt asked Jamie.

'Because you're a psycho, Matt.'

We took our place near the back of the queue, and watched as the men picked their walk-out songs – a selection you might expect, featuring a lot of US Gangster Rap, UK Drill music, and classic American Rock 'n' Roll from some of the older participants. Jamie panicked, realising we'd have to come up with a song we could easily license to play in our documentary, meaning anything too popular was off the cards. We had an idea. Matt would choose an Andrew Tate original. (A lesser-known fact about Tate is that he loves music and makes his own rap songs.) We opted for the track 'Broke Boys', which we found unironically hilarious. The chorus embodied the general sentiment of the song, and indeed of much of Tate's life: 'I been flexin' on the broke boys (That's right) Flexin' on 'em, flexin' on 'em (Woo)'. The music video was like a hustle-culture fever dream, with shots of Tate around the world in nightclubs, driving supercars and surrounded by beautiful women. The verses were just as on brand as the chorus, with lyrics like, 'First class every time I fly out. Lookin' for a property to buy out (Woo). High class hoes wanna ride out. But us only real Gs at the hideout.'

Veru was sat in front of an open laptop, bringing up each fighter's song on YouTube before copying it over into a spreadsheet. Matt's turn arrived and he sat down in front of Veru.

'Song?' Veru asked.

'Yes, can I please have "Broke Boys" by Andrew Tate?'

Veru looked Matt straight in the eye, then burst out laughing. He pulled up the song on YouTube and the poorly produced trap beat emerged from his laptop speaker, accompanied by Tate's opening hook. This caught the attention of the men in the room, many of whom turned to look at Matt, some of them starting to sway with the music, rapping along to its lyrics. Matt finished with Veru and moved to the next station to have his blood taken. As soon as he left, men reappeared at Veru's station, asking to change their song selection to another track from Tate's repertoire.

As if on cue, Tate arrived to meet us in the room. He brought another five War Room members with him, from the 'no' group who had now changed their minds and wanted to fight. Jamie checked with Tate that he would license us his song 'Broke Boys'.

'Of course,' he laughed, 'it's a good walk-out song, actually.'

We were keen to ask some of the men in the room why they had decided to fight, but dutifully following the chain of command, we first asked Joule if this would be ok. It would be, came the answer, but they would pick who we spoke to and supervise the questioning. This wasn't ideal, but it was all we could get.

Joule made a beeline for a tall, muscular man. 'This guy's a doctor,' Joule said, introducing us to him. 'Just to show you the kind of calibre of men we have in our War Room.'

Before we began our interview, Joule gave the man a piece of advice: 'Clear, concise answers. You're a doctor, you felt something was missing. Speak about the value that the War Room has brought to your life. Show that you're not some sort of right-wing extremist for this.'

'So, why did you join the War Room?' Matt began.

'I don't want to be stagnant. I need to grow. It was just a fundamental shift in my mindset,' the man replied. 'What I thought could be bad is actually good. Before the War Room, I used to think, "Why is this happening to me?" Now I think, "What is this trying to teach me?"'

Matt looked puzzled. Everything he thought was bad before, he now thinks is good? That didn't sound like a sensible position to be in. Matt pressed him: 'What about the negative publicity that Andrew gets – for some of the things he says about women?'

Jamie glanced at Joule, who looked slightly concerned but allowed the question to proceed. 'I don't know, man . . . Positive and negative. People have their own opinions. For me, it's positive and he has improved the quality of my life in all metrics possible. It [the War Room] has given me an opportunity to get better. Why would you not want to get better?' A politician's answer.

'But what about Andrew Tate more specifically, and the things he says online?' Matt pushed.

The man took a deep breath in, scrunching up his lip and looking at Joule before responding. 'I think he's speaking the truth.'

'Really?' Matt asked.

'Yeah, we live in a politically correct world, and society would be so much better if we were, like, honest with ourselves and cut through all the bullshit.'

Looking out the windows and down into the main hall, we could see the remainder of the War Room; the men who had said 'no'. They were seated in a large circle of chairs, facing outward, and with a two-metre space between each chair so that each man faced the wall.

Tate re-entered the room. 'What's happening to the guys who said "no"?' Matt asked.

'They're doing something slightly different,' Tate answered, beginning to gesticulate. 'Describing the reasons they didn't do it, how that affects their life as a whole, whether they're going to make any changes in the future to be more ready for opportunities. That's where honour comes from, right? From victory.'

Later on, a War Room member, unbeknown to Tate, spoke to Jamie about what they were put through. The men who said 'no' were assigned to Iggy, and their first task was to face a wall for hours, making a list of all their inadequacies, and the ways they felt they had failed as men.

Following the prescribed chain of command again, we asked Joule if we could interview one of the men who had said no. After an hour, he and Andrew returned, accompanied by a muscular man in his twenties, wearing a skin-tight grey t-shirt and black tracksuit bottoms. The man, who was German, was one of the longest-standing members of the War Room, having joined in 2019, the year of its inception. Before the War Room, he claimed, he was a different man – nervous about everything, even about speaking in public. But Tate had changed everything for him. The young man now made his money running his own private network, which he described as 'similar to the War Room, but German'. It was a paid-for subscription which gave customers access to articles on subjects like 'confidence', 'public speaking' and 'fighting'. If this man sold advice on how to fight, and he had chosen to say no to Tate's Test, perhaps Matt really was making a huge mistake.

'I have huge respect for you right now,' he told Matt. He seemed visibly disappointed with himself.

'You look like you might have some experience fighting,' Matt began. 'You look very strong . . . and I don't! Why did you say no?'

The young German took a moment to think. 'Because . . . I have been in the ring before, but just sparring. And . . . I don't want to scare you . . . at the end of the day, it's just . . . you're getting punched, right. That's it; you're not gonna die . . . But I was like, fuck, professionals? And they're Russians? Like those guys are serious. I can give you all the explanations, but at the end of the day . . . it was just because I was scared. Honestly. I was too scared to do it.'

Matt nodded, trying to show the man that this was a perfectly normal response. 'And afterwards,' the man went on, 'I saw you saying yes, and I was like fuck, the Vice guy is saying yes! So, I felt bad about myself. I really felt pissed about myself. Later when I was by myself, I felt angry at myself. Because I came here to be tested, and I thought we'd be in the mountains, running and doing all this stuff, and I can show everyone how fit I am, right? But then it got to fighting, and fighting is real. Everything else is easy compared to fighting. That's real pain.'

We were told there was no shame atop Wudan, but that didn't seem to be the case.

The young man ended the interview with a direct insight into Tate's appeal for a generation of dissatisfied young men: 'I used to play video games all the time. I played all day, that's what I did. And it felt great while I was doing it, but afterwards, at night, I was like fuck – what am I doing with my life? This is not getting me anywhere. What am I going to tell my kids? That I played video games all my youth? What can I show them? I want to show them experiences! I want to tell them, "Hey, back then in the day, I went to Romania," and do you know what I would have loved to tell them? That I had a one-day-notice fight with a professional, and I fought him. But I will not be able to tell them that now.' He then raised his hand, pointing a finger at Matt, 'But you will. And I think that probably feels great . . . Right?'

CHAPTER SIX

Fighting Talk

The Piatra Mare hotel towered over the ancient Transylvanian pine forests that covered the mountains high up above Brasov. The cool and misty air was a respite from Bucharest's heat. The forest was home to Europe's largest population of brown bears, and residents frequently received 'bear alert' texts from the government after a spate of deadly attacks. Two thousand years ago, bears were driven out of their dens in these forests, tied to planks and carted off to Ancient Rome where they were killed in gladiatorial combat.

Matt woke and glanced out at the trees through his window, wondering if there were any bears there now. Normally, the forest would fill him with calm, but this would be the second day he'd spent in a remote hotel with a hundred men, many of whom distrusted and disliked him, all the while anticipating a brutal beating orchestrated by a man who was eager to see the liberal media brought to its knees.

Jamie asked Matt why he wanted to fight. Matt responded that it was to get more access to Andrew Tate's War Room and continue the investigation. A good answer, Jamie thought. But he also saw something else in Matt's eyes: a familiar look that Jamie had last

noticed one evening at the pub when Matt had been dared by colleagues to climb a lamppost. By the time Matt was ten metres up,
no one could convince him to come down.

Throughout the day, along with everyone who had agreed
to fight, Matt was subjected to a series of anxiety-inducing pro-
cedures. He had his blood tested for HIV and hepatis B and C,
got a mouthguard fitted, was officially weighed in and had his
photograph taken.

Some of the othermen poked fun at Matt. When participants
were asked to fill out their previous fighting experience, one recommended he write 'dancing'. And when the shirtless, pre-fight
photos were taken, revealing Matt's average-sized body, there were
murmurs of 'he's fucked'.

But other men respected him for saying 'yes' to the fight. These
yes-men, and Matt, felt they were part of a group that was superior,
because they had agreed to be filmed getting the shit kicked out of
them (the fights, we were told, would be televised).

Striding back and forth through this pressure cooker of male
insecurity, in camouflage combat fatigues, was the 'commander of
the War Room', from whose brilliantly twisted mind this insane
spectacle had been born: Andrew Tate. A visionary, if nothing else.
He had corralled a hundred men into a hotel in Romania where
half of them had paid $5,000 to be beaten to a bloody pulp, and
the other half had paid $5,000 to feel ashamed. How must he have
felt seeing his plan coming to fruition? Probably not far off how the
creators of *Big Brother* felt when the first episode aired. Outwardly,
Tate projected an air of knowing how things would turn out, but it
seemed as though inwardly he was giddy with excitement that the
mad experiment was actually happening.

Tate sauntered over to Matt with a grin. 'Show me your moves. What's your plan?'

Matt said with a tense smile, 'I was thinking as soon as he blows the whistle, I might just sprint directly at him and go for the legs before he has time to think.'

Tate joked, 'He's fucked. Why are you assuming the gender of the person you'll be fighting? You should know this as a liberal.'

'You did get me there. I'm worried when I take off my shirt everyone's gonna see all my rainbow tattoos and my nipple piercings.'

'Well, you'll be all right.'

At this point our minder Sartorial was pulled away by Tate, but not before introducing us to his temporary replacement, a middle-aged man called Alpha Wolf. Matt's mouth twitched almost imperceptibly upon hearing this moniker. Like all War Room leaders, Alpha Wolf's tight suit, clasped hands, raised chin, furrowed brow and soldier-like step all strained under the constant effort to emit a stern gravitas. He claimed to have worked for Canadian intelligence, once 'enduring torture at the hands of his enemies'. He recounted a story about working as an extra on a Michael Bay film several times throughout the day. It was, we complained to each other, impossible to distinguish myth from reality at this stage. The only option was to nod politely and press forward.

As part of The Test, Tate had told participants that they would be interviewed by Romanian media. Alpha Wolf ushered Matt over to his first interview.

A bearded man with a tangled mass of brown hair sat, holding a microphone, in front of a backdrop that read 'The War Room'. Two news cameras stood on tripods. Beckoning Matt onto a chair opposite him, the man claimed to be a Romanian TV reporter, but his wrinkled shirt and scruffy appearance made us suspicious. Had he been hired by Tate to fuck with us?

'So, Matt, if we were to meet on the streets right now, and someone said, "Ok, you two – do you wanna fight?" I'd look at you and say, "Ok, I'll fight". But have you seen the guys? These guys, when they're in the ring, are animals. For them it doesn't matter if you're a beginner or if you're a pro. They will hit as hard as they can. What's your training?'

'I have no training.'

'What's your background?'

'I'm a reporter.'

'So you'll hit back with some questions?

'I like you,' Matt laughed. 'I'm here from Vice to make a documentary about Andrew Tate and the War Room. And I want to ask Andrew Tate some questions. I want to get him in my version of the cage. But to get to that stage, I know I must play his game. My main hope is that I survive not too incapacitated to interview him afterwards.'

'But the cage is a very dangerous place.' It was as though, Matt felt, they were desperate for him to be afraid.

The interview concluded, Alpha Wolf ushered Matt over to a second interview set-up. 'Different questions,' he explained.

A second, female reporter apologised to Matt as he sat down. 'I'm sorry, I'm nervous.'

Strange, Matt thought, that a professional reporter was nervous to conduct an interview. 'Are you ready for your fight with the professional fighter?' asked the reporter.

'No.'

'Are you ready to take a knockout?'

'No.'

'Ok. But when you will lose, and you probably will do because you will fight with a professional fighter, the images will be everywhere. How do you feel about this?'

'Nervous.'

'Do you think your family knows that you are here?'

'They've specifically asked me whether I'm actually going to get into the ring, and I've said, "Of course not". I've lied to everyone.'

'Ok, good luck.'

As Matt was subjected to the pageantry, Jamie was becoming increasingly concerned for his safety. Over a buffet lunch in the Piatra Mare's food hall, he tried to get assurances from the War Room leadership that Matt wouldn't be seriously hurt, leading to a confrontation in which Tate yelled at Jamie across the table: 'We aren't giving your guy any different treatment than any of the other guys. Either he fights and risks his life like everyone else, or he says no to the fight. I'm not having you make my guys look like pussies.'

Later that evening, Tate threatened to have Matt fight a professional female MMA fighter. Tate's intention seemed to be to force Matt into some kind of moral quandary caused by what Tate perceived to be a contradiction in liberal values – that women were equal to men, but you can't hit them. Matt assured Tate that it made no difference to him whether the professional fighter who would be pulverising him was male or female.

Our team at Vice also expressed concern that Matt was in danger. They saw the War Room as an extremist organisation which, especially after Matt's critical questioning of Tate, might be motivated by a desire to see a Vice journalist humiliated and hurt. Again, Matt told Jamie that he intended to go ahead with the fight regardless of what he or their bosses said. Finally, Jamie accepted the inevitable: Matt was going to fight.

In order to assuage the Vice team's concerns, Jamie arranged a call between Vice's security consultant and Sartorial Shooter. In the call, Sartorial Shooter agreed to have a professional MMA fighter – War Room member Luke Barnatt – teach Matt how to safely fall when grappled. Sartorial Shooter accompanied us.

Would being thrown on the floor by a 6 foot 5 trained killer make Matt feel better? Yes, it turned out. It made it feel more like sport and had the secondary effect of humanising Barnatt, the giant nicknamed 'Bigslow'. Afterwards, with the cameras still rolling, Matt began to ask him some questions, 'What is your mentality when you go into a fight?'

'This may not be what you want to hear, but it's not about winning. It's about intimidating the next person. So, I want to hurt and damage that person as much as possible, so the next person I fight is intimidated.'

'But surely you trained and sparred before entering the ring?'

'Yes, but in my first ever fight I was super, super scared. In the first round I got hit with a lot of big shots. I told my coach I thought I broke my jaw. My coach took a look and said, "No, you've just lost a few teeth". I went back, won by knockout, and then my coach said, "Right, we need to go to hospital immediately. You've broken your jaw." I had broken my jaw in the first fight. I ended up eating my Christmas dinner through a straw.'

Sartorial Shooter interjected, 'Luke – we want him to get in the ring, right?'

We all laughed, Matt a bit too hard. 'Could that happen to me?' asked Matt.

'The worst that could happen is you leave with a couple of broken bones. I mean the worst, worst, worst is you could die.'

'I'll try to push these thoughts out of my head. Why do you like fighting?'

'It's the realest thing you can do. You get to show the world who you are.'

Barnatt spoke about Tate with real reverence. 'He's an actual genius. He's the real deal. A lot of people think it's an act, but then you meet him, and you think, Maybe he's just putting it on. But the more time you spend with him, you realise he's just being him. That's what the War Room is about: be yourself.'

Matt asked about the more controversial things Tate said. Sartorial Shooter, aware of our cameras, interjected to guide Luke in his response, advising him that, 'The main criticism is about misogyny. Speak to that. We've seen how he treats his women. The man is the provider and protector. He's anything but a woman-beater. And he needs to stop saying stupid shit!' For Sartorial Shooter, the criticism of Tate appeared to amount to the simple fact that he had made jokes about physical violence towards women.

'I've been around his girls,' Luke said. 'He's been with the same girls for a long time and they're super happy, super fulfilled. There are lots of other guys within the War Room who have got the same set-ups.'

Matt glanced at Jamie, both wondering what, exactly, this 'set-up' was.

'Do you think all men should know how to fight?'

'It's better to be a dangerous man that's kind than a useless man that's kind – he's got no other option. If you have the capability to kill someone physically in the street – which I have, and I don't – then that's much better than someone who doesn't have the capability and doesn't, because he can't anyway. I believe every man on the planet should be able to go to war—'

Sartorial Shooter interrupted, 'Sorry could we redo that, guys? Let's not talk about violence, man, let's keep it sport-related. I just don't want this stuff about killing in the street. Your point's valid – it's gold. I just wanna avoid those words.'

'Every man should be able to protect themselves,' Luke continued. 'Protect their women. Protect their family. I'm prepared for anything. If I had a problem with anyone, then I could solve it. Me and you, we go to a bar, trust me, I'm the more confident guy (every bar is a battleground when you treat life as a competition between all men). Because I know I can handle every situation that's thrown at me. You can't. You're stepping up, and from this experience, you will hopefully gain some clarity.'

Sartorial Shooter seemed proud of Matt, and keen for him to understand the philosophy of the War Room. He offered to take Matt for a ride in his Ferrari.

Sat in the parked sportscar, with Jamie filming them through the window, Sartorial Shooter explained, 'I have a theory that struggle builds a man, but it breaks a woman. I've yet to see one woman in the corporate world who isn't deeply unhappy in herself. Whereas when I see a woman who submits to a man she respects, I see her femininity flowing. Happiness.'

As operational manager of the War Room, he claimed to immediately kick out any member who displayed 'signs of sexism'. Who knew what, if not his previous two sentences, constituted 'sexism'?

Sartorial elaborated, 'There are many clips of Tate out there saying, "I'm not a misogynist. I provide for my women. I protect my family. I would stand up for my women in a violent situation." That's the reality of who he is.'

'And what', Matt asked, 'do you think his detractors would say about, for example, the phrase "my women"?'

'The phrase "my women", for me, ties into the very traditional values that we have. We believe that for a man to be fully fulfilled, he should do what a man is biologically designed to do. To conquer, to protect, to provide. And equally, for a woman to be fulfilled, we believe that you'll be better served in terms of your happiness if you listen to the oestrogen and the oxytocin in your blood, which lead you towards feminine-based gender roles: which is nurturing, which is caring, which is listening, which is raising a family.'

Matt countered, 'What about a situation where I want my girl-friend, who I love, to be a kept woman, but she doesn't. She wants to pursue a career or something like that?'

'Then find a different woman. Very simple.'

'Andrew is well known for talking a lot about his multiple girl-friends. How does that tie into this idea of a traditional relationship?'

'Well, firstly, I can neither confirm nor deny any allegations. However, in very traditional religions, such as Islam, a man can take on multiple wives. Now, that's not because he wants to have casual sex with many women.'

Matt suppressed an eye roll.

'It's because men', continued Sartorial Shooter, 'at certain levels, can provide for multiple women. Are we going to say that the entire Islamic world that partakes in that practice is bad? I mean, even we can go back a hundred years ago – kings, you know, wealthy men, they would support multiple families. If a man is at a level where he can take proper care of multiple women and multiple families, how is that a bad thing?'

Matt felt a familiar sensation on hearing these arguments. It was the sensation of needing too long to explain why something was wrong, because it was more deeply wrong than most arguments he was used to hearing. To put it in the words of left-wing

YouTuber Hasan Piker when he livestreamed himself watching this very interview after our documentary was released, 'My man thinks *kings* are good'.*

What piqued our interest, though, wasn't their views on gender roles. It was the notion, now expressed by numerous War Room leaders, of 'having multiple women'. Sartorial Shooter tried to characterise this practice as a kind of religious polygamy, but we weren't convinced. After the interview, he told us, 'I also have multiple women whom I take care of on a long-term basis. If a man has an urge to be with multiple women, isn't it healthier to maintain a long relationship where they know about it than just fucking randoms?'

Sartorial showed Matt a picture of a woman who had his initials tattooed near her genitals. These initials, in the same typeface, were embossed on the hood of his Ferrari.

Sartorial felt the interview had gone well, but there were some sticking points. He complained to Jamie: 'It blows my mind that in the West, you can't say "my woman". That people think that's sexist. Would your girlfriend get annoyed if you called her "my woman"?'

Jamie pretended to contemplate the answer when it couldn't have been more obvious. 'I don't think she'd love it, no.'

Sartorial looked puzzled. 'But, man to man, are you genuinely happy in your relationship?'

'Yeah of course, very happy. We get on very well.'

Sartorial's look of confusion hadn't left his face. 'But does she give you blowjobs on demand? Does she proposition other women for threesomes with you? Does she make money for you?'

Now it was Jamie's turn to look confused. 'They're not really my priorities in a girlfriend, to be honest.'

---

* https://www.youtube.com/watch?v=Nkbn5GpL2D8&t=2931s

Sartorial chuckled, 'Don't knock it until you've tried it!'

As promised, Sartorial Shooter took Matt on a ride through the winding Transylvanian roads, hitting 100 miles per hour on sharp turns. He was a keen tutor, educating Matt as they drove: 'Ok, so this is not a normal Ferrari. It's got a full Novitec exhaust and a few other bits and pieces. The engine is a V12, so that's why you get that operatic flavour going through the ribs.'

Sartorial Shooter screeched round a final bend, returning to the Piatra Mare's front steps. Several War Room members were stood smoking cigars on the steps like proud dads at a barbecue. Tristan Tate, who had begun to respect Matt for agreeing to fight, spoke to him about Sartorial Shooter's Ferrari.

'I've got the same car in blue.'

'Well, I'd be lying if I said I didn't want one of these,' Matt admitted.

'I think everyone does. A lot of people pretend money doesn't buy happiness. I would say to people, "What would you do more of if you had unlimited money?" They'd say, "I would travel more. I'd take care of my parents." How is that not happiness? Best purchase I ever made? Eight years ago, when I called my mum and said, "You don't work anymore". Just bought her a new car. The look on her face? That makes me happy. Money absolutely does buy happiness.'

'And can I ask how you managed to get your money?'

'How I managed to make my money?' He hesitated. 'Um. Mine and Andrew's story is linked. Every business we've run together. Every company. Fighting was something we both did together. So, if you know Andrew's story, you know mine.'

This seemed like a deflection.

'I don't know how much he wants to tell you,' he quickly added. 'That's down to him.'

'Got it.'

'But nothing illegal. We're not criminals.'

'Right.'

It was time for the men who chose to fight to participate in their 'face off' – a typical promotional event in combat sports when opponents come face to face to taunt each other before the match begins. Matt and the others gathered outside the lobby. Andrew told them to wait for their names to be called before entering the NATO room. They could either take their shirts off before walking through the doors or as they walked through, but they had to be shirtless.

Andrew's demeanour had changed, and we couldn't tell why. His giddiness at pulling off the event had been replaced with anxiety. He seemed to want to get things moving.

Matt and the other fighters waited outside the NATO room. Every so often, the lift would ding, and bewildered hotel guests in bathrobes would walk out into a crowd of shirtless, posturing men. He felt anxious, but mainly ridiculous.

Matt's name was called. He went through the doors and ripped off his shirt, feeling sillier by the second. As he walked onto the stage at the front of the hall, he noticed that the men who had said 'no' were made to sit and clap for him as he entered, in a final bit of playground cruelty. Once Matt was stood on the stage, between Tate and Luke Barnatt, his fighter appeared. He was shorter than Matt, but much wider. He had a friendly face, and, perhaps sensing Matt's scepticism towards the whole event, shared a brief, knowing look. Matt smiled at him, and he betrayed a fraction of a smile back. Then he shoved Matt in the chest, almost knocking him over.

Matt – 10th August 2022

The next morning, Alpha Wolf greets me outside the Piatra Mare hotel, where I am ushered onto a coach with around twenty other 'fighters'. Each of us has been issued with a t-shirt bearing the War Room's chess-piece insignia. We begin the drive to Brasov, where the fight will be held.

'Keep your chin up,' Alpha Wolf tells me. 'You're going to do great.'

On any other day, his name alone would make me laugh, but on this one I appreciate each word of encouragement from him.

The bus stops, and Alpha Wolf leads me into the venue. Inside, around forty War Room members sit at a dozen tables arranged around an octagonal fighting ring. The Test participants have to wait their turn to fight from behind a curtain. Some try to poke their heads through it, but Sebastian Veru and Andrew Tate yell that they will be kicked out if they do it again.

An oily, grey-haired referee in a suit introduces each fight over the loudspeaker, claiming that if any of us beats our fighter, we will 'win all their girls, all their money'. Some fights are more brutal than others. One fighter doesn't stop beating his War Room member after the bell goes, and Tig has to jump in. Sartorial apologises to Jamie afterwards about this, blaming it on 'roid rage (an outburst of aggression caused by the use of anabolic steroids) and claiming Veru will never let him fight again. Most end in seconds. On one end of the room sit the Tate brothers, flanked by the War Room leadership and a few women we had never seen before. Tate stares at his phone with a look of deep concern. I know why.

Over the past twenty-four hours, the global media have

been running a torrent of negative stories about Tate. Social media platforms have begun to ban his account and some of his content. The War Room leadership, who until now had possessed a sense of momentum and invincibility, were panicking for the first time.

Their quickfire solution was to have Tate donate to a 'women's charity'. Sartorial Shooter implored Jamie, 'How can we kick this misogyny thing? Do you know any women's charities who will take a £200,000 donation from Tate?' When Jamie explained that he thought this unlikely, Sartorial was taken aback. 'Why wouldn't they want £200,000?'

Moments later, a story appeared on Tate's Instagram account. 'I have decided to show what a loving and nice man I am and donate $1,000,000 dollars to charities which support domestic violence against women'. The message continues, 'I will however also donate $1,000,000 to charities which help men with mental health issues. I support men and stick up for men, and the haters and liars think this means I hate women. No. WE CAN BOTH WIN. PEOPLE need support. Not just men or women. Top G has kindness for all.'

All of a sudden, I see one of the War Room attendees get knocked out during his fight. His blood is splattered across the octagon. Sartorial Shooter stands in front of our cameras and demands we stop filming. An ambulance arrives to take the injured man away.

I try not to let the sight of his bloody face psyche me out. I open my phone to see more news stories pop up about Tate's cancellation on social media. No doubt thousands of print and TV journalists are right now reaching out to the Tate brothers for comment. And I, the one journalist in the world with access to Andrew Tate, can't ask him a single question, because I am about to get into a cage fight at his behest.

At this moment, just as I begin to question how I have found myself in this situation, 'Broke Boys' by Andrew Tate begins to play on the venue's sound system, signalling my turn to fight. I walk, shirtless, into the octagon. This is happening.

As I shake hands with my opponent, I remember some advice Sartorial Shooter gave me earlier today: 'Never let him close distance, move backwards and from left to right'. Ringcraft, he called it. That way, the fight will last longer.

'As soon as the bell goes, Matt has passed The Test. I know he's going to lose, but wow, he's actually in there,' Tristan commentates.

My opponent is initially confused, unused to my 'fighting' style of running away from him in an ever-expanding circle.

'He doesn't know how to throw. He doesn't know how to jab,' shouts Tristan.

At this point, my opponent begins to get frustrated at my evasions and so begins hitting and kicking me. I don't enjoy this. Recalling Sartorial Shooter's advice that MMA fights tend to end on the ground, I manoeuvre to 'grapple' my opponent in order to get the kicking and punching to stop. My version of a 'grapple' is to slowly hug my opponent, almost physically requesting him to end the fight on the floor.

Which he does, with considerable force.

'And it's gonna be a ground-and-pound finish. And that is it! The referee calls it. Good decision; he was unable to defend himself. I hated these guys when they turned up. I almost punched Matt myself when he was in my house. But you know what? He's officially won me over,' Tristan beams.

It's over in about thirty seconds. I come out with what feels like a cracked rib, but the other novices have had it much worse.

Andrew is grinning wildly. Each of the War Room leaders shakes my hand. The brothers hug me. 'I'm proud of you,' Tristan says. 'I mean that.'

It feels good to win their favour. A momentary fantasy flashes before my eyes, where I bin my values and ethics in favour of a career as the Tate brothers' third wheel. My conversion would garner so much publicity that we would go on to dominate the alt-right. Maybe I could pull them closer to the centre. Maybe I'd get my own Bugatti. Then I remember why I am here.

The attendees were bussed back to the hotel to listen to concluding speeches. Many had dark bruises and swollen faces. But they seemed to have gained a life-affirming boost of confidence from the experience.

One attendee with long dark hair and thick glasses, who looked to be in his early twenties, stood up to share what he had learned. 'If you take the easy route, it can become a habit. This is the first time where I haven't quit to avoid suffering the sting of the proverbial punch in the face. Because losing sucks, and no one wants to do it. But I'm glad I did it because I feel like my word to myself matters more. I can take myself seriously when I say I want to become a certain type of man.'

In this sense, The Test could be seen as a positive experience for men who used it to overcome self-doubt. But those who opted out of fighting were made to feel ashamed, and the War Room leadership actively reinforced this insecurity in a way that felt harmful.

Luke Barnatt addressed the group. 'The guys who said "yes" – I just want to say, as a professional athlete I was extremely proud of you having the balls to step in and do what you did. Congratulations, guys. For the guys who said "no", we offer you redemption. You get an opportunity to get in the cage and to prove yourself as a man against another opponent. So, we're launching the War Room's fight club today.

'Right now, the guys who didn't compete might be feeling shame and anguish. Might be looking at the people who said "yes" and feeling jealousy. Remember that feeling. You might go home to your family, go on Instagram, and as you're walking the streets you might think, I'm a man. You're not. The only way you can redeem yourself is by stepping up. Don't let this feeling of shame leave you, because it's very easy to let it disappear.'

A nineteen-year-old – the youngest attendee – stood up to say: 'Didn't it feel like a movie these last few days? I feel like that's a great metaphor for life. You know, we shouldn't be slaves. We shouldn't be working nine-to-five jobs. We should actually make our lives into . . . I guess, a movie.'

While his explanation wasn't the most eloquent, there was truth to it. Many of these men had come here to escape the mundane in search of the action-hero type of masculinity promised to them by movies and video games. Tate had once told us that he was 'selling the James Bond lifestyle'. This wasn't just what attendees felt. As we were about to discover from Iggy, it was the intended purpose of the experience. The War Room leaders weren't just teaching men to bring their action-hero fantasy to life; they were telling them to distrust and bend any reality in which that fantasy wasn't true. In fact, Sartorial Shooter would later call his tailoring company 'Custom Made Reality'.

Iggy now addressed them. 'We knew that some of you would say "no". We also knew that some of you would say "yes" for the wildest, craziest, weirdest reasons, but it didn't matter.' He paused for an entire ten seconds as he looked around the audience. 'It was all about your mind,' he said hypnotically. 'To change your perceptions, your relationship with what you perceived as reality. It was engineered. All of it. Including the insurrection. Including the negation. Including the positivisation. All of it.'

The event, it turned out, had not been broadcast live, and the 'interviews with Romanian journalists' were also a sham.

Iggy continued, 'Scintillating tales is what makes the man. Not millions of dollars, not a litany of items. Flashy cars, cool accessories – those are extra. Doesn't matter if you have those, if you don't have great tales to tell. Many of you came to me. Many of you asked for my opinion as to whether or not you should do this. Some of you didn't listen. That made all the difference in the world. My position here in the War Room is unique. I'm not your ally. I'm not your friend. My operations are beyond all your comprehension. But I am damn proud of all of you.

'This was a test. Some of you failed. Some of you passed. But that in of itself – the fact that you stood up and came into it, eyes open, bringing your best self to it – will change your lives.

'As always, I thank the master and the commander of the War Room for giving me this opportunity to work with all of you. It's an honour and a privilege, sir. And it's an honour and a privilege to have watched all of you go through The Test. Thank you.'

Earlier that week, Sartorial Shooter had told Matt, 'Andrew is the most driven and disciplined man I've ever met. He's an expert at creating a tailor-made reality, and his ability to do that in his own life is something that can be replicated and taught. I didn't have supercars before Andrew Tate. I didn't train two or three times a day. I didn't work the equivalent of three or four working days in one day. That's the norm now. His passion to build a tailor-made reality is something that other men, first of all, they see it and they wonder if it's true, then they feel inspired by it. Then, through the guidance of the War Room, they can get out and they can create that tailor-made reality themselves. So, Andrew Tate, for me, to use the Matrix analogy, has learned how to rewrite the Matrix, and that's something that other men can learn from him.'

Tate closed the speeches by inviting everyone, except us, to a party in the hotel bar. 'For the people who want to stay and relax, there's some chicks. Dunno where they're from. Let's have fun.'

Before we left the NATO room, Matt made an attempt to speak to Iggy. Throughout the week we had been told unequivocally that Iggy would not speak to us. But that was before Matt had passed The Test. Now he walked over to Iggy and introduced himself, suggesting that they could speak without recording it to begin with. Iggy gestured at Matt's lapel microphone and pantomimed throwing it away. Matt obeyed. Iggy then did something very Iggy.

He began to walk around the perimeter of the conference room, hands clasped behind his back. Matt followed, imploring him for an interview, saying things like, 'While you may not agree with us being here, this is a chance for you to defend and counter some of the negative press around Tate and his circle'. Iggy remained silent the whole time, walking in long, perfectly even strides. Matt was compelled to keep following him. Once Iggy had led them back to where they started, completing a perfect circle, he turned to Matt and held out his hand. Matt took it.

'You are a brave man,' said Iggy. Then he walked off, leaving a trail of expensive-smelling, patchouli-based cologne.

Had he just cast a spell on Matt?

*

Despite Matt gaining the Tate brothers' favour by fighting, tension was still high as the negative press continued to roll in. Disallowed from the hotel party, we lingered around the hallway and lobby, imploring Sartorial to find Tate for us. At midnight, Andrew agreed to sit and speak to us. There were unanswered allegations we had to put to him, and unless we addressed them, Tate and his team might have been thinking that the experience of The Test had converted us to their way of thinking. We realised we might not get another chance to interview Tate, and this time it was bound to turn ugly. So, we made up a lie that our batteries needed charging and went back to our hotel to pack up our car for a quick getaway.

When we returned to the Piatra Mare's lobby, we could clearly see topless women through one of the hotel windows. They were being photographed. Were these the 'chicks' Tate had referred to?

We walked back in and set up for this final interview. For the first time since we had met, Tate looked afraid. We saw in his wide eyes the face of a young boy holding back tears after realising he has made a big mistake. But he still had a ton of fight in him.

Matt began: 'The first thing I'd like to say is, I think it took a lot of courage from you to let us in here. And I think any time anyone lets someone into their organisation and their life it shows that they're confident in what they're saying and doing. And I really respect that. And I respect the ritual that I've been through. And I do think that having something difficult that you think you can't do and then you do it can benefit people. I'm going to ask you questions about the negative stuff. And I want to give you a chance to respond, because that's my job.'

'That's fine. I appreciate you respecting me for letting you guys in. I do that because I genuinely, genuinely believe I'm a force for good in the world. There's a lot more to the story of Andrew Tate and the War Room and the things I'm doing than the very shallow, fictitious versions you're going to read online. We try and build people up and show them that, you know, a lot of these issues, they're internal, but you need to do external things out in the outside world to feel differently about yourself inside. And I know it may look a bit crazy or a bit extreme, but I really believe that the only way to happiness as a man is to face some fears and then look at yourself in the mirror and say, "Yeah, I'm that guy".'

We discussed the negative publicity he had been getting. 'Would you accept that some of the things you say online could actually cause harm?'

'As a professional, you must understand that your things, the things you publish, can be taken out of context as do some of mine, which is something I will certainly take into consideration moving into the future. Absolutely. But I'm not going to sit here and say that the things I say are purely damaging and that I shouldn't say anything that can inspire people because one per cent of the population might misunderstand it. That doesn't make sense, and that's a very unprofessional way to view the world.'

Matt and Tate went back and forth on this. Tate was beginning to get genuinely upset.

'So,' said Matt, 'the main defence that you've given to me so far is that you think these things are taken out of context. But I think to some extent they are in context: in the context of you and your views. For example, you often talk about "high- and low-value women". How would you describe a "low-value woman"?'

'That's a very specific question to paint a narrative that I support misogyny. It can't be misogynistic if it's not gendered. It's about people. It's about low-value people. I'm happy to answer your questions about anything, but I just find it disingenuous.'

'You have, in my presence and publicly, spoken about unattractive women being of less value than attractive women.'

'The media is so obsessed with purported misogyny and obsessing over one per cent of the things I ever say. And it's very strange. Most of the questions you're asking ignore ninety-nine per cent.'

Matt homed in on a final line of questioning: he asked Tate to explain why he was arrested as part of a human-trafficking investigation.

'The truth is that the police came to my house looking for a girl. At the time they came, I wasn't even in the house. The reason they came is because my brother and I were hosting a party at our house. We had fifty people there. The girl put up some Instagram stories, and her boyfriend in another country called her at the house, said, "Why are you having a party in another man's house?" She said, "Oh, I didn't want to come here. I had to come here. And they won't let me leave." From my understanding of what I've been told by the police, he called the embassy and escalated it. The police saw there was absolutely no crime and within forty-five minutes they said, "Oh, sorry, we just had a call we had to come check out". I was formally arrested. I was not formally charged.'

'Why, then, have the Romanian police said the investigation is ongoing?'

'I don't know the specifics of Romanian police investigations,' said Andrew, now visibly stressed.

Sartorial Shooter, who was chaperoning the interview, stood up, almost in tears, looking utterly betrayed. 'I'm shaking, I'm so angry,' he said and walked out.

Something felt dangerous in Sartorial Shooter's loss of composure. Considering his size, we didn't want to imagine what happened if his tears turned into fury.

'We let you in,' Tate said. 'We tried to take care of you and you're just sitting here attacking us for three hours' [in reality, it lasted an hour and fifteen minutes]. He threatened to take us to court. 'We have a lot of money and a lot of time. You're not interested in the truth.'

We ended the interview in whatever way we could. Tate sat in silence while we removed his microphone and then walked out of the room.

As we left the Piatra Mare hotel for the last time, Tristan was drinking whiskey on the steps with a crowd of War Room attendees. Andrew and Sartorial Shooter now believed that we were enemies conducting a 'hit-piece', but this was unknown to Tristan, who still beamed with pride at Matt. We walked down the steps and Tristan suggested we meet for a drink in London, inviting us to stay with him if we ever came back to Romania. He then made the entire War Room do three cheers for Matt. 'Let's hear it for Matt!' The knowledge that in mere moments his brother, just steps behind us, would tell him about our turbulent final interview, made this one of the strangest and most awkward experiences of our lives.

We wouldn't find out what was really going on in the War Room for several months. We were just happy to be done with it. We drove through the entire night to get to Bucharest, eager to get as far away as possible from the Piatra Mare hotel.

CHAPTER SEVEN

Testimony

We got back to London twenty-four hours later on 12 of August 2022, and, surreally, Andrew Tate was everywhere. Schoolteachers were beginning to complain about his impact in their classrooms, various charities were expressing concern about the nature of his content, and the press and government bodies around the world were starting to take notice. Tate had now been banned from almost all major social media platforms; but perhaps more worryingly for him, Stripe, the digital payment provider for Hustlers University, were threatening to pull their services (something they would go through with around a week later, on 20 August).

All this attention seemed to be compounding Tate's anxieties about the documentary he had just participated in, particularly the final interview. Waking up after his first night back in his own bed, Jamie picked up his phone to find a slew of WhatsApp messages from Tate:

> Everybody wants to remove consent. Everybody. I'm talking
> to them now. If you give us a full and uncut version of the final

interview, for our own records to hold, I will convince everybody
to stay part of the piece. Without that film I can't protect myself
from the hit-piece you're about to do. Let me know.

This demonstrated a surprising level of panic and vulnerability
from Tate. Even him stating 'I can't protect myself' seemed so
wildly out of character that it threw Jamie more than the implicit
threat. He replied, 'I'll get back to you', and forwarded the messages
on to the legal team at Vice. Jamie knew full well that these men
could not withdraw their consent, which they had given knowingly,
particularly because there was a growing and important public-
interest case building around Tate and his War Room.

By the afternoon, Tate had sent another message: *'Need your
email. Legal letters incoming.'* Jamie sent him his email (despite
them having been in email contact previously), but Tate continued ruminating on the issue for the rest of his day. At 8pm he
forwarded Jamie a TikTok video from a controversial influencer
Shannen Michaela, in which she listed the ways that feminism had
ruined life for modern women. *'Do a hit piece on her too'*, Tate messaged. It was 11.10pm, and he was still persistent. His next message
read, *'Lets do a phone call tomorrow with you and perhaps a boss.
Spoke to some war room guys, I'm trying to keep the documentary
together and everyone participating, but need to clarify a few things
with you.'* He seemed desperate to retain some control over our
documentary, but his tone was beginning to soften.

Five minutes into his walk to work the next day, Jamie received
a call from Tate. It was the most cordial he had been since Jamie
had first spoken with him. He was glad we'd made it home safely,
and hoped the journey hadn't been too much trouble. He then
began yet another request for the footage from our final interview,

but this time taking a new tack. Tate told Jamie that he felt he had actually done very well in the final interview, but as a professional, he wanted a chance to review it, so he could improve for his next encounter with a journalist. To us, it sounded like he might have wanted the interview to cut up and release himself. It wasn't a convincing sell and given that the day before Tate had been threatening legal action and predicting an impending 'hit-piece', Jamie wasn't buying it. Regardless, he informed Tate that Vice had a policy of not giving their footage to anyone else, and that he'd have to speak to his managers. Tate pleaded with Jamie to emphasise with the Vice management that he had opened his home up to us, told us about his life and, in return, we should do him a favour.

These conversations would continue in the weeks that followed as we began our edit. But we weren't the only people looking into Tate now – suddenly, everyone was. While the 'mainstream media' grappled with how to discuss Tate, constantly weighing up his growing impact on young people and its significance as a news story, against their fears around platforming his views, content creators on YouTube took a much more liberal approach. Tate had achieved maximum relevance, particularly on the internet, and as a result, YouTubers now covered him with an intensity rarely seen before.

In a matter of days, opinion pieces and reaction videos about Tate appeared on the channels of huge numbers of popular YouTubers. Most of the videos were fairly inane, in which people filmed their reactions to Tate's rants, allowing his clips to circulate further around the internet. Some YouTubers were more considered. Hasan Piker, known as HasanAbi, was one of them, using his videos not only to make jokes at Tate's expense, but to systematically break down some of his arguments and views. Another was Daz Black, known for gaming and reaction videos, who took a similar approach to Piker. Black had millions of followers, and we knew his video on Tate would do well, so we decided to reach out to him.

Matt sent Daz's team a message, explaining who we were and what we were working on, and asked that if he was contacted by anyone from Tate's past in response to his video, he should pass on a message from us, along with our emails. Daz's agent called Matt and agreed. 'Just one thing,' she said, before hanging up. 'We're a little bit worried because of the reaction from Tate's fans after Daz spoke out about him. It has been intense. They even tried to create a fake story that Daz was a paedophile, and it has been picked up by a few websites in America. So, be careful.' Daz's video went on to get millions of views within a matter of days, and shortly after its release, some emails started to come through.

We received a flurry from women from the UK who had known Tate back in 2015 and 2016, mostly from the areas surrounding Luton, his hometown. Jamie called each of them, and the stories they told all sounded relatively similar. They were in their early twenties when they had been approached by Tate, either online through social media, or through a male friend who claimed he was 'friends with Tate', recruiting models for his new business. In their conversations with Tate, which followed similar patterns, he would switch between flattery, control and insults, calling the girls beautiful one moment, then making demands or calling them stupid the next. However, none of these women had actually met up with Tate or gone through with his proposals of work. All of them had felt something was up, or, in some cases, the conversations just died out.

Then, roughly three days after we'd spoken to Daz's team, we received an email from a woman who claimed to have been Andrew

Tate's 'girlfriend' in 2015 (she placed the word girlfriend in inverted commas herself). She gave us her phone number. This would be the first time we would speak directly to a woman from Tate's past. Jamie immediately ran to an empty edit suite to call her.

This woman, who we'll be calling Sally, told Jamie that she first met Tate when she was nineteen. They messaged on Facebook, and Tate eventually asked her out for a drink. 'He was really, really cocky, like he is now, but he could also actually be quite nice and sweet.' After a successful date, they continued their relationship, and, Sally told us, he began speaking to her about his webcam company. Tate bragged that he was making huge amounts of money running the company out of a studio in a luxury penthouse apartment with his brother, and he promised her that if she worked for him, he could make her incredibly rich. She wouldn't even need to sleep with anyone, he said – all she'd have to do was perform by herself on webcam. Tate would even do the typing, speaking to the clients himself using a keyboard that would be off camera.

Sally had never done anything like webcam before, but she was young and working a minimum-wage job, and the proposition sounded interesting. Tate continued to sell the idea to her, guaranteeing that with her good looks, they would both make huge amounts of money together 'as a couple'. Sally agreed, and Tate took her to a pub to loosen up before her first 'show'. Sally claimed he then bought her several drinks, before taking her to his 'luxury apartment', which turned out to be a dingy two-bedroom flat above a Londis mini-market in Luton. When Sally arrived at the flat, she was dismayed, but said Tate plied her with more alcohol, and she drunkenly performed her first show, with Andrew and Tristan Tate watching over. Sally claimed that on that first night she got a glimpse of what was to come. 'We were just sitting on the bed and Andrew punched me in my arm and I was really confused because there was no real need for it. It was completely out of the blue. I went to the bathroom and cried,' At this point in the call, Sally began to cry. 'But then, when I came out of the bathroom, he was super, super nice,' she continued. She didn't know what to make of Tate, or the situation she was in. This, she alleges, is when the horrors began.

In the days that followed that first show, Sally says Tate convinced her to quit her job to work round the clock for him on webcam, not leaving his flat for three days. Sally was told not to message her friends, and that as Tate's girlfriend, she would no longer be able to speak to any other men. Though Tate had told Sally that he had an existing successful webcam business, when she arrived in the flat, the brothers appeared to have no other workers. However, after Sally had been there for a couple of weeks, new women began to arrive. They were split into groups, she said, either 'managed' by Tristan or Andrew, and the women would be required to sleep in their respective managers' beds. When the Tate brothers were away for a fight, their mother and stepfather would show up to watch over the webcam flat.

Sally claimed that Andrew Tate usually started to abuse the women verbally, 'calling us lazy hoes, dumb hoes, stuff like that', but quickly progressed to using physical violence. 'I saw him smack women with a belt because they wanted a lie-in,' Sally went on, her voice cracking. 'He used to strangle us, like, choke us as well.' Sally quickly followed up: 'And not in a sexual way either, it was like completely random. He would just walk up to you and grab you by the neck, or come into the room and say something like, "Which bitch am I gonna strangle today?"' Sally recalled one time where Tate had strangled her so badly that she'd woken up with red spots around her eyes from where the blood vessels had burst. Tristan was kinder to her than Andrew, but according to women we spoke to, he too could be deeply unpleasant to his own 'employees'.

One memory that stood out for Sally was Tristan roaming the flat wearing a pirate hat and wielding a plastic sword that he would hit the women with, bragging that he was 'captain of this money ship'.

Sally had been working for Tate for around six weeks when he brought in a new young woman, whom we'll be calling Helen – someone Sally recognised from school in Luton. As one of 'Andrew's girls' she was required to sleep in the bed with Sally and Tate between cam sessions. However, unlike Sally, Helen had a boyfriend and refused Tate's advances. For Helen, she said, it was strictly about the money: the £15-an-hour wage seemed attractive to her and Sally, despite the fact that Tate himself would regularly earn £500 for each of their online sessions. They knew this because the earnings popped up on screen.

Sally recalled waking up in the bed with Tate and Helen one morning, before going to the bathroom to shower. She reiterated, '[Helen] had a partner, so she was not interested in Andrew at all'. Sally took a deep breath before continuing: '. . . and I had gone to the shower. I came back, and I noticed he was like, he was behind her, and I saw him . . .' Sally struggled to finish her sentence, beginning to cry. 'I saw him raping her.' Sally apologised for losing composure. 'She left the house almost straight away, but I stayed for a bit longer. It was different, though. I didn't want to work for him at all, I just needed the money. I remember suggesting to him and Tristan that I could work from home. I told them that I'd still give them a share of the money, and they wouldn't even have to do anything. They just laughed at me, called me a dumb hoe, saying this was their business, and they had trained me, and why would they let me leave . . .' You could hear the frustration in Sally's voice building as she reflected on the way the Tates had treated her.

'Then one day, I was in bed, and I was really tired, I didn't want to get up and webcam, and Andrew was just really angry at me, saying I had to. I hid in the bathroom and he was threatening to beat me up, saying, "Oh, I don't give a fuck if you call the police. I'm going to beat the shit out of you." That's when I knew I needed to get out of there.'

Jamie was reeling from what he'd just heard. There had always been questions around Tate and his behaviour towards women, particularly the ones who 'worked' for his webcam company, but here was someone giving us a direct and detailed account of physical and sexual abuse. What's more, these allegations dated back to before Tate was a celebrity, even before his appearance on *Big Brother*. Jamie asked Sally if she had reported it to the police and to his surprise, she said that she had.

A few days after leaving Tate's flat Sally had called the Sapphire Unit – a division within the Metropolitan Police that specifically dealt with rape investigations. The unit came out to interview her at her home, but nothing further came of it. That was until Helen also came forward, reporting her alleged rape to Hertfordshire Police. It was at this point, in the summer of 2015, that an investigation into Tate was opened, and he was arrested by the police for questioning before being released. Sally going to the police at the time would make it a lot easier for us to stand up the allegations she was making to a level where we could publish them. She told us that that she was still in contact with Helen, and that Helen might be interested in speaking to us.

Two days later, Jamie managed to get on the phone with Helen. She was nervous, and found it difficult to recall that period, taking long pauses as she spoke. Whereas Sally had given us lots of detail, Helen spoke in a more detached way, rarely going into her emotional state at the time. But she confirmed what we had heard from Sally: that she had been brought into Tate's webcam studio in Luton, where Sally was already working at the time. Helen also confirmed the allegations of physical violence and verbal abuse, before coming to the moment in question that Sally had told us about. Helen recounted that day, eventually managing to say, 'That's when he raped me,' before bursting into tears.

Before Jamie could try to comfort Helen, the line had gone dead. She had hung up. He sat there for a moment, trying to process what had happened. Guilt washed over him. These women owed him nothing, so did he even have the right to ask them about things that had happened to them five or six years earlier? Jamie sent Helen a message to say that she needn't speak to us again if she didn't want to, but that we were always here if she felt she did. He heard nothing for weeks, but then received a message from Helen saying that she was free for a call.

She explained in this subsequent call that it was still extremely difficult to talk about what happened, and in addition that she was dating someone who wasn't comfortable with her ever mentioning it. She said that a few months before, as Tate was becoming famous, she'd tried to share her story on TikTok, only to find hundreds of Tate supporters abusing her and then reporting her account, leading to it being removed. Helen didn't think she was in a place to be able to go on camera, but she was keen for Sally to speak publicly about what had happened to them, including Helen's allegations that Tate had raped her, and Sally's account of having witnessed it.

We invited Sally to the Vice offices, so the three of us could meet in person. She was nervous, but warm and open with us. We explained to her the risks of participating in the documentary – primarily, that even though we would conceal her face and her voice, we could not guarantee her complete anonymity. It is a criminal offence to identify a sexual assault victim from the moment they make an official allegation, unless they explicitly waive this right. She gave us written permission to publish her interview, despite Matt telling her: 'When this film comes out, even if we hide who you are, Tate himself will know exactly who you are. We would have no control over whether he chooses to name you, and what his fans may do with that information.' It was a daunting prospect, publicly speaking out against one of the most famous men on the internet, whose fans had developed a reputation for regularly harassing and doxing his critics online. We told Sally she could take all the time she needed to think about this, but her mind was made up: 'I want people to know what he did to us'.

A week later, Sally returned to give a filmed interview recounting her story, having decided that she would not allow herself to be intimidated by Tate and his followers. As she took Matt through what had happened to her, it became clear that she felt let down. Hertfordshire Police's investigation into Andrew Tate began in the summer of 2015, so when Sally received a call a year later from one of the officers, informing her that Tate would be appearing on *Big Brother*, she was horrified. 'How could *Big Brother* agree to have someone who was being investigated for all of this terrible stuff on their show?' she questioned. Although Tate hadn't been charged at this point, and there was no way that the allegations would have shown up on any checks during the show's casting process, Hertfordshire Police confirmed with us that once they knew Tate was on the show, they had contacted the production company,

Endemol Shine, and informed them of the ongoing investigation. The producers had decided to keep Tate on the show for a further five days, before removing him for undisclosed reasons, relating to events 'outside of the Big Brother house'. During those five days, he was shown playing truth or dare in the hot tub, and kissing a topless female contestant. Channel 5 said publicly at the time that Tate had been removed from the Big Brother house because of 'information which came to light', and the press reported that his ousting was linked to a video that had surfaced of him slapping his ex-girlfriend, and then beating her with a belt. Tate himself endorsed this version of events, and public outrage eventually simmered down after he released a video on his Facebook showing the woman in question saying that it was all part of a consensual kinky game.

Speaking to Sally, we started to understand that Tate's ability to spin public narratives long preceded his real rise to fame. Despite being removed from *Big Brother* due to an ongoing police investigation for rape and physical assault, Tate had the public believing it was because he had made a 'consensual' BDSM video with his ex-partner. This new false narrative, now being amplified by some of the UK's press, is what took hold, and no reporter at the time uncovered that it had in fact been these ongoing criminal allegations of rape and abuse that led to Tate's eviction. It was no doubt an easier narrative for Tate to explain away, when compared to the ongoing criminal investigation.

After interviewing Helen, we approached Banijay UK, the company that owns Endemol Shine. They said that after being informed by police of their investigation on 8 June 2016, they 'began a process of extensive consultation with Channel 5, and legal teams, including the lawyers representing Andrew Tate'. They told us that Tate was 'closely monitored at all times' during this period while they sought to clarify the detail required by Channel 5 on the police investigation. He was removed from the house on 13 June. Sally and Helen were angry with the *Big Brother* producers for confronting them with their abuser by putting him on one of the biggest shows in the country, but their real frustrations lay with the police.

The two women had filed their criminal complaints with the police shortly after the alleged events occurred in 2015, then undergone their police interviews, handed over their phones (at the time it was common for police forces in England and Wales to demand that sexual-assault survivors hand over their phones to the police) and shared their sexual health records (both alleged that Tate had given them an STI). It wasn't until almost four years later, in July 2019, that the police passed their cases on to a lawyer at the Crown Prosecution Service (CPS), who would choose whether or not to proceed with a charge and take the case to court. Sally says that in this time they rarely spoke with the police, although she was contacted by an officer in 2018 who informed her that he was 'reopening their case', despite the women not having known it had been closed. According to Sally, the officer told her that the case had inadvertently been shut while an officer was on maternity leave, but that he was now looking at it carefully himself.

We contacted Hertfordshire Police about this. They denied that the case had been inadvertently closed and emphasised that officers in charge of investigations regularly change for routine reasons. They did, however, admit that the investigation had suffered delays, and that apologies had been made to the women at the time.

'They told us they believed us,' Sally said, referring to the police. 'They believed that Andrew was guilty. But there was nothing they could do.' For her, this only made things worse.

In 2019 the CPS decided not to prosecute. When we contacted the

CPS about this in late 2022, they told us that the case 'did not meet our legal test, and there was no realistic prospect of a conviction'. It is extremely unusual to have a witness in rape cases, but Sally said she had witnessed Tate raping Helen. Why then were the CPS reluctant to prosecute? In 2019, Helen had received a letter from them informing her that voice notes that she and Sally had exchanged had informed the decision not to charge Tate. In these voice notes, they had discussed whether they should tell the police that Tate had plied them with alcohol. 'We decided to tell them because it's the truth. Andrew did used to get us drunk, and we thought they should know that,' Sally told us. 'But they said that it could look like we were working together or something, coming up with a story to tell the police.'

The whole experience had left Sally and Helen devastated. Sally ended our interview with a message to Tate's followers: 'All these young men follow him, and think he's such a great guy, and he's their idol and stuff, and that's so difficult to see . . . There are better role models out there; don't be fooled by all the money, and the nice cars and all the women. Working on yourself and becoming a better man with a better mindset, yeah. But real men don't lay their hands on women.'

We spent the remainder of 2022 editing our film, going back and forth on various legal points, and doing our best to fact check the allegations that were being made. Tate continued contacting Jamie throughout October and November, asking about the film and trying to leverage a further interview with him in exchange for a viewing of the cut. We told him this wouldn't be possible. We knew that we would have to put Sally's and Helen's allegations to Tate before we released the film, to give him a chance to give his side of the story, or to deny it altogether. Vice scheduled the film's release for mid-January 2023, and we began to discuss when we should approach Tate with the allegations. We needed to give him enough time to properly consider them and come back to us; but on the other hand, we didn't want to allow him too much time to sit with the allegations, or give him an opportunity to try to intimidate Sally and Helen, knowing what was about to come when the film was released.

Meanwhile, Tate's sensational ascent was still facing serious hurdles, primarily his bans from social media. Journalists pointed out that Hustlers University looked like a pyramid scheme. His income would be taking a hit. But Tate and his team were masters of manipulation when it came to his image.

In October 2022, a video appeared on Instagram and YouTube of Tate with a rabbit emoji over his face, walking beside a turquoise pool. Palm trees and violet desert sky clouded by light pollution indicated that he was now in Dubai. He was preaching a reinvented creed to his followers, karate chopping the air with each word, as if striking down evil with his wisdom.

'You need your hand held, because when you first escape the Matrix, you're lost in the ether. You understand you're living inside of a mechanism which is designed to control you, but you don't understand exactly how to escape it.

If I were to tell you there were ways of making money that are so foreign to you, so alien, that you've never even heard of them, you'd sit there and go "no, that can't possibly be true".

If you've heard of it, why are you still broke? The Real World: the real key to understanding finance is just like everything else. There are secrets which are held from you on purpose, because they need the backbone of the slave force.'

Shortly after this video was released, a new website appeared, called 'The Real World'. A separate video on the landing page explained to viewers that the Hustlers University had been forced offline by some kind of attack, and then invited them to join The Real World, which appeared to be Tate's new online university platform. This video showed a screenshot of the Hustlers University homepage and clips of Tate talking about getting his followers rich. The screen was then taken over by falling green computer code and the words 'The Matrix Attacks'. News clips about Tate being de-platformed and testimonies from people talking about cancelling their Hustlers University subscriptions were shown. Then, in a clip taken directly from *The Matrix*, Morpheus says, 'This attack is an act of desperation', and Tate appears on screen doing more mock kung-fu moves, this time in sunglasses and a black leather trench coat.

The video claimed that this new platform, The Real World, was uncancellable, employing 'completely self-sufficient hardware and infrastructure'.

It went on, 'Without any matrix-controlled infrastructure, we can teach things we've never taught before. Join the resistance.'

Tate and his team had used his 'cancellation' to rebrand him as a resistance fighter. By merging conspiratorial thinking with economic aspirations, they were able to drive thousands more young men to a new online course subscription.

Hundreds of newly made Instagram accounts posted a series of videos and images of Tate in Dubai: Tate lounging in a pool on a yacht, his face obscured by a bear emoji; Tate being shown exotic animal collections; posing with a boa constrictor; buying a new sportscar; diving into a plunge pool . . . Some of them were soundtracked by a song called 'Top G in a Bugatti', which they had got an amateur dancehall artist to produce. In one clip, a man in a traditional Arabian thawb handed Tate a phone, revealing Steven Seagal on the other end of a video call. 'I'm a huge fan,' Tate claimed. Sartorial Shooter appeared at another point, revving the engine of a Lamborghini Huracán STO. Even banal events like Tate getting a haircut were given the cinematic treatment of a Michael Bay film, the camera panning 360 degrees around his freshly shaven head.

In some of these videos, Tate seemed deflated and preoccupied, like he was forcing his smiles. The momentum for his media circus seemed to now come from those around him: Tristan, Sartorial Shooter and an assortment of muscular sycophants. At a party atop a yacht, a bored-looking Tate went through the motions of flirting with women on camera and smoking cigars. The upper deck offered a photo-opportunity installation: a golden archway with the words 'billionaire' spelled across the top. Tristan and Andrew posed in front of it. Andrew seemed to disappear from the party before the sun set, while Tristan provided all the enthusiasm and good humour, ordering 'big whiskies' and regaling the crowd with stories of his brother. But even his tipsy anecdotes appeared a little bit forced.

In another video, the Tate brothers attended an event in the desert with the same people from the yacht. At one point the War Room leaders did archery, but the arrows had the suction cups you'd find on kids toys instead of real arrowheads. It's unclear where these women and other hangers-on came from, but their demeanour showed that they didn't just happen to be there. Like everything else in the videos, they had been procured. Once everyone was filmed arriving, they sat down and scrolled silently on their phones. A woman arrived at Tristan's side with a saxophone and played

'Mr. Saxobeat'. The Word 'Tate' was lit up in flames on the sand dunes. No one seemed happy.

When Matt called Tate during this Dubai period to ask for another interview, he was full of disdain. He started his sentences with 'Game theory':

'Game theory. Why would I give you another interview for you to ask shallow and fictitious questions when I have every media outlet in the world wanting to speak to me?'

It was difficult to understand the change in Tate's mood, because things appeared to be looking up for him. He had used his de-platforming to increase his allure to far-right audiences. The Tate brothers were very much not banned from Rumble, an alternative media website backed by the conservative libertarian tech billionaire Peter Thiel. After Tate signed a lucrative deal with Rumble in 2022, their daily active users soared 45.3 per cent. And he appeared on Tucker Carlson's Fox News show, saying, 'All these social media platforms pretend to care. As soon as somebody [young men] resonate with stands up and champions their issues, they mass blanket-ban me. They think that by banning me I'm just going to vanish, and the young men are just going to start eating the gruel that they're fed on their YouTube feed. They don't want to see transgender people wearing make-up. They want an action hero.'

In a surprise move, Tate publicly converted to Islam. A boxer and Dubai-based influencer named Tam Khan released a video of Tate praying in a mosque, and he appeared on a podcast with Islamic influencer Mohammed Hijab, which was listened to millions of times. His support among Muslim schoolboys soared in the UK, making him one of the most famous Muslims in the English-speaking world. Hope Not Hate polled sixteen-to-twenty-four-year-olds in the UK and found that 61 per cent of Muslim males in this age group had a positive view of him.* What's more, non-Muslim Tate fans began to consider converting, including one we met in Northumberland who was 'working on his beard'. In one of the year's most bizarre moments, Tate appeared to have been endorsed by the Taliban.[†]

Though he had been banned from TikTok that summer, Tate's content was still appearing on the platform via his army of followers. Two weeks after his ban, the Center for Countering Digital Hate (CCDH) found that videos of Tate posted by other accounts had been viewed hundreds of millions of times. In one of these, Tate said, 'Virgins are the only acceptable thing to marry'. In another, he said women who do not want children are 'miserable, stupid bitches'. TikTok removed these videos, but Tate was still appearing – quickly and frequently – on teenagers' feeds.[‡]

Tate claimed at this point that The Real World now had more than 200,000 members, which could have made him $11 million in the first month after he was de-platformed. But in November 2022, his fortune increased even more dramatically.

In 2017, Tate had been banned from Twitter for posting harmful tweets, including one that claimed women who 'put themselves in a position to be raped must bear some responsibility'. On 27 October 2022, Elon Musk bought Twitter, firing 80 per cent of its workforce and inviting election deniers, white supremacists, climate-change deniers and other conspiracy theorists back onto

---

* https://hopenothate.org.uk/wp-content/uploads/2023/02/state-of-hate-2023-v7-1.pdf

† https://www.newsweek.com/taliban-worried-about-andrew-tate-they-ask-his-freedom-1770693

‡ https://www.theguardian.com/technology/2022/nov/06/tiktok-still-hosting-toxic-posts-of-banned-influencer-andrew-tate

the site. He claimed he was doing this to promote free speech, though he also suspended the accounts of several journalists who had covered his takeover of the company. On 18 November, he reinstated Tate's account, along with a few others.

Tate immediately posted a photo of himself sat in his cigar room, wearing a white blazer, muscles fully tensed and face screwed up, intending to look tough, but in reality looking somewhat constipated. The caption read, 'Mastery is a funny thing. It's almost as if, on a long enough time scale, losing simply isn't an option. Such is the way of Wudan.' He gained a million followers in forty-eight hours and several million more over the following months.

Tate was back, and Musk's version of Twitter – renamed 'X' in July 2023 – was his biggest platform. Many journalists reached out to Twitter for comment on this. They received a single poo emoji in response, which was the press office's automatic reply at the time.

CHAPTER EIGHT

The Real World

In February 2023, frontline workers from the UK government's counter-terrorism Prevent programme warned of a rapid rise in the number of referrals coming from schools about Tate. At the time, misogynistic extremism was not considered within the remit of counter-terrorism in the UK, unless the person in question was also an incel – a classification that did not apply to Tate supporters who often boasted about the number of women they slept with. Nor is misogyny included in hate-crime legislation in the UK.

Throughout the making of our documentary, we had been contacting DIICOT, the Romanian Directorate for Investigating Organised Crime and Terrorism who had raided Tate in April of 2022. They were guarded in their responses, but in mid-December, we decided to have one last attempt. In his email, Matt made reference to past statements Tate had publicly made about Romania, including claims that it was easier to get away with crimes relating to the abuse of women there than in the 'West'. DIICOT again declined to give us an interview, but confirmed once more that their investigation into Tate was ongoing. Five days later, everything would change.

Feeling confident, on 27 December 2022, the thirty-six-year-old Tate had decided to go after the environmental activist Greta Thunberg, who was nineteen at the time. 'Hello @GretaThuberg,' he tweeted. 'I have 33 cars. My Bugatti has a w16 8.0L quad turbo. My TWO Ferrari 812 competizione have 6.5L v12s. This is just the start. Please provide your email address so I can send a complete list of my car collection and their respective enormous emissions.'

Thunburg's reply soon became one of the most-liked tweets in history. It read, 'Yes, please do enlighten me. email me at smalldickenergy@getalife.com'.

Tate continued the spat by tweeting a video in which he tried to counter, through cigar smoke, that 'Greta doesn't realise she's been programmed. She's a slave of the Matrix.' At one point, someone off camera handed him a stack of pizza boxes from a Romanian company called Jerry's Pizza, revealing to viewers that he had returned from Dubai to his compound in Bucharest. 'Make sure', he jested to the off-camera presence, 'that these boxes are not recycled.'

The night of Tate's spat with Thunberg, several armed police from Romania's Gendarmerie Special Intervention Brigade (BSIJ), who combat terrorism and organised crime, stormed into the Tate compound. It was widely reported that the police had been alerted to Tate's return to Romania by the pizza boxes in his video retort to Thunberg, but Romanian authorities denied this. They had been planning this for a long time.

Jamie first saw the videos emerge on Twitter, in which masked officers frogmarched Tate into a police van, as he declared to the bevy of news reporters present, 'The Matrix is attacking me.' Once inside the van, he looked directly at one of the cameras and formed his hands into the signature triangle shape that has been dubbed his 'illuminati gesture'.

The authorities seized all fifteen of the Tates' cars, as well as ten properties, watches and millions of dollars. They had been arrested as part of an ongoing investigation into human trafficking and forming an organised crime group. DIICOT accused them of recruiting women through the Loverboy Method and coercing them to create explicit content. Tate himself was also being investigated for rape. Two women were arrested with them. We recognised one as Tate's girlfriend/personal assistant from our first visit to his compound, Georgiana Naghel. The other woman, Luana Radu, was a Romanian ex-police officer who had allegedly worked with Tate as a webcam performer and 'manager' of other women.

Our suspicions about Tate using the Loverboy Method might have been correct. Jamie quickly sent the posts to Matt. 'Dude, I think they've actually been arrested . . .' By the morning, Andrew Tate's face was on every news channel around the world.

'#FreeTopG' quickly became a top-trending hashtag. Groups of teenage boys gathered in Athens and Bucharest to protest his arrest. Teachers in the UK began reporting pre-teen boys chanting 'Free Top G' in the classroom. Nightly discussions about Tate's arrest were held on Twitter's live audio function, Twitter Spaces, giving rise to a new cadre of Tate sympathisers, many of whom masqueraded as 'journalists', 'experts' and 'lawyers'.

We'd always wanted to put Helen's and Sally's allegations to Tate directly, but that would no longer be possible – the legal case against him meant we'd have to contact him via his lawyer. Under investigation but not charged, Andrew and Tristan Tate were to be held in police custody for at least the next thirty days, but more likely for the next six months. This has become relatively standard practice in Romanian human-trafficking investigations, due to fears that the accused will either harass the alleged victims or attempt to flee the country. With Tate behind bars, our original plan of a surprise phone call was off the cards, so we were forced to send him the allegations via his legal representation.

Shortly after Tate's arrest, his lawyer Eugen Vidineac made his first public statement to the press, professing his client's innocence and denying the allegations. Vidineac had been practising in Romania for around fifteen years, having qualified from the Transilvania University of Braşov, a short drive from where we had gathered for the War Room Test. Vidineac didn't look like your typical defence attorney. He was young, with an overly groomed beard, and during his press appearances discussing the Tate's case, he developed a reputation for unconventional outfit choices: expensive designer shoes, trench coats with fur lapels, and flamboyant suits. We confirmed the allegations with our legal team at Vice that we would need to put to Tate and shortly after Tate's arrest, Matt called Vidineac.

The lawyer was perturbed, not so much by the allegations, but with the fact that he was having to spend his time speaking with us. 'The Tates are very fucking busy,' Vidineac began. 'They don't have time to respond to some issue from years ago.' This wasn't the sort of reaction we'd expected.

'So that's the response to the allegations?' Matt asked again.

'I told you that in good faith,' Vidineac quickly shot back, 'and anyway, our conversations should be off the record.'

Our conversations were, of course, not off the record, because nothing of this nature had been agreed before we spoke, but we still didn't feel we had an adequate reply from Tate, despite going through his own lawyer. We decided to give Tate one last chance, sending Vidineac the allegations in writing, and giving him a further forty-eight hours to respond. Within twenty-four hours we received an email from Tate's team, and their statement made it clear that, at least this time, Tate had been contacted and given the allegations.

Tate, perhaps unsurprisingly, denied all the allegations that we put to him. He accused Sally and Helen of wanting money because he fired them. For Tate, it appeared that the decision not to charge him by the CPS was all the evidence we needed that these allegations were false. *'The police understood after the investigation that I am innocent and the police found messages from the girls' phones where they were talking between themselves and planning to lie about me'*, he emailed. We took this as a reference to the voice notes in which Helen and Sally had discussed whether or not they should tell the police about Tate giving them alcohol.

According to Rape Crisis England and Wales, only 2.6 per cent of reported rapes results in a charge, let alone a conviction.[*] So, for every 100 people that are accused of rape, fewer than three will ever face these allegations in a court of law. In 2019, the same year the CPS declined to bring charges against Tate, the *Guardian* reported on a CPS seminar during which the CPS director of legal services, Greg McGill, and the director of public prosecutions' legal adviser, Neil Moore, urged prosecutors to take a proportion of 'weak cases out of the system' to improve conviction rates. One prosecutor who attended the seminar claimed staff were told, 'If we took 350 weak cases out of the system, our conviction rate goes up to 61 per cent'. Rape cases are typically some of the hardest to prove and, therefore, are more likely to be considered 'weak' by the CPS. In trying to increase their conviction rate, the CPS may have inadvertently, or not, made it near impossible to take an accused rapist to court.

---

[*] https://rapecrisis.org.uk/get-informed/statistics-sexual-violence/

We had our allegations, and now we had our response from Tate, so by 4 January 2023 we were ready to publish. Along with our colleague Tim Hume, we penned an article revealing that Tate had been arrested on suspicion of rape in 2015, including Sally and Helen's testimony, and a filmed interview with Sally. It was published at 8:44pm on Vice's website, and the public reaction was near immediate.

By the time we woke up the next day, the allegations had spread all over the world. Newspapers across Europe and America began to republish the claims, and ardent Tate supporters clamoured to put forward alternative explanations. Some said Sally was an actress we had hired, while others held that we had approached all of Tate's ex-girlfriends with offers of £50,000 to speak badly of him. We had no idea where these claims came from, but many of them were accompanied by statements such as, 'I have it on good authority that . . .' or 'confirmed, Vice paid this woman . . .' These false accusations gained most traction on Twitter, which was beginning to look more and more like a Tate propaganda site.

Despite this, we felt positive about what we'd published, and we still had around ten days until our full documentary would be released. Along with the backlash from Tate supporters, we received numerous emails from women wanting to pass on their support to Sally and Helen, many of them having also had negative experiences when trying to report allegations of sexual abuse or rape in the UK. Buried among them was an email reading: 'Hi, I'm one of Andrew's ex-girlfriends and the other woman in the police case. Can you call me please?'

The other woman in the police case? We had been back and forth with Hertfordshire Police, the CPS, Sally and Helen, and none of them had mentioned a third woman. Within minutes we were on the phone with her. We'll be calling her Amelia.

Amelia was exasperated and confused. 'Why didn't the other girls mention me in their interviews?'

We waited for a moment, hoping she would elaborate. 'What do you mean?' Matt asked.

'Well, I was part of the same investigation. I was the third woman in the police case.' When we then told Amelia that neither we nor Sally nor Helen knew that there was a third alleged victim in the case, she was dumbfounded. We made a plan to meet Amelia along with a friend in Bedfordshire two days later.

Amelia grew up in Luton and had known Tate since 2009. 'He was a well-known guy in Luton back then. Everyone knew who the Tates were,' she told us on the phone. After she bumped into Tate at a nightclub in 2013, their relationship became romantic, and they started dating. Amelia was twenty – seven years younger than Tate at the time – and had only been in one serious relationship. Tate was sweet at first, she said. 'I can understand why people find him funny, because I did for years. And that's very enticing: an intelligent, tall man who's a kick-boxer – that's funny . . . Why would you not want to spend time with them?

'He was always quite forceful about coming to meet him. He'd message me stuff like, "I'll be at yours eight o'clock. Be ready."'

A few months after they'd been dating, she met up with Tate at his flat. 'He said he'd just come from training, and he was wearing a ripped hoodie. He goes, "Look at me. I'm a tramp, but I'm still a G." I remember specifically, on Facebook, there was a picture that he put up, and it was of a police officer, an armed police officer with his foot on a female's head, crushing her head. And he captioned it as "pimping".

'So, I always knew he had this horrible side. But in my head, it was always: it's for attention. It wasn't until that first time I went round. And he was dressed like a tramp. And we sat downstairs for not even five minutes, until he was like, "Let's go upstairs".'

Amelia stopped and began to cry. She apologised repeatedly. Her friend encouraged her to continue. 'Remember why you wanted to do this,' she said.

'Back then, and he knew this, I'd only been with two people. He knew what that meant to me . . . that act was very important to me.'

The pair were kissing on Tate's bed, she told us, when he began trying to take off her clothes. After a while, he went, 'I'm just debating whether I should rape you or not'.

'I didn't know what he was talking about,' she went on. 'I wasn't sure if he was just making some kind of sick joke. So, I put my hand on his chest and said, "Don't be stupid, what are you talking about?" Within an instant, he changed who he was,' she said. Suddenly, Tate grabbed her neck and 'started strangling me, forcing my trousers off me'. Tate was a professional kick-boxer at the time, and Amelia had no way of keeping him off her. 'I was trying to keep them on, and he started screaming at me, "Take the fucking trousers off, bitch". I was so scared; it was terrifying. I've never been strangled before. I don't know if he's going to stop.'

Amelia paused again, 'I'm sorry. I haven't spoken about this in so long,' she continued. 'It's like, whenever you think about being in that situation, you think you're going to fight back . . . But I'm telling you, you don't. Because if you fight back, what else is he going to do to you? He's a 6 foot 2 . . . champion kick-boxer, for God's sake.'

Amelia said Tate then went on to rape her, choking her throughout and saying things like 'Who do you belong to?' She couldn't respond – she was being strangled – but, 'He's like, "Fucking say it, bitch. You're not fucking saying my name, say my fucking name, otherwise I'll kill you,"' she told us. After the assault, Tate fell asleep with his arm across her as she lay awake trying to process what had just happened.

When she got home the next day, she called a friend, who began spelling out to her that she had been raped. Amelia couldn't come to terms with it. 'I couldn't even say the word; even now I struggle to say the R word.' Amelia was traumatised, but desperate to not see herself as a victim. 'I just wanted to pretend it never happened. I thought, if I go and see him again, and I want it this time, then I'm not being degraded, then it's not the R word,' she said. 'So that's what I did. I was like, "Right, I'll see you again . . . you haven't taken that control of me. You haven't hurt me.'

Shortly after, when out with Tate again, Amelia says she was raped a second time. She told us Tate had driven her out to the countryside in his Range Rover, locking the doors and assaulting her in the car. He told her it was his 'rape van'. Shortly after this, Tate wanted to take her away for the weekend, at which point she broke things off.

Amelia then showed us text messages from Tate in which he appeared to discuss the rape.

Amelia: What do you get from me hating it?

Tate: *Because I'm a terrible person.*

Amelia: Mr. fucking nice yeah

Tate: *And I love raping you. And watching u let me while still debating if it's a good idea or not I like the conflict you have And you do have it. Don't deny it.*

Amelia: Makes you feel powerful?

Tate: *No.*

I'm already powerful

There were voice notes in which Tate said, '*The more you didn't like it the more I enjoyed it. I fucking loved how much you hated it. Turned me on. Why am I like that? Why?*' In another, he said, '*Are you seriously so offended I strangled you a little bit. You didn't fucking pass out. Chill the fuck out, Jesus. I thought you were cool, what's wrong with you?*'

It wasn't until 2014, about six months after the first alleged rape, that Amelia filed a complaint with Bedfordshire Police.

'[The police] were horrible,' she said. 'I went in with my friend, and I was obviously upset, crying and struggling to tell them what happened . . . and they asked the friend that I was with if I had learning difficulties, like right in front of me. I just felt so stupid . . . That made me feel so small . . . like, I can't even be emotional,' Amelia recalled. 'I can't even . . . feel how I'm feeling, because you're trying to put me down.' This left Amelia unable to pursue the complaint, and she instead opted to 'log' it, recording the allegation with police to pick up again when she felt stronger. To try to move on with her life she relocated to a new town and embarked on a new career, far away from Tate. So, if she didn't press charges with the police, simply logging her complaint, how did she come to be involved in the 2015 case?

In 2015, Amelia received a call from an officer at Hertfordshire Police, who told her that they were looking into complaints from two other women who had also made allegations of abuse against Tate – one of rape, and another of repeated strangulation – and asked whether Amelia would be happy with her complaint being included in that investigation. These two women were Sally and

Helen. 'I felt so conflicted,' Amelia said. 'I felt like I'd let them down. Like, if I had gone through with Bedfordshire Police, then maybe this wouldn't have happened to them,' she went on. 'But at the same time, I was, like, well now if there's three of us, we maybe have a chance,' and so she agreed to join their investigation. 'I felt stronger. I felt, like, ok, I'm not alone now. I've got two other girls.' She handed over all the evidence to the police, including the text messages and voice notes from Tate.

In late 2019, when the CPS decided not to prosecute, Amelia was called in to Hertfordshire Police station to be given the news. 'I went [to the police officer], "Well, explain to me why you're letting a monster on the street?"' We could still hear the anger in her voice. 'He even told me, "It's not that the police don't believe you. It's not that the CPS don't believe you. It's the fact that there's an ounce of doubt in the case.' The ounce of doubt that the police were referring to was apparently the fact that Amelia had been to see Tate again after the first alleged rape – something she herself had told them. They only wanted to go forward with cases where they felt there was a 100 per cent chance of a successful conviction.

'They told me, these things are very traumatic for victims of rape, so we don't want to put anyone through it unless we think we will definitely get a conviction, because we don't want to traumatise you further,' Amelia told us. 'But I wanted to go to court, I was devastated by the decision.' Amelia, Sally and Helen would join the tens of thousands of women who report their alleged rapists to the police in the UK, never to see them face charges in court.

Having tried to move on with her life, Amelia went in to work one day and was sitting at her computer when she heard a distinctive voice playing out of one of her colleagues' phones. Amelia froze. 'Who is that?' she asked her colleague.

'Oh, this guy called Andrew Tate. He's crazy. He's like really big on TikTok or something.'

Amelia was in disbelief. 'I'd had it before, when he went on *Big Brother* in 2016. I was so angry when I found out, and it was me that called the police and told them he was going on the show.' But this time it was different. 'He just kept appearing everywhere. I couldn't even go on social media without seeing his face.'

As Tate's fame grew over the coming months, Amelia's mental health worsened. But after seeing Sally go public with the allegations, she felt emboldened to go public, too, wanting to stop the same thing from happening to other women.

'When I saw he'd been arrested in Romania, I was relieved,' Amelia explained. 'But I was also so, so angry.' We asked why, and her response was emphatic. 'I was angry at the police here. We gave them all this evidence. There was three of us, and yet they let him get away with it. He was able to just go on with his life, hurting however many more girls . . .'

Over the following days, we worked harder than we ever had in our careers to get our film – and Amelia's story – out as quickly as possible. It was released on 12 January 2023. Almost immediately afterwards, an onslaught of abuse and attempts to discredit us began on social media. Tate and his fans portrayed us as traitors. We were 'snakes'. They had let us into their own home, helped us to become better men and, in turn, we betrayed them with a hit-piece that was intentionally released while they were trapped in prison.

Usually, when famous people are accused of rape, the world shares in the victims' fury. After we released our film featuring our first interview with Sally, she felt like the masses were taking Tate's side. His fans were all over social media claiming it was an 'attack by the Matrix'. When an American, far-right 'masculinity influencer' named Sneako, who at the time had millions of followers, live-streamed himself watching that interview, he scoffed, 'Yeah, women crying . . . but there is zero evidence. And why is she only coming out now?' At one point in the interview Sally says, 'He used to strangle us as well.' Sneako questioned, 'Ok, was it strangling or consensual choking during sex?' His fans echoed his disbelief in the chatroom, asserting she was a paid actor. 'Drop a 1 in the chat if you'd rape Sally,' one said. 'Don't care if he smashed your dumb ass, whore' wrote another. 'This bitch needs to be hung' said a third.

A right-wing 'masculinity' podcast called 'Fresh and Fit', whose hosts were long-time supporters of Andrew Tate, did an episode discussing our work. They filmed themselves leading a chant of 'fuck Vice' at a party and released it to their followers. Sartorial Shooter appeared on the podcast in his new thawb and repeated exclamations of 'Mashallah' announcing to the world that he had followed his beloved leader in converting to Islam. He claimed that we had manipulated our documentary because our superiors demanded a hit-piece. (He also admitted to Matt in a phone call that the tattooed woman he had shown us was actually his wife – and she was not happy when she saw the documentary and found out what her husband had been up to).

War Room general Dylan Madden released a viral TikTok video that portrayed Jamie as Matt's sinister 'handler'. Matt had apparently been enjoying the experience of The Test, until, all of a sudden, Jamie was seen 'whispering in his ear' to attack Tate.

Other videos went viral where supposed 'experts' claimed that the voice notes in which Tate had apparently discussed raping Amelia were 'faked with AI'. Amelia and Sally, who had given us filmed interviews, were still being accused of being paid actresses. A news website called Poptopic published a piece claiming that an

inside source revealed to them that Sally was 'played by' the in-
house Vice reporter Sophia Smith Galer.

On the hugely popular Twitter Spaces show 'The Roundtable',
(given a plug by Elon Musk himself), nightly live discussions were
held in which speakers attempted to discredit our work. Then, when
Vice Media went bankrupt soon after the documentary's release due
to long-standing financial issues, many on Twitter believed Tate's
narrative that this was because our documentary was 'debunked'.
On 2 May, one viral tweet about the bankruptcy read, 'Vice News
made headlines with their hit-piece against @cobratate, but the
documentary was debunked upon its release'. It was viewed 1.6
million times and retweeted by Jordan Peterson.

Then death threats began to appear in Matt's inbox:

> You fucking snake if I catch you in England I will strangle your ratty
> neck till your blue in the face you fucking 2 faced fucker.

> Better hire bodyguards for yourself or else you will be found dead by
> July 2023 ☺ Better apologise for what misinformation you bastard
> scripted for Andrew Tate through Vice News or Wait for a terrific
> brutal death you Ugly MotherFucker.

> Hey Matt I recently seen your interview with Tate and I believe you
> made an effort to damage is look in the public eye because of this
> I would like to inform you that the day I find you I am going to put
> a knife so deep into your neck it comes out the other side I will be
> waiting out of the London vice office everyday looking for you stalking
> you I will find you and I will be there to witness your last breath.

There were about a hundred more of these. And as Daz Black's agent had warned, they began contacting Matt's bosses claiming to have 'evidence' he was a paedophile.

Soon Tate fans began to appear in Matt's life offline too, almost every time he went out in public. At Caffè Nero, while he waited for his coffee . . . The caterer at an award ceremony for our film . . . The air steward on his flight . . . At least three Uber drivers . . . At Glastonbury Festival, on the way back to his tent, three official security guards surrounded Matt and accused him of 'stitching Tate up'. Some people just wanted to name-call, but most felt entitled to a debate. And they all had the exact same look and mannerisms – muscular, perfect posture, speaking in short, terse sentences as the War Room instructs, domineering body language and formal attire. It was as though an army of robots had been unleashed.

Every single one of these Tate fans believed the narrative they had been fed on Twitter: that our film had been debunked, our sources were fake and Tate was totally innocent. Yet when Matt engaged them, it became clear that they had neither seen our film nor read our articles. They had only seen the reactions to them from Tate's supporters on social media – especially Twitter. As far as they were concerned, the film had ended our careers and made us the laughing stock of the world. On Elon Musk's Twitter, we were losing the battle.

CHAPTER NINE

Keep the Receipts

Along with the trolls, in the weeks that followed the release of our first documentary, people started getting in touch with information. Some emails contained fanciful stories about Tate with all the authenticity of a message from a foreign prince offering millions of dollars if we would just share our banking information. From a reporting perspective, these were too good to be true, and although the false flags were relatively easy to spot, we began to feel a little paranoid. We knew Tate had a huge following that he could mobilise through his Real World platform, and we became wary of them feeding us anonymous 'poisoned pills', or fake stories about Tate, in a bid to have us report on one of them, so that they could then discredit us as journalists.

This had long been the practice of Project Veritas, a US right-wing activist group founded in 2010 by James O'Keefe, who ran the organisation until February 2023 when he was removed, to the dismay of his many acolytes. In the thirteen years that O'Keefe was at its helm, Project Veritas amassed a huge following for its 'undercover operations' in which members would try to discredit the 'mainstream media' and charities they deemed overly progressive, such as Planned Parenthood (which delivers reproductive health care and education). We began to read every email through a lens of suspicion, knowing that a takedown of a right-wing 'hero' like Tate by 'woke-agenda' Vice, would be a prime target for the group to discredit.

Buried among the hate mail and obvious fabrications, however, were some emails that caught our attention. These included one from a young woman in the US, who we'll be calling Amanda, which read: 'I am reaching out because I have information about Andrew Tate and his webcam business and the violence, abuse and exploitation that occurred within it. I never met Andrew Tate or worked with him directly, however for a period of time he sold courses on how to get girls to webcam for you and I was a victim of this.'

Jamie – 6 January 2023

It's late in the evening when I see the message from Amanda. I'm already in bed, scrolling through our inbox of tips, trying not to wake my partner with the brightness of my screen, but I know it's earlier in the US, so I sneak out of my bedroom to call her. The Tate story has now taken over almost all of my mental space, and I know I won't be able to sleep until I hear what she has to share with us. After a few rings I hear a bright, American 'Hello?'

After a hesitant start to the call Amanda starts going into her story, without divulging the identity of the man she is talking about. Three years ago, she tells me, when she was nineteen years old and working as a barista in Starbucks, she met the person she refers to as 'Ryan', a seemingly successful and handsome older man, almost twenty years her senior. They spoke online for months, and eventually he asked her out on a date. 'It was a very interesting date, if you could even call it a date,' she tells me.

'What do you mean?' I ask.

'He picked me up and we went straight to a hotel. We didn't have dinner. We didn't get drinks. Didn't chat basically at all. And as soon as we got to the hotel room, he like, shoved me onto my knees and, like, started having sex with me for, like, hours. And it was . . . it felt pretty horrible, to be honest. Like, I had been chatting with him for months and he [had] seemed really sweet and charming and into me.'

After that night they continued speaking, and Ryan suggested she work for him on webcam, 'and I instantly was like, "No," I'm like, "I don't want to do it. I have no interest in this".' Certain things had happened in her life, she explains – things that she doesn't want to go into right now – but 'he kept selling me this idea of how great it would be and how good I would be at it, and if I would complain about anything in my life, he'd be like, well, I have a solution for you'.

Eventually, Amanda agreed, at which point Ryan was ecstatic, but didn't have anywhere for her to webcam, and Amanda still lived at home with her mum. This is when he introduced her to another man. 'Hmmm,' she ums, 'let's call him Eric'. I write down the name Eric, and find myself subconsciously starting to write the word Tate, wondering when he will come into play, if at all.

Amanda started camming from Eric's house, and was allowed to keep 20 per cent of the money she earned, with Ryan and Eric splitting the other 80 per cent. Amanda alleges that

Ryan grew physically and emotionally abusive. 'They made me work like eight to ten hours a day, and if I had what they considered a "bad day", he would just be awful. He would take out his actual anger and aggression towards me in physical ways and was mean to me and would yell at me. And it was pretty hard on me.'

It all seems fresh in her mind, yet very well processed. 'I got out of there about six months ago,' she explains. 'I went to Eric's house and packed up all my stuff while the two of them were away on one of their trips.' Amanda had met a new guy, a boyfriend who was horrified by her situation, and he helped her to leave and find her own apartment.

Amanda's story seems like an interesting case study in the exploitation of women by Loverboys, who groom women into working for them on webcam sites, and relevant to the world of Andrew Tate. But at this point I am still struggling to see how he is directly connected to this story. I broach the issue with Amanda, wary of not making her feel like what she's told me isn't important, just because it doesn't involve Tate. 'And what about Andrew Tate – you mentioned him in your email?'

Amanda almost laughs, 'Oh, of course, I probably should have said this at the start. They were part of his War Room thing. I'm pretty sure that they learned all this from him.'

I pull the phone away from me, slightly reeling. It is one thing if some men watched a video of Tate's and learned from him online, but if what Amanda is saying is right, men were being taught how to exploit women within Tate's 'closed network' in real life.

Amanda says that once she began camming, the men constantly spoke about Tate as the man they aspired to be like, *the man who had made millions doing exactly this. According to her, they were constantly on their phones, on a Telegram group with other members of the War Room, discussing 'their girls'. 'Did you get any idea of how high up they might be in the War Room, like are they just paying customers?' I ask, eager to know who Eric and Ryan might be.*

'Oh pretty high up, I think. Like, Ryan would always talk about how he was, like, a master at this [webcam], and that he taught other men how to do it. They would go on these trips all the time to these, like, War Room events, and Ryan had loads of pictures of him and Andrew together. If you asked him, he was like his best friend, or one of his brothers.'

I sit there for a moment, contemplating what to do. I'm desperate to find out who the man who Amanda claims groomed her is, particularly if he could be a senior member of Tate's War Room, but I don't want to push and risk scaring her. 'This can be off the record, and we wouldn't need to publish this,' I begin, 'but for my own research, and just in terms of knowing what's what, would you be able to tell me who these men are?'

Amanda thinks for a brief moment, and then agrees, on the condition that we won't publish their names (she would later change her mind on this point). 'I guess it couldn't hurt.' I feel my stomach start to swirl with excitement.

'Ryan's name is Jonathan. I can send you his Instagram now on WhatsApp.'

I open the message from Amanda – a link to an Instagram account called '7.and.counting'. The description reads, 'Former USAF C17/757 EP/IP', followed by an emoji of a bicep, a cherry and a wad of dollars. 'Been Everywhere,

*Loved Most of It. Builder of Men. Master of Logistics.
Weaver of Legends. Craftsman of Dreams.' The account
depicts a handsome man in his late thirties, who wears a
pilot's uniform in many of his photos. It is Jonathan Bowe,
aka the Money Pilot or the Right Hand of Wudan – one of
the War Room's most senior generals, whom we'd seen in
Romania at The Test.*

*   'Would you feel comfortable sharing your story with us on
camera?' I ask.*

*   Amanda thinks for a moment. 'I don't see why not.'*

The call with Amanda confirmed our suspicions. Our first documentary had only scratched the surface, not just of Tate, but of his
ever-growing War Room. If the War Room was teaching men Tate's
methodology of misleading and recruiting women for online sex
work, it could be one of the largest grooming networks in the world.
We knew that we needed to do further reporting and get Amanda's
story out there. In March 2023, we prepared to go to Romania again,
this time for the BBC, seeking to expose the men behind Tate and
uncover what the War Room was really up to.

Early on in the process, Matt received a DM on Twitter from
another woman whose testimony supported what we were beginning to discover. The message was from a twenty-two-year-old
woman from Argentina, who we'll be calling Maria. She told us that
she too had met a guy online, 'a cute one', and they'd started dating.
Maria was twenty at the time, and it was her first real relationship.
'I remember him saying, "You seem like a girl that is going to help
me a lot". And he kept repeating that like, "You're going to help me.
You don't know how yet what you're going to do, but you're going to
be glad that you do it."' Maria didn't take this as an ominous sign,

but rather as a statement of his deep romantic intention, and she fell in love with him.

About six months into the relationship, he suggested that they make an OnlyFans page for her: 'Ok, you want to make money, too? Let's do something, it's going to be fun. We're going to spend more time together and we're going to make dollars.' They began making content for OnlyFans. Maria never controlled the account or knew the password, and she wasn't allowed to keep any of the money. At the same time, she alleges that he became more and more controlling and demanding, limiting who she could see and insisting that she follow his every order. On some occasions he became violent, but mostly resorted to what she described as emotional abuse and manipulation. 'Like, I remember not being able to see my friends, not being able to go out to, like, one of their parties, or even the park, because he was, like, "No, you're staying with me. What you want to do? What else? You have another man, probably, that I don't know. You're staying here." Not even my family. Like, not even my sister or my mom. He was, like, "You're staying here with me."'

The man that Maria claims did this to her was also a member of the War Room – a relatively senior member who, we knew from our own research, ran a programme for other members on growing their social media followings. She sent Matt a photo from his Instagram account, showing him sat next to Tate at a high-end restaurant. Maria claimed she was even taken to a War Room event at a luxury penthouse in Buenos Aires, where other men in their thirties and forties wearing suits and smoking cigars were all accompanied by young women, like her, in their late teens and early twenties. She was always told that the War Room was a positive thing – a club where men could hang out, and network with like-minded individuals. But as she came to find out more about its leader, Andrew Tate, and as her relationship became more abusive, she knew she had to leave.

Maria told her family what had happened and broke off contact with the War Room member. She agreed to tell her story on camera, as she wanted the world to know what she felt the men of the War Room were being taught by Tate: 'They find [a] woman and then they try to make them to fall in love with them. And once they are in love and they have all this control over this person, they use it for their profit.'

Since their arrest in December 2022, Andrew and Tristan Tate, along with the two people accused of being their accomplices, Georgiana Naghel and Luana Radu, had remained in prison. Every thirty days a judge was required to determine whether they should continue to be held in custody while under investigation, as DIICOT requested. Typically, with these cases, as time progresses and those being investigated are shown to be following the guidance of the judge and the court, restrictions for the accused are reduced in the lead-up to trial. On Friday, 4 August 2023, after more than seven months in prison, the Tate brothers were released into house arrest, along with their two alleged accomplices. They were still under investigation, but placed under 'judicial control', and prevented from leaving their house or contacting anyone involved in the investigation, including the alleged victims.

When the announcement was made, we were, as usual, glued to our phones, following the updates in real time. We immediately pulled up the conditions that had been published by the judge. While the Tates would be prohibited from leaving their homes, there was no condition stopping them from receiving visitors, and crucially, no restrictions around speaking to the press. Since publishing our allegations, and releasing our documentary, we had been barred from challenging Tate directly about what Sally, Helen and Amelia had alleged. What's more, since speaking to Amanda and Maria, we had further questions about the War Room that we needed to put to him. What were the chances that Tate would still answer our phone calls? There was only one way to find out.

Sitting in the BBC offices, overlooking the vast newsroom below us, Matt dialled Tate's number, and the phone began to ring.

'Well, if it isn't Matt!'

Matt looked at Jamie with an expression that said, 'He's picked up!'

'Andrew, hi!' Matt replied. 'How are you?'

Tate didn't respond to the question, but instead continued, 'Mr honest journalism!'

Silence ensued for a moment, as we waited for Tate to elaborate. Then, 'Yep, that's how I like to think of myself!' Matt went on, trying to disarm Tate as best as he could. 'How are you? Are you in your house?' he asked, aware it was the only place he was legally allowed to be.

Tate ignored the question and continued along his previous path. 'It's a shame no one else thinks of you that way, Matt. That's why you had to turn off the comments on your little video.' Tate was referring to Vice turning the comments off on Sally's and Amanda's interviews. This is standard practice when reporting on sexual violence, to prevent viewers from harassing or trying to identify the victims in the comments, which would be a criminal offence in the UK.

'Congratulations on being released under house arrest,' Matt prompted.

Tate waited a moment, and then replied, 'Thank you'.

Matt thought for a moment. 'What do you think is next?' he asked.

'Well,' Tate began, 'it's a beautiful reality. It's a beautiful life and I am clearly one of God's chosen ones. And I'm here to spread a positive message, and continue with my mission, to prevent the degeneracy that is purported by organisations like Vice, drug taking and other forms of pornography, a bunch of other stuff you lot are involved in. I'm here to combat it, and I'm going to lead people to the truth and the light. We're all going to be better people, have a better society for that. And I think you learned that when you turned the comments off on your little video. Most people understand I'm a force for good, and that hit-pieces don't really work because you, the mainstream Matrix mechanisms of the media, have lost all credibility. Unfortunately for you.'

Tate was characteristically misusing long words like 'purported', but other than that, a lot appeared to have changed. Tate was speaking of himself almost as a religious prophet, an ex-pornographer protecting the world from pornography and other evils. Matt tried to bring the conversation back on track, telling Tate that the real reason we had called him was because we felt we had been cut short and still had unanswered questions, and wanted to see if he was up for another interview.

'The problem is, Matt, everyone on the planet wants to interview me. So, the question is, why would I choose you when I have offers from people who are far more successful than you, and better at the job? Because I'd be doing . . . and I'm not trying to disrespect you, I'm just being honest . . . I'd being doing you a favour. Like Matt . . . what's your last name? Shea. That name didn't matter until it was associated to mine. You do an interview with me, and you matter for a little bit. But I can do an interview with anyone, so why would I do an interview with you? This isn't an insult, I'm genuinely asking.'

Matt responded quickly, 'Because we have a history?'

Tate laughed. 'We have a history of you doing dishonest journalism on me, so I would choose you. Interesting.' Tate went on, in full megalomania mode: 'All these reporters who want to say bad things about me, I get to choose which reporter on the planet gets to become relevant, via proxy, because I am the most relevant person, and I get to do the charitable act of allowing someone to sit next to me and ask me questions. It's kind of interesting. I need to think heavily about it. I can't just give out such a fantastic opportunity to disingenuous nobodies.'

Silence hung in the air as we waited for Tate to speak. It was difficult to know how to respond to this rant. 'I'm gonna think about it, Matt, because I'm the one who matters here. I can sit down with fucking . . . Big Bird, Oscar the Grouch. I can sit down with anybody, and it would be the most important podcast or interview in the world. I'm gonna think about it . . . Would you bring me a box of chocolates?'

Matt looked at Jamie, perplexed. 'I can bring you a box of chocolates,' he replied, while Jamie shook his head behind the camera.

'If you promise to give me a box of chocolates, that will increase your chances and you'll have an answer within twenty-four hours. But you have to promise me, Matt, don't lie to me.'

'I'll check with my superiors whether I can bring you a box of chocolates.'

'Well, you check with your bosses. Check if you're allowed to spend a large portion of your salary on a £5 box of chocolates, and you let me know. If you can, I will strongly consider allowing you the opportunity to speak with me.'

On 13 April we were on a flight to Romania. Our bosses at the BBC had determined that we were indeed allowed to take Tate a box of chocolates, to be consumed as refreshments during the interview. It was the first time in BBC history that anyone had requested chocolates in order to conduct an interview. We had our own editorial discussion with our executive producer, Mike Radford, and had agreed that we would not hand over the box of chocolates to Tate until we sat down to interview him. Given our previous encounters with him, and his demeanour on our call, we knew we were most likely being baited. Tate might try to draw us into giving him the chocolates on camera, so that he could post it online. The implication might be that Matt bought him a box of chocolates to apologise for our 'hit-piece' documentary.

We were right to assume that Tate was playing a game. When we arrived at his compound, where he was under house arrest, we weren't greeted by him, but by a young Romanian man called Alex. Over the course of the day, Alex continually requested the box of chocolates on Tate's behalf, returning inside to relay our messages to Tate, who would send him back out to demand the chocolates again.

'Can't you see how silly this is?' Matt asked Alex. 'Andrew is facing some really serious allegations; does he not want to take them seriously?'

Alex's uncompromising message was that we should hand over the box of chocolates.

We could hear Andrew's and Tristan's voices booming through the house, but they refused to come out and speak with us. We managed to get Tate on the phone, but we were only greeted with further rants about his maximum relevancy, and the claim that he 'is the culture'. Tate told us that he needed the chocolates first, to be able to muster the energy for the interview. When we reminded him that it was Ramadan, and as a now publicly devout Muslim he should be fasting, he replied that he just needed to hold the chocolates to get energy from them. After five hours of this, we decided to leave and fly home, chocolates still in hand. Tate was, of course, filming the whole affair. And, as we expected, it made good content for his fans.

Soon afterwards, Tate would release what he called his own 'documentary' – *The Comical Demise of VICE News*. The thumbnail bore a digitally altered and deformed picture of Matt's face outside the Tate compound, and read, 'Dork, Nerd, Geek. A Tate documentary'. From that day forward, Tate fans would message 'DNG' to Matt every single day, sometimes hundreds of times a day.

With Andrew Tate refusing to engage with us, we would have to investigate the new allegations about the War Room through other means.

Besides us, there was one person who had noticed the significance of Tate's story early on. @Crabcrawler was an account on Twitter that started posting about Tate, condemning some of the things he was saying online, but also drawing public attention to some of the potential red flags we had also spotted. Crabcrawler's real name was Nick Monroe, and he was a member of the hard-right online community, who had gained some notoriety in the space for his writing during the 'Gamergate' saga (a semi-organised harassment campaign that complained about the 'corrupting' force of feminism on the video game industry). In 2020, Tate had messaged both Jamie and Crabcrawler about Jack Murphy, another manosphere influencer, urging them both to write about Murphy's unfolding apparent sexual history as a 'cuck' who performed in porn. This interaction had put Tate on Crabcrawler's radar. As someone on the right, he couldn't understand why so many of his peers were amplifying or associating with this man, who he saw as scamming his followers, as well as promoting pornography, misogyny and potentially being guilty of human trafficking.

Perhaps because of his association with the political right, or because of his public denouncement of Tate, when the first War Room whistle-blower emerged, it was Crabcrawler that they went to. In early 2023, before our chocolate saga with Tate, there were murmurs on the internet that Crabcrawler had been handed something we desperately wanted to get our hands on. When Amanda told us that the Money Pilot spent all his time on a Telegram group, messaging the other War Room members, we knew we needed to get access to what they were saying. This Telegram group would likely be the only record of War Room members speaking candidly, believing that no one was watching them. A whistle-blower had decided to leave the War Room, but before doing so, he downloaded over a year's worth of chat logs from the War Room's 'Great Hall' Telegram channel and gave it to Crabcrawler. As soon as word got out about the chat log, Jamie called him immediately.

Crabcrawler was breathless on the phone, clearly excited by the magnitude of what he'd got his hands on. When Jamie told him that we were speaking to potential victims of the War Room, Crabcrawler immediately offered to help us, and on 4 May 2023 we flew out to meet him at an Airbnb in the suburbs of Cleveland, Ohio. We discussed what he had found out about Tate over a take-away burger, with Crabcrawler drinking a four-pack of beers. There were over 10,000 pages of messages to go through, and once we started digging through them, we couldn't stop.

Large portions of the War Room's Telegram chats were, perhaps as you'd imagine, fairly inane conversations about conspiracy theories, working out, the benefits of consuming meat and misgivings about the liberal Clown World. Among these, however, were some of the most revealing things we had ever uncovered about Tate and his War Room.

The first thing that stood out was that the idea of using Tate's PhD course to recruit women for webcam held a significant place in the War Room. Iggy Semmelweis spoke with reverence about the course, telling his men that the 'PhD is the prescription. The War Room is the Answer', and claiming that Andrew and the PhD had brought the entire 'Red Pill Arc under wraps', teaching men that women should either comply and make them money, or they should be gone. When one man bragged, 'We're all in here to make millions and get pussy!' Iggy corrected him: 'Actually, the PhD is about making pussy get us millions'. The PhD appeared central to the ideology of the War Room. As Iggy wrote in one message: 'It all STARTS with the PhD course. That teaches the way to screen the great ones and catch them into the WebCam mentality needed to make the money.' These men weren't just *talking* about Tate's PhD course; they were putting it into action in their lives, and believed it was having results. As one member wrote: 'My D game [dick game] has been improved massively following the lessons from the WR [War Room], PhD and Elite Channel . . . Will get a bottom bitch when I finish moving to the new country and get her on lockdown . . . more to follow.'

Throughout the chat logs, War Room members solicited and gave advice about how to recruit, 'train' and then financially exploit future girlfriends in the online sex industry. We recognised many of these methods and tips from our conversations with Amanda and Maria.

Both women had spoken about starting relationships with the men online, and here we found members advising each other on how to curate their online presence. Generals who had perfected the art of using social media to attract the 'right type of girl' were appointed by Tate to run courses. Amanda was a young service worker when the Money Pilot first approached her, and this appeared to be one of the War Room's target demographics. As one member suggested, 'McDonalds would be good for cam prospects I would have thought. Young women in lower paying service job, as long as their of age.'

American members of the War Room expressed concern for the 'legal' age of the women they were speaking to, but it didn't stop them from entertaining the idea of speaking to women who were underage. In one message, the Money Pilot sent a picture of a young woman drinking a smoothie, with the message, 'Is it November yet?' In a strange coincidence, it appears the man who recruited Maria replied first, with a series of laughing emojis. Tate responded: '*Who's this. The young one?*' to which the Money Pilot said, 'Yeah, told her to wait till she's 18. Keeps sending me pics [another laughing emoji].' A minute later, Tate: '*Jesus. Speed up time!*'

Something else that caught our attention was a series of messages referring to having the women you were trying to recruit bring you chocolate the first time you met them, as Tate had done with Matt. We asked Amanda and Maria if they had been requested to bring anything when they went on a 'first date' with their respective recruiters. Amanda said, 'Yeah. He asked me to bring him, like, a unique kind of chocolate on the date, which was a bit weird.' Shortly after, Maria confirmed, too, that she had been asked to bring a special box of chocolates on the date, which she bought on her way to meet him at his apartment. According to War Room thinking, women who obeyed this first demand would be more susceptible to manipulation, and eventually to working on webcam or OnlyFans. In asking Matt to bring him a box of chocolates, then, Tate may have been testing how liable Matt was to submit to future demands. Or perhaps, more likely, it was an inside joke for his War Room members in the know.

The chat logs were filled with insights we could have only hoped for, and this was partially the fault of the members themselves. Iggy appeared to have created the idea of 'receipts' within the War Room: the notion that if you were claiming to be doing something, then you should be able to prove it to your War Room brothers with 'receipts'. As such, the group was filled with photographic evidence of the 'spoils' these men had acquired through their training.

The men weren't just discussing recruiting, but also, as Iggy termed it, 'training'. War Room members appeared to believe, following on from Tate's PhD test, that there were certain trials or training that you could put your new 'girlfriends' through, to make them more submissive and therefore more likely to work on webcam for you. Both Maria and Amanda spoke about being given daily tasks, outside of their webcamming work. These included things like doing their recruiter's laundry, buying him things with their own money or preparing his meals. Maria recalled her recruiter waking her up at 6am to make him coffee, before she was allowed to go back to sleep. Both women told us that the men referred to these tasks as 'missions'. A message from Iggy hinted at the purpose of these 'missions':

G's gotta keep their women occupied with tasks – Missions – to keep them busy and proving their devotion. A chase cycle consists of . . .

1. You set the mission.

2. She completes the mission.

3. You reward her APPROPRIATELY for successfully completing the mission.

'Set the Mission' means you explicitly task her with doing something. That something MUST BE non-sexual in nature . . . 'make me a sammich' is a mission. 'Pick up my cleaning' is a mission . . .

Yes this is Pavlovian Conditioning.

Yes, this is operant conditioning.

Yes, this is how you train dogs.

Deal with it.

Both Amanda and Maria had told us that their recruiters were keen on BDSM, and Amanda felt at times it was to introduce violence into the relationship: 'This, you know, would come out, like, when he was like, angry or upset with me, he would bruise me pretty badly and, like, inflict pain on me.' In the chat logs, we could see members like Iggy and the Money Pilot sharing tips on BDSM practices. Some men shared photos of severe bruising on intimate areas of women's skin. One message from the Money Pilot read: 'A certain someone is still trying to figure out where a thumb-shaped bruise on her neck came from. Still has no idea.' Dylan Madden replied, 'Most girls like marks like that. As reminders and signs of ownership.' Iggy referred to these acts of 'reprogramming' a person's brain as 'spells', and suggested that some 'spells' could not be cast without BDSM being involved: '. . . there are those special spells that require electricity, nipple clamps and vibrating anal plugs to REALLY get the job done'. Amanda told us that she thought, for them, BDSM was being used as an 'excuse to get away with being abusive'.

Once the War Room members had managed to recruit a 'girl-friend', they appeared to focus their efforts on how to make them more dependent, isolated and submissive. This included having the woman tattoo the man's name on her body, a practice common among many human traffickers and pimps. Tate had bragged on Twitter that he'd had his name tattooed on multiple women, and in one podcast he claimed that *getting the girl, or fucking the girl, is the first 10 per cent of the game. Having a girl tattoo your name on her is the other 90 per cent'*. Tate boasted of this in the War Room chat logs as well, sharing photos of the women marked with his name, one accompanied by the statement: *'34 or 35 girls now. I don't even know.'*

Amanda and Maria had both told us how their recruiters were determined to have them tattooed, but that they had continually refused. One member claimed that 'tattooed girls will be G's living, walking, talking ad boards', and another responded, 'branding these bitches'. Men solicited advice from each other on how to approach or achieve this, and may have used each other's photos to further pressure their recruits, making the argument: 'Look, my friend's girlfriend did it, so why won't you? Don't you love me?' Many of them succeeded, and accompanying one photo of a tattooed woman was the message: 'Attached is a receipt: got my girl to get my name tattooed on her body. She loves it; she loves being owned by me. I would've never been able to pull this off if it wasn't for @cobratate and what he taught in his PhD course . . . I got another girl who is down for getting my name tattooed on her; we'll see how that goes but I will elaborate more in the PhD room. Eventually I'm gonna see if I can put them on cam. Little by little been making my way up the pimpin' G ladder.'

These women had no idea what they were getting into. As

Amanda had said, 'It ruined my life in a lot of ways because I was too scared to, like, date anyone else, even though I was, like, involved in this, like, not so . . . kind of . . . relationship. But I, I was scared to let anyone get close to me, like, friends, people in my life. And so, it felt very isolating.'

According to Iggy's instructions, this isolation may have been by design:

We deliberately reduce attention and note if she chases.

Then we set up a 'coffee date' and execute a move to find out if she is WILLING TO PAY for our coffee and serve us.

After that it becomes a series of gradual steps to remove her entire support structure from her life.

Then we 'punish' her for a transgression – real or imagined – by having her get our name tattooed on her, leaving her family's home/apartment/town/country, WebCamming/ stripping/walking the track for us, getting us girls, escalate, escalate, escalate.

Here's something you guys need to hear out loud because it now can be said:

The PhD Test NEVER ends.

She has to PROVE IT EVERY DAY, and PASS IT EVERY NIGHT.

And like every Test it gets 'harder' and 'more difficult' with each level.

This is the Way of Wudan.

This is The White Path.

The desired level of submission and subservience from the War Room members could be summarised with a single message from Iggy, who hints at a further stage: 'Female Sexual Slavery. Just a place-marker for what we're preparing for the next-iteration of PhD.'

We were shocked not only by the content of the messages, but also by their frequency. These men appeared to spend vast amounts of time on Telegram, in almost constant communication with each other. Tate and Tristan were revered. Tristan would post occasional 'receipts', and Tate was referred to as the 'master and commander', but they were far less active in the group than the rest of the members. Tate's participation, in particular, dropped off towards the end of 2020. There was one member, however, who appeared to be almost always online, constantly replying to messages and advising men on their next steps. He seemed to hold the power to remove members from the War Room, and bring new ones in, admonishing those who weren't 'performing' with messages like: 'I will burn you motherfuckers unless you start bringing some maximum value to the War Room, NOW!'

The man seemingly in control of the War Room, leading its members in their endeavours, was Iggy Semmelweis.

PART THREE

The Men
Behind the Men

CHAPTER TEN

The Many Names of Iggy Semmelweis

From the moment we saw Iggy Semmelweis in a War Room promotional video, bearded, wearing a trilby and shooting animated balls of fire out of his hands, we were enthralled. As we found out more – his unusual names, his claims to being a master hypnotist and the 'Grand Priest Master of the War Room' – our curiosity grew. Who was this strange man, posing as a wizard, standing by the side of one of the most controversial influencers in the world? Everything about him seemed so out of place in Tate's story – we had to understand how he came to hold such a significant place in it. His current moniker, Iggy Semmelweis, was adopted from a nineteenth-century physician Ignaz (Iggy) Semmelweis, who popularised hand-washing in the medical profession after he recognised that it was germs rather than 'vapours' that were causing infections. But why did Iggy choose to take on this new name? And who was he really?

When we'd met Iggy in Romania, he'd flatly refused to speak to us, so it was difficult to gain much insight directly from him. One

186 THE MANY NAMES OF IGGY SEMMELWEIS

huge resource we had access to was his public Twitter account, which he used prolifically. His tweets were a strange mixture of endorsements for Tate and the War Room, musings on US politics, red-pill and PUA culture, misogynistic and homophobic jokes, and retweeted pictures of cute puppies. Buried among this mass of tweets were snippets of revealing information, alongside troubling comments. One of his tweets read: 'My WebCam girl is home 100% of the time; has no time nor interest in going out. She sleeps, cooks, cleans, does her shows, gives me ALL the money, gets railed by me and our girlfriends, then smiles, thanks me, and goes and does it again tomorrow. Welcome to the War Room.' In many of his tweets, Iggy appeared to be talking about his own wife, Satchie, who, he bragged, worked for him on webcam. Another tweet read: 'Gs recognise seduction, sex & women as nothing more than tools to be utilized in order to build a man's wealth. THAT understanding is the TRUE Red Pill.'

Multiple tweets expressed admiration for Edward Bernays, an American pioneer in the field of public relations and propaganda. According to Iggy in one tweet: 'Communism is evil. Socialism is evil. Feminism is evil. Fascism is evil. Antifa is evil. ALL created by the SAME GROUP of people; designed to appeal to the greed and avarice in the weakest of minds. Edward Bernays explained how it works; how it's done. You are in The Matrix.'

Iggy's penchant for far-right views was clear from the people he admired, including the science fiction writer and 'activist' known as Vox Day, who claims to have popularised the term 'cuckservative'.* A

---

* A hybrid of conservative and 'cuck', or 'cuckold'. A derogatory term within online right-wing political spheres for a conservative who is too willing to compromise, or isn't conservative enough.

quick look at Iggy's Twitter feed showed his admiration for Trump, and his disdain for immigrants and particular people from LGBTQ communities.

In one Twitter thread, Iggy posted photos from a War Room meet-up, and Jamie scrolled through it scanning the faces, until he came to the final tweet in the thread, featuring a picture of Iggy wearing a gold-sequinned cardigan and snakeskin trilby. Above the picture he had written: 'I am the Master of Spells & Shadows, Order of The King Cobra. Keeper of the Scarlet Citadel. Inside The War Room @OfWudan. I will you to Greatness as I show you ways to unlock your potential beyond imagination.' This message stood out to Jamie. 'The Scarlet Citadel?' he said to Matt. 'We've seen that in one of his other tweets, haven't we? It's oddly specific to come up more than once.'

A Google search revealed it to be a 1933 fantasy short story by Robert E. Howard, creator of the Conan the Barbarian universe. The story, which was also turned into a popular edition of the game Dungeons and Dragons, featured Conan (the 'Cobra King'), and curiously, a dark wizard called Tsotha-Lanti, who, in the graphic novels and fan art that depicted him, bore a striking resemblance to Iggy. Tsotha-Lanti was the keeper of the Scarlet Citadel, a dungeon below his castle, where he tortured his victims and created scrolls out of their skin. Tsotha-Lanti also wore a ring with a cobra's head on it, the fangs of which produced venom that he poisoned his adversaries with. We'd seen rings that matched this description before, not just on Iggy when we'd met him in Romania, but on the fingers of the men who'd allegedly groomed Amanda and Maria, when we found images of them online. Was Iggy leaving bread-crumbs on his own Twitter, trying to signal his influences for the character of the Grand Priest Master?

Matt began to read out loud from the story:

'Men said that he had a whole library of dark works bound in skin flayed from living human victims, and that in nameless pits below the hill whereon his palace sat, he trafficked with the powers of darkness, trading screaming girl slaves for unholy secrets. He was the real ruler of Koth.'

By referencing this wizard, was Iggy making some sort of sick reference to the trafficking of women, as slaves, and suggesting he was the real leader of the War Room, as the 'real ruler of Koth'?

The comic-book adaptation of *The Scarlet Citadel* was filled with images of almost-naked women chained to stones inside dark citadels and hypermuscular men with long hair, wielding axes in a kind of pastiche of some unknown 1970s' heavy-metal sexualised fantasy. Large portions of the Conan the Barbarian books that Howard wrote focus on Conan, or other rivalling characters, stealing each other's harems. Returning to the War Room chat logs, it was clear that this reference to *The Scarlet Citadel* was no coincidence. One message from Iggy read:

It's just that men are, by nature, attracted to unlimited sexual variety.

Nature LOVES it when a guy can get his hands on LOTS of different willing women.

That's what makes a Hareem so attractive. I read a LOT of Robert E. Howard growing up and wanted THAT lifestyle – a Cimmerian Conqueror's.

Perhaps resigned to the fact that he couldn't be Conan, the Warrior King, Iggy had opted for Tsotha-Lanti.

Another lead we picked up from the chat logs was a reference to a particular online group. Iggy repeatedly complained about 'the Gammas' or 'the fucking Secret Kings', writing: 'The entire War Room flows like a river and it's always the Secret Kings – the Gammas – who insist on throwing big fucking rocks into the river. Those rocks disturb the flow, create turbulence, and next thing you know, all the water that was once flowing smoothly is now just pooling, becoming stagnant and fetid.'

The Gamma Secret Kings was a collection of accounts on Reddit, who organise under the subreddit r/gammasecretkings. The group was focused on exposing 'public-figure Political Grifters' and described itself as a 'nonpartisan Grifter news aggregator and gossip rag'. Like many groups on Reddit, they were far from 'politically correct', and many of them had come from the alt-right or manosphere themselves, but now exposed the scamming that they felt took place in those spaces. The Gamma Secret Kings had been posting about Tate and his War Room for some time, trying to convince men not to sign up. Many of their posts were compelling, pointing out contradictions in Tate's personal story and statements, but loaded with insults and memes, and coloured with the language of niche internet forums. Iggy complained in one message, 'This is why the Secret Kings and Gammas are such a fucking pain in the ass. They really are smart – but always in such a fucking retarded kind of way.'

We reached out to the Gamma Secret Kings, and one of their moderators, going by the name of E-Scorpio, agreed to speak to us on the group's behalf. He joined us on a video call from Texas, sporting black wraparound sunglasses and smoking a cigarette in his garden. E-Scorpio seemed to relish mocking the War Room, telling us: 'These men, we think it is all a ridiculous display and we make fun of them for it. That's it. Now I'm sure, especially some of these young men they lure in are convinced that this is all very real. Some of these, you know, War Room generals themselves may even believe it is real to a degree. What is he, the shaman? The priest? The wizard Iggy Semmelweis? He is playing a role. These men are not – what is it, Wudan, the Kingdom of Wudan, or whatever it is – these are not, you know, Chinese monks. These are just right-wing idiots playing games on the internet.'

But if Iggy Semmelweis *was* playing a role, then who was he really? E-Scorpio told us one of their members had uncovered Iggy's real name, and he sent us a link. We opened it up to find a blog post on a website called High Probability Selling, written by a man called Miles Sonkin, which, E-Scorpio told us, was Iggy's real name. Now in his sixties, Miles Gary Sonkin was originally from Morton Grove, Chicago, and, according to the internet, was currently living in Koreatown, LA. His father studied law, and his mother was a local radio and TV personality who presented programmes on the paranormal. Gamma Secret Kings showed us photos of Miles in various high-school theatre productions, but other than that, there was very little about him online. That is, apart from the blog post on the High Probability Selling website.

In Pennsylvania USA, in the late 1990s, a telemarketer and sales trainer called Jacques Werth, known to most as Jack, wrote a now well-known book about his personal sales technique, which was called High Probability Selling, or 'High Prob'. Jack founded a business with two partners, self-publishing the book and running in person-workshops, starting off in the US and expanding globally. He employed various independent contractors to help him spread the message of High Probability Selling, running workshops and implementing their practices for struggling businesses who would hire them as consultants. From the blog post, it appeared that in the late 1990s, Miles Sonkin attended a High Prob workshop in the US, before moving to Japan where he coordinated the translation of the book into Japanese, and began running workshops in his new hometown of Osaka. The Gamma Secret Kings believe it was pickup artistry that brought him there, as Osaka was a popular destination for Western PUAs to travel to target Japanese women.

When we reached out to see if Jack Werth would be interested in speaking to us, we received a response from one of his business partners, Carl Ingalls, who informed us that Jack was now suffering with dementia and would not be able to talk. Ingalls was one of the longest-standing associates of High Prob, and when we mentioned Miles Sonkin to him, he agreed to set up a call between us, himself and Paul Bunn, who would have known Miles back then, he said.

When we got Bunn on the phone, however, he was less emphatic than Ingalls. 'To say that I know him would be a bit of a stretch . . . I talked to him twice in the late nineties, way back.' Bunn told us that he remembered that Miles was indeed living in Osaka, Japan, around that time and that he was primarily making a living selling offshore financial investments to expats. 'We spoke about his experience with martial arts, aikido specifically, and I got the impression he was quite good at that.' As well as helping us to confirm some basic details about Miles's life, the more we spoke to Ingalls and Bunn, the more it became clear that Miles's time in High Probability Selling had influenced his teachings as Iggy Semmelweis.

The basic premise of High Prob is that rather than wasting time convincing everyone to try and buy your product, you should instead filter your prospective customers down to those who, as Bunn put it, 'want what the person is selling'. To do this, you ask them lots of potentially disqualifying questions, and leave at the first indication that there is not a 'high probability' that they are a true 'prospect'. Werth wrote in his book: 'Only High Probability Prospects – those who are willing to commit step-by-step to the buying process – are worth the salesperson's time, energy and resources.' And as Bunn elaborated, 'The whole process itself is a series of micro-commitments or disqualifications. We're not calling someone and asking if they'll buy whatever we have, like, no matter what; we're calling them and asking them, basically, are they likely to buy, or do they want the outcome that our product or service provides?' In Jack's book, he tells us that the disqualifying questions that you ask may seem blunt or rude, but that they would only appear so to those who were not real prospects. While asking these questions, Ingalls told us that as practitioners of High Prob, 'we are constantly testing and evaluating the probability that there will be an outcome that we want . . . It's like playing poker; you are constantly looking at the hand that you have and the information you see, and working out: what are the odds that this is gonna be a win, or not?'

When Iggy instructed War Room men to request that the women they went on dates with bring a special type of chocolate, he knew this would disqualify a good number of them, leaving only those who would be good 'prospects' for Tate's PhD programme. When we asked Ingalls and Paul if they thought High Probability could be applied to meeting women, Bunn shared a story that Jack Werth had told him, from his youth in New York in the 1950s. Werth told Bunn that he would go to a bar and approach women in extremely direct terms, 'the epitome of cut to the chase', and then say to them, 'Is that something you want?' Bunn laughed. 'He'd get slapped, say ok, move on to the next one, get slapped, say ok' – and again and again, 'until eventually someone said yes, and he was all set!' Ingalls told us that Werth had, in fact, once spoken on the topic of High Prob and attracting women at a conference in Canada, but that his experience had been negative. According to Ingalls, Werth supported using High Prob in a non-manipulative way, but the audience he encountered was more interested in using manipulative techniques, often taught by practitioners in neuro-linguistic programming, or NLP.

NLP is the pseudoscientific belief that you can use your language, delivery and tone of speech to influence people's neurological pro-cesses, and therefore their decisions and actions. Many liken NLP to hypnosis, and since its creators first wrote about it in 1975, it has been used by celebrity figures such as Derren Brown, Paul McKenna and Tony Robbins. NLP was big in both the pickup-artist commu-nity and the sales community, and Paul Bunn told us it was likely that many of the salespeople who attended High Prob conferences would have also looked at NLP for sales. Iggy's Twitter made it clear that he took a keen interest in NLP, with frequent references to it and claims that he had studied directly with Richard Bandler (one of the founders of NLP), Robbins and other major proponents. When Iggy calls himself 'the greatest hypnotist in the world', he may really believe it, and when he calls himself 'the Master of Spells and Shadows', these are presumably the spells he is referring to. Ingalls insisted that Jack Werth always opposed NLP unless used by a med-ical practitioner, claiming 'it can be used by psychotherapists quite effectively, and also by megalomaniacs quite effectively'.

Referring back to Iggy, and his adoption of what he learned from High Prob as Miles, Bunn told us, 'I can see some of the aspects of High Prob, the directness and all that, combined with NLP, com-bined with the underlying fundamentals of aikido as a martial art, not meeting force with force . . . and if you're a charismatic person, yeah, I could see him using it for that . . .'

Ingalls butted in. 'If the person was also a con artist,' he added.

As our conversation drew to an end, Bunn added something else. 'It's kind of neat that he borrowed Semmelweis's name. That's kind of a cute one.' When we asked him what he meant, he explained that when they discussed High Probability Selling, they would talk about it in the context of a 'paradigm shift'. Their theory was that High Prob would cause such a dramatic shift in the way you viewed sales, you would now view everything related to sales through this new paradigm. In the seminars, Bunn explained, they would give different examples of paradigm shifts. 'One of them was, we had this little chart, and it said "vapours which cause disease", and then showed Semmelweis coming along and saying "No, guys, it's germs", so Semmelweis caused a paradigm shift in medicine.' Miles saw himself as a man like Semmelweis, who would cause a paradigm shift, affecting the people who encountered him so dramatically that they wouldn't be able to view the world in the same way again.

We asked Bunn and Ingalls what had happened to Miles, but neither of them could be sure. 'There was a period where no one could contact him,' Bunn explained, 'around 2005.' Bunn told us that Jack was worried about Miles, and desperately tried to find him, sending someone from the US to look for him, and even going through the American Embassy in Japan. 'Nobody could find him, he literally just disappeared.'

It turns out, however, that Miles hadn't disappeared. He was still in Japan. It also seems that Iggy Semmelweis wasn't the first character he created.

After leaving High Probability Selling, Miles decided to combine what he had learned there with his love for NLP and pickup artistry. He founded his own company, Date Masters – an online dating coaching company that taught men how to pick up women. Here, Miles went under the name Douglas Hall, claiming to be an infamous PUA with a long history in the scene. (Douglas Hall is the name of a university building in Miles's hometown of Chicago.) Miles also authored a book called *How to Meet More Women* as Douglas Hall, which he sold on the Date Masters website, and which was written in similar language and tone to Werth's *High Probability Selling*. As Douglas Hall, he ran seminars in Japan targeting Western men, who could fly out to Japan and be shown how to 'date' Japanese women. The website was still archived, and alongside its blog posts and now defunct links to buy the book, was a picture of Iggy's wife, Satchie, much younger than she is now, accompanied by the caption 'The current Sexual Mastery Seminar co-trainer at Date Masters Japan'. Date Masters, like Tate's businesses when they would appear almost twenty years later, appeared to have an affiliate marketing scheme built into it, whereby subscribers could earn a fee by marketing and selling the scheme to future members. It was becoming clear to us that Iggy Semmelweis, or Miles Sonkin, or Douglas Hall, had developed both the skills and knowledge that Tate would later use, and, in many ways, there were echoes of Miles's past in Tate's present.

Douglas Hall achieved a degree of underground 'success' and notoriety, attracting some attention for his blogs, but this was almost nothing compared to what Miles would achieve when he created Iggy Semmelweis and started working with Andrew Tate. E-Scorpio thought Miles had needed someone like Tate and was waiting for him. 'Iggy is not a very appealing man at all, in my opinion', he told us. 'Whereas Tate, you have to admit, you know, is a man who is at the peak of his physical prowess. He's an attractive-looking man.

So, why not have that as your as your honey to lure in these men that want to have that? That want to be that image themselves. They don't want to be like Iggy. They want to be like Tate.'

Shortly after speaking to the Gamma Secret Kings in May 2023, Matt was able to make contact with a family connection of Miles, who spoke to us anonymously. According to him, Miles was extremely intelligent as a young man, but had little interest in school, skipping classes whenever he could. The family member told Matt that Miles was extremely paranoid right now, and had told another member of his family that he was being investigated by the FBI for potential financial crimes, and was planning on going into hiding. Perhaps most revealing, however, was what he told us about Miles before the days of High Probability Selling and Douglas Hall. In the 1980s, Miles had been a member of a fairly notorious cult, the Rajneesh movement – an Indian-based meditation cult, perhaps best known today for featuring in the 2018 Netflix series *Wild Wild Country*. Its leader faced numerous criminal allegations, including the sexual abuse of his followers.

We'd long started to feel that the War Room resembled a cult, and given that Iggy, who seemed to be playing a central role within the organisation, had previous experience in two alleged cults, as well as an interest in mind control and hypnotism, it was starting to look as though he had created this cult intentionally. In chat-log messages, Iggy refers to 'Tateism', speaking with an almost spiritual reverence for the War Room and its objectives. In May 2023, not long after our initial discoveries about Iggy, Crabcrawler reached out to Jamie to let him know that he had been approached by a disgruntled recent ex-member of the War Room who was willing to speak to us. This would be our first chance to hear an insider's perspective.

'J', as he asked to be referred to, was in his thirties and had been a member of the War Room for around a year and a half, before leaving towards the end of 2022. With the gift of hindsight, J believed the War Room was a scam, aimed at tricking him into parting with thousands of dollars. J worked in sales, and had joined the War Room to try to learn some new skills about business, keen to generate the large streams of passive income that Tate had promised. However, upon joining the group, J said he found that one of the only ways to make money they actually showed you was having women work on webcam and OnlyFans, something which J said he, a happily married man, had little interest in. J had also joined the War Room with some expectation that it would be a chance to get close to Tate, spending time and perhaps even working directly with him. In reality, J told us, time with Tate was very rare; and it wasn't Tate who was primarily guiding the men in the War Room Telegram groups, but rather the 'generals', in particular Iggy Semmelweis.

'He never sleeps,' J told Jamie. 'He's online all the time, constantly replying to every message.' When Jamie asked J what he thought of Iggy, he replied sternly: 'He is strange. He scares me.' According to J, Iggy appeared to believe that the War Room would have a monumental impact, with the ability to change the very way that millions of men viewed the world. 'He has very dark ideas, to be honest with you. I think he might be a Satanist.' According to J, Iggy saw women as the root of evil in the world, referring to them as 'dragons' that must be tamed.

J told us that when you joined the War Room, you were presented with a document from Iggy, entitled 'The Survival Scrolls', which opened with a reading list curated by him, aimed to 'reprogramme' readers' brains. This included classic manosphere titles such as *The Predatory Female* by Rev. Lawrence Shannon and *The Manipulated Man* by Esther Vilar, which argued that women were not oppressed by men, but control men for their own advantage. A message from Iggy in the chat logs reads: 'Gs are men of purpose, men of will and men of power that the War Room builds. All women are merely dragons chasing them. Gs understand this reality and use their power and purpose to bend dragons to their will and get them to give over their hordes of treasure while never letting the dragons catch them.' Although Tate was the figurehead of the War Room, used to sell membership to prospective customers, J was adamant that Iggy appeared to be its leader in practice, and he was building a cult of sycophantic followers.

Messages in the chat logs appeared to confirm the War Room members' perception of Iggy, with one writing that 'Iggy is the man who keeps the War Room as the ultimate filter. If you post 0 value, he mentions it. He is the moderator.' Iggy's posts admonished the men, inducing feelings of guilt in them – a typical control tactic within cults and one we'd seen in action in Romania. Many of the men appeared to thank Iggy for their punishments, with one writing, 'Thanks very much for breaking my balls Iggy, I deserved it and it was a good lesson.' Iggy simply responded, 'You have much of value to bring here, do it'.

Another feature of cults is the 'restructuring of members' thought processes',* and as well providing his reading list in the Survival Scrolls, Iggy appears to have tried to use hypnotism to achieve this with War Room members. Dr Steve Hassan, an ex-member of the Moonies turned academic and cult expert wrote: 'In a sense, NLP teaches in a systematic way what many cult leaders and con artists

---

* Steven Hassan, *The Cult of Trump*, Free Press, 2020, p. 75.

do'.[*] In one message, Iggy told a follower, Joshiah, to 'Re-code memories. Go back in time and tell the younger Joshiah what he needed to hear back then with the wisdom you have now. Deep trance work. Tons of fun. I'm in the middle of re-coding everything with what I've learned here in The War Room from all of you guys and Andrew and Tristan. Trippier than any drugs on the market.' He seemed keen to impress on the men that the War Room would cause a 'paradigm shift', revealing their futures in a spiritual sense, writing of the Romania summit in 2019 that 'THERE WILL BE, The Arc. The entire ARC OF YOUR LIFE Presented to you so you can KNOW, REALLY FUCKING KNOW, where you are going, AND HOW YOU ARE GOING TO GET THERE.'

When we saw Iggy delivering the story of Wudan to the men in Romania, was he using brainwashing and hypnosis techniques to try to lure them further into a cult? It's not hard to imagine the self-styled 'Master of Spells and Shadows' reading the earliest NLP book, which is called *The Structure of Magic*. The strange, hypnotic speech patterns that he adopted could be seen not just at War Room events and in his tweets, but also in the messages he sent to men on Telegram:

And we always move forward – carried by the current, the stream, the flow.

The flow that takes us to Wudan.

The flow that IS Wudan.

That which calls us is Wudan . . .

More than a person, more than a place, we are ALL Wudan.

---

* Ibid.

A significant observation we made was that Iggy seemed to encourage War Room members to isolate themselves, just as he appeared to be in favour of removing women from their support networks, making them entirely dependent on the men who groomed them. When one member complained that his friends did not seem to support his new life path, Iggy replied sternly: 'Get new friends. They're lost and they're pulling you down. If you had a different class of friends you'd ALL be soaring by now. Imagine having ALL those guys here together in The War Room – then taking EVERYTHING you learn in here and APPLYING it on your REAL WORLD all together as a team. BUT. They'll never come in here, because they are not bred for it. Their DNA is worm DNA . . . You've got to walk on.'

This distinction between 'us' and 'them', War Room vs worms, War Room vs Clown World is yet another identifying feature of a cult.

Iggy also made direct comparisons with organised religion. One message read, 'The tales of Jesus able to feed multitudes with just bread, turn water into wine . . . When Men of Power are among us, eating only bread is a BANQUET, drinking mere water in their presence makes us as giddy as if we'd drunk wine.'

But why would Miles Sonkin create the character of Iggy Semmelweis, and use Andrew Tate to create this cult of radicalised men? What did he hope to achieve with it? According to J, Iggy's motivation was clear. It came from a desire for power, and a genuine disdain for women: 'He really does see women as different from men. As less than men. They're dragons.'

A further 'scroll' of Iggy's, titled 'How To Train Your Dragon', was given to men in the PhD room and dealt specifically with how they should handle women. In one chat-log message, a War Room member refers to Iggy as Merlin, training an army of King Arthurs.

Buried in the Survival Scrolls, within a curious section titled 'Scrolls for the Sexual Adventurer', Iggy listed three works relating to BDSM that he designated 'required reading' for anyone on the 'God Mode' course and recommended reading for anyone on the 'PHD Program'. Below these titles, he wrote: 'NOTE: even if you are NOT interested in BDSM or Anal, you will still WANT to read Screw the Roses, Send Me the Thorns, and The Ultimate Guide to Anal Sex for Women because they train you in setting up the Female Sexual Slavery Frames and the Female Sexual Progressions'.

Was Iggy's dark and twisted fantasy to use NLP, hypnosis and dark psychology to create female sex slaves? If he was using Tate's image to build a cult for this purpose, we needed to confront him.

We booked an Airbnb fifteen minutes' drive from the large, old apartment complex in Koreatown, LA, where Iggy lived. Accompanying us was our producer, Tashi Hanlon, who was working with us on our new documentary for the BBC. Without permission to enter the complex, we wouldn't be able to go directly to his front door. So, with limited time in LA, we decided to search other haunts where we might find him: a hotel where we knew he held business meetings and a burlesque bar that hosted magic shows where he had been photographed holding a War Room event with Satchie, his wife, and Jonathan, the 'Money Pilot', who Amanda claimed had groomed her. We also found a photo of Iggy at what looked like a fetish party in LA the summer before, pictured with his wife and two other women. One of them was tagged. 'I could just DM her?' Matt suggested. She replied within a minute, and Matt's phone began to ring. We asked her if she knew Miles Sonkin, but she seemed confused by the name. 'He was with his wife, Satchie. He might have used the name Iggy Semmelweis?' Matt suggested. She still had no idea. Matt forwarded her the photo, 'Oh,' she replied. 'You mean Sean and Rose?'

The woman on the phone had first met Iggy at a fetish party, and he, using the name Sean, learned that she was a 'bling artist', who bejewelled various items of clothing. Iggy had commissioned her to make him a velour tracksuit bearing a large jewelled chess piece on the back. It was the now familiar War Room logo, and this was the very same tracksuit Iggy had worn during his speech at The Test. She began to get the vibe that Iggy and Satchie were trying to proposition her for a threesome. 'It was very obvious they were kind of angling for something, which I was not interested in . . . They were definitely trying to get me alone in a room with them. One hundred per cent.' When Matt asked her what 'Sean' or Iggy was like, she told us, 'He thinks he's really really smart. And he thinks he's like five steps ahead of anybody else, and kind of has the book of secrets or something. Anytime he was talking about anything that he disagreed with, viewpoints, he completely discounted it as unintelligent and misinformed. Very arrogant.' She didn't know where Iggy was now, or even if he was still in LA, so our only option would be to try to catch him at his home.

The next morning, we parked fifty metres away from the front gate of Iggy's apartment complex, which we'd determined was the only way he could leave the building, and we began a stake-out. Stake-outs might seem exciting in police films or TV shows, but in reality, this one involved sitting staring at a single point for hours, drinking absurd amounts of coffee and constantly worrying about needing to go for a piss. Five hours in, there was still no sign of Iggy. Our producer Tashi walked to a convenience store to use their bathroom, and called us fairly distressed, saying she'd just seen a young trans woman being attacked by a man outside the store. Moments later, this young woman, bleeding from the head, pulled up on her skateboard by our car, still parked outside of Iggy's home. A car then drove up, and the driver began shouting transphobic abuse at the young woman, threatening to 'fuck her up'. When she picked up her skateboard and said she would hit his car, he pulled away, shouting, 'You're a man, not a fucking woman'. She sat down on the pavement, in tears, and we jumped out of our car to check that she was ok. It transpired that she lived in the same block as Iggy but given the immensely stressful situation she was currently in, we didn't think this would be the right time to start asking her about a potential sex-trafficking wizard living in her building.

A small crowd of neighbours had gathered to watch, and we began to worry that Iggy might appear and spot us outside his home, helping this young woman. She didn't have a phone and asked us if she could call her partner on one of ours, as well as asking us to call the police. We of course obliged, but were now in the rather surreal situation of having called the police to our own stake-out, drawing huge amounts of attention to ourselves, when we were supposed to be hiding. When the young woman's partner arrived, we gave her our phone number in case the police needed any information from us, then retreated to our car, reversing another thirty metres down the street.

Eight hours into our stake-out, and still no sign of Iggy, we began to wonder if he was in LA at all. Then, just as we were considering leaving to get dinner before heading to the bar we knew he frequented, a tall, thin figure emerged from the apartment block and crossed the road. Sporting a beanie hat, with his long beard poking out beneath, was Iggy. He was more dressed down than we were used to seeing him, but wore a leather jacket and shoulder bag, both bearing the War Room's logo.

'Fuck, it's him, it's him,' Matt said.

Adrenaline pumping, we followed him in our car as he walked down the road. Then we pulled up and jumped out.

'Iggy Semmelweis!' Matt exclaimed, walking straight over to him.

A shocked expression briefly appeared on Iggy's face, before he shook his head and continued with his determined stride.

We followed, Jamie holding the camera, and we asked him the questions we desperately wanted answers to. 'Is your real name Miles Sonkin? Are you the leader of the War Room? Do you teach men how groom women? Are you creating a cult using Andrew Tate's image?'

Iggy continued resolutely, giving no answers to our questions, but grimacing slightly when our questioning revealed that perhaps he had been caught out.

'What did you mean by the words "Female Sexual Slavery" in the Survival Scrolls? Did you learn this method when you worked at High Probability Selling? Or was it when you were Douglas Hall?'

We'd always assumed that if we did find Iggy outside his home in LA, we'd be able to ask him one or two questions before he either turned around and went back inside or jumped into a car and drove away. Instead, we found ourselves walking for eighteen minutes through Koreatown, as Iggy continued to ignore our questions, seemingly focused on reaching his intended destination. The journey through Koreatown, as the sun began to set, felt long and surreal, and we began to run out of questions. Eventually, after walking over a mile, we arrived at a burger restaurant and Iggy opened the door and walked in. Now he'd entered private property, we couldn't follow him in with our camera, so we were forced to wait outside. Iggy whispered something to a young member of staff, before sitting down at a table, intently messaging someone, his mouth twisted in frustration as he repeatedly glanced from his phone to us.

Jamie began to get worried, asking Matt, 'What if he's messaging someone to come and get us?'

Matt replied, 'Just film him'.

The young staff member Iggy had spoken to came out of the restaurant. He was in his early twenties, with long hair and a typically relaxed Californian manner. 'Hi, er, this guy says y'all are bothering him?'

When Matt explained that we were from the BBC, and were investigating this man on suspicion of running an organisation that teaches men how to groom women, his answer showed that he wasn't shocked: 'For real? Yeah, I got that vibe. He comes here a lot.'

Wait, what? He told us that Iggy came into the restaurant frequently, wearing his velour tracksuit and accompanied by various middle-aged women, all 'heavily dressed, very rich-looking'.

Matt asked him upfront: 'So, when you say that you got the vibe that he might be doing something like that, what do you mean?'

His answer was revealing: 'I thought he was a pimp.' Iggy had far bigger ambitions than mere pimping, though. He was gearing up for a war, one that he hoped would tear 'Clown World' apart. The wizard had already found his warrior king; he now needed to assemble his generals.

CHAPTER ELEVEN

Generals in the Culture Wars

We were beginning to pull back the veil of secrecy surrounding the
War Room, but there was still a lot we didn't know. How big was it?
Was it as powerful as Tate and Iggy claimed? Who were the mem-
bers who made up its ranks, but weren't admitting this publicly?

Another whistle-blower, who did not want to be named, came
forward with something that would help to answer some of these
questions. We'd spent time building a relationship with this source,
and late one night in mid-2023, a folder appeared in our inbox. It
contained a number of spreadsheets dated from August 2022, with
a list of the members of fourteen different Telegram groups for various War Room 'rooms': one for discussing the PhD course, one for
webcam and others with more cryptic names, such as the 'Sha Do
Room' and the 'Brothers Money Room'. Perhaps most notable was
the 'Great Hall', the main Telegram group for the entire War Room
whose chat logs we had already seen. This was our first chance to
see a comprehensive list naming all 433 members of the cult of
Andrew Tate. Some had signed up using pseudonyms, but by cross-
referencing these usernames with other social media accounts, we
were able to identify many of them. Some were foolish or brazen

enough to sign up with their real names. This list of War Room members, combined with the two sets of chat logs we had been given by whistleblowers, one through Crabcrawler, and another set of logs from the War Room's 'PhD' chat room given to us by an ex-member, would give us new insights into how the War Room worked, and who made up its ranks.

Now that Tate was world famous, his coverage in the media boomed. One trend, picked up by the British press in particular, was the flooding of social media with 'mini-Tates' – new influencers who seemed to parrot his views and adopt his grandiloquent rhetoric and tactics to build their own social media followings. It was working, and many of these accounts gained thousands of followers by adopting Tate's viewpoints and approach. Think-pieces were written in the 'mainstream media' highlighting a growing number of manosphere/hustle-culture influencers, blaming Tate for inspiring them. Little did they know, Tate had done more than inspire them – he had helped build their ideology directly through his War Room.

Looking through the list of members, we noticed a number of these mini-Tates, emerging stars in Twitter's manosphere, in their ranks. They included the British influencer Hassan Haider, known as @MrOverpaid, who, like many of the manosphere and red-pill grifters, had recently relocated to Dubai. Going back to our chat logs, we found that Hassan had joined the War Room on 30 August 2019, as a nineteen-year-old Finance and Accounting student at Loughborough University. When Hassan joined the group, the first thing Iggy asked him was if he had bought the PhD course. Hassan replied that he had not, claiming that 'girls aren't a focus right now, trying to make money'. Other members were quick to tell him that the PhD and webcam course were a path to making money, and by the end of his first day in the organisation Hassan was convinced, stating, 'Yeh maybe I should focus on girls then because I'm quite good with them', and promised to buy the PhD course as soon as he had the money. It was easy to see the influence the War Room was having on Hassan as time progressed, particularly when it came to how he viewed women. When he asked the group for a recommendation for a film to watch with a girl he had coming over, Iggy responded, 'Sure. The porn we made together 20 minutes earlier. That, or horror. Sometimes they're the same thing depending on the mood I was in.'

By February 2020, Hassan appeared to be fully immersed in the mythology and culture of the War Room, repeatedly using the phrases 'trust in Tate' and 'such is the way of Wudan'. Two months later, he bragged to the group that he had managed to recruit his first woman for his new OnlyFans and webcam business. When the girl he had enlisted left him before he could get her account up, he told the group, 'She just sent me a bunch of nudes for the only fans so now ik [I know] after quarantine I'll meet her she'll fall in love then I'll get her on webcam,' followed by an emoji of the devil.

What interested us more than how the War Room had shaped Hassan's views on women, though, was how Tate and his generals had taught him how to go viral online. Early on in his membership, Hassan claimed, 'Outrage addiction is real'. Hassan would adopt similar shock tactics to Tate's, playing to the public's outrage addiction, achieving Twitter fame with videos like 'Why men don't want to date black women' and 'Why Indian men are the smelliest', along with a live Twitter update of how many women he claimed to have had sex with. Like Tate, Hassan's content led to a pay-to-join network called New Money, and also like Tate, his target audience and primary customer base was teenage boys. As of January 2024,

Hassan had over 100,000 followers on Twitter, and claimed to have over 1,300 members in his group.

Looking through the list of War Room members, it wasn't just the new generation of mini-Tates that we found, but a host of names we recognised from the so called, alt-light, alt-right and far right. This included men like alt-right fitness influencer and pickup artist Alexander 'AJA' Cortes, who once declared 'leftism is for ugly freaks'. It seems Iggy wasn't the only member with an affinity for far-right politics. Tate's association with figures on the right and far right had long been on our radar, and from the first time we spoke to him about them, he had denied that he or the War Room had any political affiliation. In one candid off-camera moment in Romania, as we sat on a bench overlooking his pool, we saw Tate admitting to broadly libertarian views: 'Keep your hands off my shit. I don't want the government having their hands on my shit.' But that was about as far as it went.

The first extreme political figure that Tate publicly associated with was Stephen Yaxley-Lennon, better known as Tommy Robinson, the far-right British activist and co-founder of the English Defence League. Robinson was four years older than Tate, but both grew up in Luton, and Robinson claims they had mutual friends through Storm Gym, the kick-boxing gym where Tate trained throughout his professional fighting career. Robinson became a celebrity figure within the global far right long before the internet knew who Andrew Tate was, so when Tate began to cultivate his brand online – as a brash ex-kick-boxer turned pimp – he began talking to Robinson, and, as we saw in Chapter 1, even publicly harassed journalist Mike Stuchbery on Robinson's behalf.

A connection of Tate's from that time who we tracked down was Caolan Robertson, a filmmaker and ex-member of the British far-right who spent his early twenties making video content for Yaxley-Lennon. We met him at his new office in Bermondsey, London, where he at the time ran the successful news company Byline Media. It was hard to imagine how this young man, courteous and friendly and now in his mid-twenties, had once made shockingly offensive content for one of the country's most hated figures. Robertson told us how he had first met Tate through Yaxley-Lennon in 2018, when Tate and Yaxley-Lennon had briefly looked at setting up a right-wing media company together, similar to Breitbart in the US. Yaxley-Lennon was apparently keen on the idea and claimed that Tate would be able to help them secure funding. Robertson told us that in reality, Tate had little interest in the company or any grandiose political aims, but saw it as an opportunity to help him achieve fame.

Tate had already had a taste of how becoming involved in political debates and supporting contentious narratives within them could help him to gain new followers and forge useful connections. In 2016, Tate had secured a meeting and photo-op with Donald Trump Jr at Trump Tower in New York, after Trump Jr had liked a viral tweet from Tate, supporting Trump. When Tate posted the photo of the two of them, he gained thousands of fans, and would go on to use it as the thumbnail for his 'Networking Excellence' course, bragging about the relationship in the War Room group.

Tate continued to appear on far-right and conspiracy-laden podcasts, including 'Prison Planet', the YouTube channel of the then editor-at-large of Infowars, Paul Joseph Watson. Watson had achieved a massive following, reporting on conspiracy theories such as chemtrails (the belief that the condensation trails planes leave in the sky are part of a government plan to poison us) and the 'New World Order', and criticising 'leftism', Islam and feminism, and he would go on to be one of the first billed speakers at a War Room event in 2019. Watson introduced Tate to his boss and conspiracy-theorist-in-chief, Alex Jones, who became one of Tate's most important allies in the conspiratorial alt-right. Tate appeared on Infowars on numerous occasions, in front of millions of viewers in the US. In the age of Trump, political conspiracy theories and distributing misinformation were becoming the best way to gain engagement on social media.

In 2019, shortly after Tate and Iggy first began interacting on Twitter, Tate appears to have continued making useful alliances within various factions of the right. In particular, he befriended alt-light superstar Mike Cernovich, a broad and burly figure who would be invited by Tate to speak at the first War Room event in Romania in 2019. Our list of members from August 2022 showed that Cernovich wasn't just a guest speaker, but a member of the War Room, too. On 2 July 2019, Iggy added Cernovich to the 'Great Hall' chat, with the introduction: 'Mike Cernovich . . . as Mike has his hands quite full covering the craven attack on Andy Ngo in Portland, Oregon this past weekend by Antifa scum, he will chime in when he can. We wanted him in The Great Hall as soon as we could, knowing full well his schedule might preclude his joining us tonight.'

Cernovich first developed a reputation in the burgeoning manosphere with his blog 'Danger & Play', which courted controversy with articles such as, 'When in Doubt, Whip it Out' and 'How to Choke a Woman'. Ironically, Cernovich's 'journalism' was initially funded by money he had acquired through his divorce from his first wife, a successful attorney. Cernovich would go on to carve out a space in the US political right by supporting Donald Trump in his first run for presidency. Through his mastery and dissemination of social media narratives, Cernovich is credited by many as having helped catapult Trump to the White House.

These methods would be echoed by his new friend Andrew Tate. Cernovich had perfected the skill of mobilising his followers to flood social media collectively with a coordinated narrative, allowing their hashtags to trend at the top of Twitter and forcing their views onto people's feeds. On 11 September 2016, when Hillary Clinton fainted after a memorial service at Ground Zero, Cernovich mobilised his followers on Periscope (a now defunct live streaming app owned by X, then known as Twitter) to get their hashtag #SickHillary trending on Twitter, with the story eventually being picked up by the *Washington Post*. Tate would go on to employ the same tactic on TikTok, but on a much larger scale, mobilising an army of teenagers. Cernovich has claimed that he perfected the technique of 'rage-bait' to make himself too big to ignore, something which Tate appears to have admired, and which Cernovich taught in the War Room.

In July 2019, when Tate's following was still small, Cernovich told the War Room, 'Cobra has the look/vibe right now. Only issue is distribution/exposure.' Cernovich then linked to a tweet of notorious MMA fighter Conor McGregor participating in a viral internet challenge involving kicking the lid off a water bottle. He then shared a video of Tate breaking a baseball bat with his shin, and told him to 'splice in Conor McGregor's kick. Tag him and say, "Nice try". That'll wind up Conor's fan boys and get crossover engagement.' Tate replied: '*30mins. On it.*' As other members of the War Room tried to join the conversation, Iggy admonished them: 'I swear I will SHOOT any guy here who interrupts this discussion between Andrew and Cerno. Just STFU and let the adults talk.'

Further on in the conversation, Iggy asked Cernovich for more advice: 'Mike, can members of The War Room work in unison to boost Andrew's signal on Twitter in any way?' Cernovich responded: 'If there were one tweet or so, it would be within twitter rules for 25–50 guys to RT it in close succession. You don't want "inauthentic behaviour", but the tactics of influenced rooms are allowed. IOW [it only works], if everyone has an account, there could be a side room where people agree to RT certain especially good tweets . . . Since it's real people with real accounts, then the RTs aren't bots.' When Tate extended this tactic to Hustlers University, it helped him achieve his meteoric rise to fame.

From the moment we first were in contact with Tate, he seemed to know that we might latch onto his connection to these alt-right figures. When we asked him about these affiliations, he said that he had simply appeared on their podcasts, but that he featured on left-wing and 'feminist' podcasts as well. The obvious difference was that when he went on the platforms of figures like Stephen Yaxley-Lennon and Alex Jones, he was deferential, constantly agreeing with them. His presence on 'left-wing' podcasts seemed to have been devised with the sole purpose of trolling the hosts in order to create viral clips for his ever-growing audience. When we started speaking to Tate to gain access to the War Room, one of his conditions had been that members could remain anonymous if they wanted to. When Jamie suggested that they could wear masks, trying to avoid the unsightly and costly process of blurring all the men, Tate refused, claiming that we would use that to make them look like some sort of 'right-wing militia'. Given his concern, it was perhaps unsurprising when we found both ex- and current US militia members in the War Room's ranks.

A lesser-known manosphere figure who went by the pseudonym Ivan Throne was also a guest speaker at the War Room's first meeting. When he joined the Telegram group in June 2019, Tate's introduction to him read, 'Please welcome the dark triad man. Mr Ivan Throne.' Within psychology, the 'Dark Triad' refers to a rare subset of individuals who combine narcissism, Machiavellianism and psychopathy – all traits that Throne appeared to view as useful weapons. Iggy in particular seemed thrilled at Throne's new membership of the War Room: 'I am honored to have you here, My Lord . . . We have been hoping to have you grace us with your feared wisdom and perspective.'

When Tate asked the group for advice on what to do with the spare room in his Bucharest home, referred to as 'War Room HQ', Throne suggested that he put 'three men with pistol' and one woman with a gun to her head in there. The group eventually decided that the room should be a 'Chapel of Wudan', with Throne supporting its use for 'magic'. Tate agreed, telling the men the messaging group would become the 'closest terrestrial representation of Wudan Mountain'. Throne told us he had no contact with the Tates from 2020 onward and had 'no inside information on their subsequent global notoriety or their criminal indictments in Romania.' Our records indicate he was still a member of their Telegram group until at least 2022, though.

Before meeting Tate, Throne was a prominent figure within the Tyranny Response Team, an American Second Amendment activist group that protest against gun control legislation. His book *The Nine Laws*, in which he pushed the idea of the Dark Triad Man, made its way onto Iggy's Survival Scrolls reading list. Throne now runs a new company, called Throne Dynamics, whose website confusingly describes it as a company that trains 'capable leaders to deliver global eternal legacy . . . provide[ing] full spectrum dominance consulting to qualified clients in critical continuity industries'." In reality, the company appears to offer consultancy to other right-wing groups, and the logo on the homepage of their website bears a striking resemblance to the Reichsadler, the Nazi war eagle. (Throne told us that the logo was not adapted from the Reichsadler but was modelled after the Roman *aquila* symbol – itself an insipiration for the Nazi Reichsadler – and his own 'hereditary family arms'.)

Jay Stang was another acquaintance of Throne's who turned up in our list of War Room members. Jay, often pictured in a suit and smoking a cigar, entered the War Room in August 2019. He appears to have joined numerous groups under the name 'Animal Mother' throughout his life, including the Tyranny Response Team and manosphere godfather Rollo Tomassi's paid network, but tells the men that the War Room exceeds them all: 'Other groups I am in are useful, but are just missing something. The War Room isn't missing anything. It is complete.' One notable group Stang was in was Oath Keepers, a far-right patriot militia, now infamous in the US for their role in the January 6th Capitol riots, for which a number of its members were charged and imprisoned. Stang at one time claimed he was the head of of the Texas chapter, one of the group's most active subsections.

When Stang joined the War Room, he introduced himself to the other men as a forty-three-year-old working in oil and gas sales and an ex-member of the US military, with aims to start his own company with the help of advisors like Ivan Throne. He told his fellow members: 'Brotherhood, networking, and financial success are my goals here, in that order. To be among a group of men who are just as hellbent as I am on becoming successful both in building

---

* https://www.thronedynamics.com/company

businesses, organizations, and value, as well as getting paid. I am grateful to Tate for the opportunity to contribute to the War Room and to join you.'

Conversations with fellow members cover topics including firearms and abortion, which Stang saw as 'murder'. A father of two, he also espoused 'traditional' family values, speaking positively of his wife, telling his fellow members to 'get you women who will stand behind you'. It was perhaps surprising, then, that we also found his name listed in both the membership of the PhD chat and the webcam chat.

In early 2023, we were able to get our hands on yet another valuable set of documents: chat logs from within the War Room's PhD room, covering a two-month period in mid-2021. In these messages, it becomes clear that after almost two years in the War Room, Stang's views on women and their use to men became more aligned with Tate's and Iggy's visions. Stang began to lament his wife, telling the other men that he was doing all he could to assume total control over her. On 21 May 2021, he wrote: 'Today I have completed a critical move along this path. The house is now in my company's name, and out from mine and her names. I am positioning the pieces one by one. The cars will be as well very soon. I am now the direct and only source of funds for her. "May I have some money?"' Stang began referring to women as dragons, but was also an avowed and public Christian. Despite this, he seemed to believe his religion could co-exist with this new world view.

In one section of the chat logs, Tate talked to his fellow members about 'Jasmina', a woman the Romanian authorities would later claim was a victim of trafficking and exploitation at his hands. Jasmina attracted headlines when she released a video claiming that she was not a victim, but a close friend of Tate's, and this was why she had his name as well as a cobra tattooed down her left arm. But Tate shared messages from Jasmina with the group from early on in their 'relationship', in which she complained that she didn't want to do webcam because of her religious beliefs, something that she said Tate was aware of when they started their relationship. Tate, however, told the men: *'She never believed in god. Women never believe in anything. Women are programmed. Just have to replace the programming. Remember that. Even when she's doing what you want her to. There's outside forces trying to rewrite the code. I never believed her shit. I knew what she was trying to do. Make me think she's a better girl than the others. We swapped that out for Cam making her better. Done deal. Identified the objections and destroyed them. I've done this with over 100 girls. I've seen it all . . .'* Stang was the first to reply, agreeing that women are 'empty vessels'. Stang also seemed to support Iggy's philosophy of slavery, claiming, 'It is painfully obvious to me from just being alive and noticing things that women want to be a man's slave to various degrees. How can anyone deny it? But here we study how to unlock it.'

This ideology, which saw women as targets to be exploited or subjugated, wasn't just confined to the small cult-like circle of War Room generals. Some of them hatched a plan to spread their message to millions of young men across the world. This would be done through content featuring their new icon, Andrew Tate, and a new group of young men who understood how to harness the power of social media.

CHAPTER TWELVE

Out the Other End

In March 2023, Thomas Bayne, aka Bayneframe, a rising figure in the manosphere, began preaching a new gospel of how to seduce women on social media. He claimed that pickup artistry was 'cringe', but that he had a new 'framework' for 'unlocking top-tier girls', centred on being genuine and approaching them in shopping malls, rather than nightclubs. This led to a dispute within the higher ranks of the War Room.

Like many War Room members, Bayneframe's criteria for 'top-tier girls' included being attractive, verifiably unvaccinated (even the saliva of a woman who'd had the Covid vaccine could 'damage your body') and of a young age and naivety that made them easy to manipulate. He once bragged about testing women for the latter by asking them to find France on a map. 'If she can't find France, she is certified low-exposure retard and wife material. If she finds France straight away, she has seen too much.'

When Bayneframe criticised a high-ranking War Room member Ethan Evans (aka Evo) for trying to seduce women in a nightclub, it quickly escalated into a public spat. 'Going to the mall and approaching girls is the only way to get real results like

I do,' he tweeted. In response, Evo posted a seven-year-old picture of Bayneframe, in which he was slightly heavier and wore glasses. The pair then proceeded to share photos of women the other claimed to have seduced, with disparaging comments about their appearance.

On 16 March, one of Evo's associates passed on a death threat to Bayneframe, saying Evo had family 'high up in underworld/politics' and could have him 'dealt with'. Shortly after, Bayneframe noticed two masked men on CCTV trying get into his apartment (Evo later denied that he sent these men). Bayneframe retaliated by 'rating' more of 'Evo's girls' and calling out the War Room specifically.

Worried about a fellow manosphere influencer questioning its legitimacy on a public platform, the War Room demanded that Bayneframe delete any tweets mentioning it. Negative comments began to appear on all of Bayne's social media profiles. It was as though an army had been mobilised.

While the rest of the War Room quickly closed ranks against Bayne's heresy, one high-ranking member, a man who went by the name of EliXAnpa, seemed to have been convinced by Bayne's thinking. Eli claimed to be a Duke University dropout in his twenties who worked in the marketing and sales team behind Tate, The Real World and the War Room. Eli told us he had been Andrew Tate's head of sales and marketing, but a spokesperson for the Tate brothers said he was simply part of their affiliate programme.

Eli was drawn to Bayne's notion that 'high-quality women' were attracted to genuineness, rather than manipulation. Like most members of the War Room, he had joined to learn how to attract women. But it was only when he used this new method – of being 'yourself' – that he saw results. He began to challenge the War

Room leaders about this, and they promptly kicked him out and began a campaign of online harassment.

Eli had always been a free thinker. Every day he ate a kilogram of raw meat – often not fillets but minced beef, directly from the packet, as well as oysters. He would wash these down with litres of unpasteurised milk and Red Bull; he eschewed water even in extreme heat. The idea behind this diet was that it would increase his testosterone levels, a notion popularised by another of the TikTok algorithm's favourite monstrosities: the Liver King. With over five million followers, the Liver King became famous for posting videos of himself gorging on bull testicles and raw liver as part of an 'ancestral diet'. His huge beard and cannonball-like muscles made it hard to argue with the results, until leaked emails revealed that, as well as kilos of offal, he was ingesting $11,000-worth of steroids every month.

Eli's was the first public denouncement of the War Room from someone who appeared to have been high up in the organisation, so we gave him a call.

'People think Tate just became famous one day, but there's an art to it,' he told us. 'We were able to make him famous by using a deep understanding of what social media algorithms respond to. We were able to create content that triggered them perfectly.'

Eli claimed that the War Room had brainwashed him over the course of three years before kicking him out. On 18 July 2023, we flew him to London for an interview. He was wearing sunglasses when he arrived at the empty office block we had rented for the meeting. He refused to take them off. 'They're part of my brand.'

The sunglasses weren't the first thing we noticed about him, though; it was the smell. It had a potency to it, reaching several metres ahead and filling up entire rooms. Oysters, raw minced beef, milk – they were all there – but there was something else, too. A sulphuric top note. This was because, along with his raw carnivorous diet, Eli had not brushed his teeth in two years. (He had recently posted a picture of his gums to Twitter. 'Yes, slightly inflamed,' read the caption. 'My body is getting rid of brain toxins and old fillings. A natural, healthy process. Entire dentistry industry is a sham.') Matt wanted to ask him whether he might have solved his struggles with women not by joining a misogynistic internet cult, but simply by using a toothbrush and not consuming the diet of an urban fox. Jamie forbade it.

Instead, Matt opened with: 'So, what first appealed to you about the War Room?'

'It goes back a long way,' Eli responded, in the businesslike tone we recognised from our conversations with other War Room men. 'I joined the War Room in September 2020, and before that I had never really consumed any manosphere or red-pill stuff online. Tate was the first person that I came across. His appeal was sort of becoming "the man". And at the end of the day, what men want is girls. And you see this guy that, based on what he's shown, can get the best girls. Then you think, ok, let's follow him.

'But that comes from a place of insecurity. And I was one of those vulnerable men that fell for the marketing. And I helped propagate that with my sales and marketing efforts all this time.'

'Given that it's run by a guy who pretends to be a wizard,' Matt probed, 'and another guy who pretends to be a character from *The Matrix*, did you ever think to yourself, "This is all a bit cringe?"'

'Well, you know what? When you're inside, you don't see the craziness, right? You only see the cringe just once you're outside.'

Eli began to explain how he and his marketing team invented the six-month plan that made Tate famous. 'We played into the insecurities of men. Meaning that when you saw Tate with a Bugatti, for example, or when you saw Tate call you a "brokie", he made you believe that he was the ideal that you needed to become in order to get a woman in your life.'

Cousin Luc (who we'd come across in Romania) was the one in charge of the marketing programme, he explained. Luc had been adrift in California, working at Chipotle and sleeping on friends' sofas. Andrew and Tristan invited him to Bucharest to work in their webcam studio as someone who chatted to users online (often one man would pretend to be several different webcam performers, chatting to male customers and manipulating them into sending money). Seeking to expand the Tate brothers' grifting operation, Luc, said Eli, created a strategy to make them famous and convert that fame into money.

Luc hired a crew of videographers to get B-roll of the brothers and then filmed Andrew giving his take on as many different topics as they could imagine. The marketing team prioritised controversial and aggressive views because that's what most social media algorithms prefer. These videos were edited for maximal manipulation of the viewers' emotions through music, data analysis of viewers' responses and pseudoscientific beliefs about hypnosis and neuro-linguistic programming (NLP).

This formula, which was dependent on 'clip length, editing style, hook power, energy crescendo and eye direction' triggered the algorithm perfectly. The arsenal of edited clips was then fed to Eli and a few dozen marketers, many of whom were recruited through the Hustlers University affiliate programme that Luc had come up with. They were told to post four to six videos a day to TikTok and two to Instagram.

The videos generated 1.1 billion views. These shorter clips were then used to funnel viewers to Tate's online platform, which grew so fast that it earned 'over a hundred million dollars a year'. Luc and Eli also employed this marketing strategy to discredit Tate's critics and sow mistrust in the media and justice system.

'They would take very real-looking accounts and they would comment on your posts, which is why on every single one of your posts, they call you DNG (Dork, Nerd, Geek). They go and they counter the narrative that you're pushing because, at the end of the day, it's narratives that fight against each other. And they do it very successfully.' (Since publishing our findings about Tate, Matt has received a daily onslaught of comments on all forms of social media – mainly variations on 'DNG', as mentioned earlier, and 'Where's my chocolate?')

'How are these attacks orchestrated?'

'We have a PR campaign team. We look for all media, whether positive or negative, that mentions Tate and send people to comment on it from very real-looking accounts.'

'So, are they real people or bots?'

'Partly real people, partly bots – very, very highly trained.'

The campaign began encouraging people to distrust institutions, and reality itself. Lots of content describing 'the Matrix' and its conspiracy to silence the Tate brothers appeared on social media around the time of their arrest.

Cousin Luc released a statement saying 'the Matrix' had a three-phase plan to get rid of Tate. First, 'they' would try to cancel him. Then, 'they' would try to jail him 'just like they did with Julian Assange'. If that failed, 'they' would 'Epstein him', i.e. kill him.

In an audio file that was leaked to us, Cousin Luc appeared to address the marketing team:

> 'Whenever there's someone who makes a hit piece on the War
> Room, or anything negative about the War Room, you always need
> to discredit the person who made the video. You need to make the
> person who made the video be a loser. They need to be a dork, nerd,
> geek, liar. You need to destroy the source. Because if people truly
> believe that that person who made the video is a horrible human
> being, why would they give any of his information any validity at all?'

Matt realised why the dozens of Tate fans who confronted him in real life seemed so immovable: their trust in the media had been eroded by Tate's marketing team. Sowing mass disorientation and distrust through social media is a common tactic of conspiracy theorists, summed up by Steve Bannon's notorious quote: 'The Democrats don't matter. The real opposition is the media. And the way to deal with them is to flood the zone with shit.' Their marketing campaign was a huge success, in part thanks to the AI-driven TikTok algorithm. TikTok is used by 58 per cent of American teenagers daily, and one in six say they are on it 'almost constantly'.*

The scariest part about Tate's rise to fame is that three chancers – Tate, Luc and Eli – were able to pull this off with such ease. The potential for people with more manpower and funding than him to wreak havoc in our world through social media is truly terrifying.

Much has been published about how social media virality favours content that triggers outrage, creating political polarisation by turning people against each other. The idea is that algorithms reflect, and then amplify the animosity that is already present in

* https://www.axios.com/2023/12/11/social-media-teens-pew-tiktok-youtube-instagram-facebook-bereal-snapchat

human nature. But Tate's marketing operation suggests that this process doesn't just happen – it can be easily orchestrated by a small number of people intent on manipulating the algorithms for self-interested goals.

A common misconception is the idea that people are crueller on the internet because there is no face-to-face interaction to dissuade them, known as the 'mismatch theory'. Political scientists Alexander Bor and Michael Bang Petersen tested this theory and found no evidence for it. Instead, they discovered that 'political hostility reflects a deliberate strategy among individuals with particular personality traits' – in particular, 'individuals predisposed to be hostile in all (including offline) contexts'.[*] Their research showed that online spaces favoured aggressive bullies seeking to gain status.

Developer Chris Wetherell, who helped launch us into a world of social media virality when he built Twitter's 'Retweet' button in 2009, later recalled thinking, 'We might have just handed a four-year-old a loaded weapon'.[†]

According to Eli, though, the real manipulation began inside the War Room. 'You become so dogmatic in what they call "Tateism",' he explained. 'It damages relationships with women because the War Room is all about you getting women that serve you in your life.

'The War Room has a methodology. The philosophy is that women want attention and men want sex. So, once men get the sex, then the power balance is flipped in your favour. Now, where she's coming to beg for your attention, she has to complete bigger and

---

* 'The Psychology of Online Political Hostility: A Comprehensive, Cross-National Test of the Mismatch Hypothesis', *American Political Science Review*, Volume 116 , Issue 1 , February 2022 , pp. 1–18
† https://www.buzzfeednews.com/article/alexkantrowitz/how-the-retweet-ruined-the-internet

bigger tasks, and eventually her whole world becomes you. And she has nothing else except you. And eventually you put her through a sort of Pavlovian conditioning, and she completely serves you. You can call it a slave. She has to do more things for you, whether it's, you know, wash dishes, do errands for you, or eventually do OnlyFans and webcam.'

Matt pointed out, 'A lot of people might say that to teach men to coerce and manipulate women – to use Pavlovian conditioning, like you said – into working in the sex trade is not only illegal but immoral and wrong.'

'I would never do it personally. I've never done it personally.'

'But that was a big part of what the War Room did?'

'It was.'

'Do you regret that you played a part in it?'

'I don't regret it. Why would I feel guilty about something that I had no control over?'

'Well, you were part of the marketing team, right?'

'Yeah, absolutely. But during that time, I was brainwashed. They actually encourage you to cut off the support network in your real life, and you start cutting off friends. They tell you a very scary thing. Iggy basically tells you to metaphorically kill your parents – he tells you that your new brothers inside of the War Room are your new life. Everyone else before that doesn't matter. "We have here the truth of life. Your parents may not agree with the things that you are learning here, but it will impede you from moving forward inside of our organisation if you do not kill your parents."'

'It sounds like what you're describing is a cult.'

'Well, absolutely. And it's not just you describing it like that. They literally describe it as a cult. Shi Yan Hui, [aka] Iggy, basically said, "Let's not kid ourselves. This is a cult."'

'Who's in charge?'

'Of the War Room? Iggy is at the top. And I would say when I met him, he's one of the most interesting men that I've probably ever met. He can captivate an audience. He's a very good storyteller. He's funny, he's witty. And yeah, I would say overall that's what it was. But when you spoke to him, he definitely had an agenda. He definitely influenced you in ways that were not of your own thinking.'

'How do you mean?'

'He really would tell me that he went inside of my brain and rearranged things. "I went in the attic and I started moving the furniture around" is how he would describe it. So, he was very good at reprogramming brains.'

'And what's his agenda?'

'I couldn't really tell you exactly what the agenda would be, other than "take over the world", I guess.'

The next day, we went through an audio file that had been leaked to us, in which Iggy Semmelweis addressed a group of War Room men:

'It is both my sacred honour and an incredible privilege to have this opportunity to talk with all of you. I'm so proud, and I'm so amazed at the assembly of talent and power and ambition that I see before me. I can open up the news and read about Clown World and shake my head and go "you have no idea what's going behind the scenes".

I know men in the War Room that are doing amazing things, that are becoming amazing men. Truly amazing men. And you wouldn't even know it from reading the papers or watching the news or talking to idiots in Clown World. But it gives me incredible energy, and it gives me incredible hope when I have a chance to meet up with you guys. Just go into the War Room and drink energy. Pure nectar. Pure

228 OUT THE OTHER END

power. It's all great, and we've only just begun. Where we've come from a year ago, you won't even believe where we're gonna be a year from now. It just keeps expanding.'

Iggy went on to speak about the comparative mythologist Joseph Campbell, author of *The Hero with a Thousand Faces*. In the book, Campbell determines that there is one single 'monomyth' story structure that remains constant across myths and stories in every different culture around the world, from Christianity to Navajo tribes. This is 'the hero's journey', which he describes as: 'A hero ventures forth from the world of common day into a region of supernatural wonder: fabulous forces are there encountered and a decisive victory is won: the hero comes back from this mysterious adventure with the power to bestow boons on his fellow man'.

Campbell's ideas were especially important to Iggy because they outline how mythology taps into every human's subconscious. A myth can be a way to get inside our heads and rebrand our internal struggles as a conquest – a 'battle against dragons'. The nature and shape of that conquest, though, is in the hands of the myth-maker: the shaman, the priest or (in Iggy's case) the wizard.

In the seminar, Iggy related the hero's journey to the story of Tate:

'When we are reading the tales of Wudan of the acolyte Cobra with his Master Po – that is echoed in the mentor and the student who then must become the master at the point of death of his master. He becomes the greatest man alive. We are going to be the greatest men alive to our sons, and when we die, our sons will become the greatest men alive. This is something that Emory Andrew Tate II put into full force into Andrew and Tristan. That they are the greatest men alive. That was a conscious decision on Emory Andrew Tate's part. Those boys grew up believing that no matter what their situation was, no matter how broke they looked on the outside – on the inside they had warrior spirit. That's what Emory Andrew Tate put inside his sons: that they were kings. And that their lives were a huge chessboard, and they had to learn how to motivate and manipulate and control their position on the board. And marshal their forces.'

Matt realised that the test he had been put through must have been based on these ideas. Campbell called that stage in the hero's journey 'The Trial'.

To Iggy, to be a man was to go on some kind of quest that involved trials, changing the 'hero' internally, and then society around them externally. In the audio file, he said to one member, 'Come forward, my brother. You've been doing well. You've been a busy bee. You've lost weight, you're looking strong. That's good. Big changes since that time we sat by the fire talking.'

So, it wasn't just about making money or manipulating women. Iggy was trying to make men undergo a spiritual transformation.

CHAPTER THIRTEEN

Real Mafia Shit

Tate once said that he moved to Romania because 'corruption is accessible to everybody'. In interviews, he bragged that he was a 'mafia-associated criminal', and given these claims, we'd long since been curious about Tate's casinos.

In December 2019, when Tate was still wary about giving us access to the War Room, he suggested to Jamie, 'Why don't we do this . . . A first part about me and Tristan in Romania and the casinos and our secret organisation.' He sent Jamie a video of the opening of a new casino in January 2020, bragging about another opening the next night. By July 2022, after his first raid by the Romanian authorities, Tate had changed his mind about letting us film at the casinos, for fear that we would upset his co-investors.

But Tate said a lot of things, and it was difficult to distinguish reality from fantasy. We worried that we were being swept up in a conspiratorial whirlwind, much like many of the countless online sleuths who had become fixated on the Tate brothers. The brothers provided a visual feast, courted intrigue and frequently hinted that they were part of something darker and more sinister. Maybe we were falling for it.

But then something happened that wrenched the Tate-mafia connection out of the realms of conspiracy and into possible reality.

A husband-and-wife Romanian journalist couple named Victor Ilie and Luiza Vasiliu had spent several months looking into the Tates. On 16 June 2023, they met us at a café in Bucharest to tell us what they had found.

Victor showed us an early interview in which Tate was asked how he generated his wealth. 'The first thing is, I own a bunch of casinos in Romania,' he responded. In the same interview, he said, 'Three brothers, mafia guys, they own 400 casinos throughout Eastern Europe. I came up to them and said "I want to do a franchise with you. They agreed."'

'But Tate is someone who kind of exaggerates,' Victor said, rolling a cigarette. 'It's frequently unclear where the mythology ends and the truth begins.'

To try to find the truth, he and Luiza searched Tate's name in the Romanian government's official gazette of Romania (the official legal publication of the Romanian State) and filed a petition with the National Commercial Registry, which led them to documents that mentioned a company called Talisman Enterprises.

'They were joint-venture contracts between Talisman Enterprises and a company called DMS BET LIVE. They split the profits fifty-fifty. These documents contained some peculiar addresses in Bucharest,' they said, which they determined to be branches of Romanian casino chain Las Vegas Casinos. They visited one. 'It was not a fancy casino. This was in a run-down, communist area of Bucharest, where people come to gamble their minimum wage or pension on slot machines. It's not Top G.

'According to one interview Tate did, these casinos were run by three mafia brothers and "turned over 18 million a day".' 'Typical Eastern European mafia,' Victor told us that Tate had said. 'Imagine: fat, bald, cigar.'

But would the Tates really brag that they had partnered with the mafia?

'We looked back at the company Talisman Enterprises was part-nered with – DMS BET LIVE. That's when we realised what DMS stood for. Doroftei, Mihăiță, Sorin.'

'What does that mean?'

'Mihăiță and Sorin Doroftei are two mafia brothers. Not much is known about them. Except we had identified only two brothers – so who was the third "mafia member" Tate spoke about?

'The one thing the Doroftei brothers are known for is founding the Romanian mixed martial-arts brand RXF.'

Jamie and Matt looked at each other – RXF organised The Test that Matt had participated in.

'Their cage fights are typically sponsored by their casinos, Las Vegas' said Victor.

Victor and Luiza found a video of Mihăiță Doroftei on Facebook paying a *manele* (Romanian pop folk) singer in a restaurant to do a shout-out to his family – the 'DMS family'. He also had DMS tat-tooed on his hand, while the same letters were shaved into the back of the head of one of Mihăiță's associates in a social media photo.

In the video of the *manele* singer, Florin Salam, paying tribute to Mihăiță, he calls the brother 'Mihăiță the Pole'. Mihăiță, they found out, had Polish citizenship.

This then led them to an old court file – a transcript of a wire-tapped meeting between a drug trafficker and his lieutenants. It said that in 2019 a 'Polish investor' brought together several mafia clans from all over Romania to launch a casino business together.

This Polish investor wanted to open casinos in every major city in Romania, with himself as the kingpin. A source they had in law enforcement was able to confirm, off the record, that this wiretap was about the Las Vegas casinos.

'But it gets more interesting,' Luiza said. 'These mobsters used to 'protect' the Tate casinos. If you were a legitimate gambling winner, they would lie in wait for you, beat you up, and hold you in a basement until you gave back your winnings. The Romanian authorities first found out about this case through these victims, which led them to find out about the huge, organised crime partnership under the umbrella of Las Vegas Casinos.'

'Each mob in each county has some particular dealings,' Victor explained. 'Smuggling drugs, money laundering through construction sites, human trafficking abroad including organised "beggars" and women forced to have sex. The Doroftei brothers built a way for them to launder money through gambling venues. And the Tates joined in on this.'

'Here in Romania,' Luiza chimed in, 'for the very first time, all the mobs were being brought together. Like the Italian Mafia did in the US, in the 60s, when they built Nevada from scratch. And at the same table we find these two British brothers, alongside all these very tough mobsters. Guys who burn each others' houses down and fight with Samurai swords.'

'Are you serious about the Samurai swords?' Matt asked.

'Yes,' Luiza laughed.

Victor added, 'Just before the Tates were arrested on charges of human trafficking and rape, police raided what prosecutors say was an organised crime group behind the Las Vegas casinos. In fact, they raided over 120 people and companies as part of an organised-crime investigation. They found several weapons. According to the police, most of the mobsters they raided were fictitiously hired by the casinos as tech guys to repair the slot machines. But in reality, they were the hired muscle who beat up legitimate winners.' He explained they had obtained documents from one of the Tates' casinos, 'which displayed an insane winning percentage. You would put €1000 into a slot machine and win €1000 back. All they would have had to do is change the programming on the machines. The government taxes the winnings, which are now clean money. But they don't monitor the amount of money that goes into the machines.'

The two Doroftei brothers were charged with being part of an organised-crime group in November 2022. 'Mihăiță Doroftei is officially a wanted man in Romania.'

When Victor and Luiza went to the Doroftei brothers for comment on this, Mihăiță 'the Pole' Doroftei insisted that he was not running away from the police, but merely living his life abroad in Poland. He also said that Las Vegas Casinos paid taxes, hired real employees, and was a respectable company.

'Law enforcement is always one step behind here,' Luiza lamented. 'I mean, many of these mobsters have many trials going on at the same time. They run PR campaigns to help their image while on the run abroad, living it up. Even if someone gets to jail, they'll be out in two years.' The Tates declined to comment on any of this, but repeated their assertion that they were innocent of sex-trafficking charges. But why would Tate incriminate himself by bragging about mafia connections?

It reminded us of one of the messages Tate had sent to Amelia. It contained a video of him breaking a baseball bat over his shin, along with a voice note: *'I thought I'd remind you of the calibre of man I am. I am one of the most dangerous men on this planet. Sometimes you forget exactly how lucky you were to get fucked by me. Don't forget, I'm a bad boy. Baseball bat – I broke it with my shin, no. I'm not limping. Yes, my shin's fine, I'm a G.'*

What kind of person sends a video of themselves breaking a baseball bat over their own shin and then, for added clarity, an explanation as to why that act makes them hard? Was it all part of his desperation to be perceived as a gangster? Like a stunt performer, he lived constantly on the edge, becoming more and more daring in exchange for the world's attention.

But even he must have known that it would all come to an end one day.

CHAPTER FOURTEEN

Indicted

Tate's biggest battle to date began when he was formally indicted in Romania on charges of human trafficking, rape and forming an organised-crime group. On 23 August 2023, eight months after his arrest under investigation, Tate was formally charged alongside his brother, Tristan, his 'personal assistant', Georgiana Naghel, and ex-police officer Luana Radu. According to the indictment, Tate and his brother Tristan used 'deception' to recruit multiple victims, 'by falsely inducing (them) about the intention to establish a family/marriage relationship and the existence of false feelings'. Essentially, they were charged with using the Loverboy Method, as we had long suspected.

The indictment stated that they subjected their victims to physical violence and psychological coercion, including constantly monitoring and intimidating them, with the aim of forcing them to engage in 'pornographic activities' on both webcamming sites and OnlyFans. It was alleged that Naghel and Radu assisted the two men in their operations, inflicting acts of violence on the women and, in some cases, 'invoking false debts' – a popular tactic among pimps and human traffickers. Tate was also indicted on the charge of 'rape in continued form', meaning he was accused of using violence and psychological pressure to get one of the victims to perform sexual acts with him on at least two occasions.

The alleged crimes are some of the worst a person can be accused of. They are crimes that almost any public figure would find it difficult to avoid being publicly shamed for, at a minimum. Tate, however, knew he had a loyal audience, and one that was primed for manipulation. All he had to do was offer them an alternative reality, a different viewpoint through which to process the criminal charges and still see him as an innocent man, a martyr.

The indictment also stated that Tate and his criminal group subjected his victims to 'forced labour', using TikTok. This claim is listed separately from the charges of exploiting women on web-camming and porn sites. It's a line that stood out to us. 'Forced labour' tends to conjure up images of impoverished agricultural or factory workers. How could this apply to young women on TikTok? Tate and his team picked up on this, too. Throughout his time in prison, and after charges were levelled against him, Tate's account remained active on Twitter. When the charges came through, Tate began tweeting incessantly about this line in the indictment, making it appear as if it was the only charge levelled against him. In one tweet he wrote: *'I spent 3 months in a Romanian dungeon, and to this day remain locked in my house because I am accused of forcing girls to make TikTok videos for money'*. In a reply to a tweet of Elon Musk's declaring that 'The media lies constantly . . .' Tate responded: *'TikTok is human trafficking'*.

Tate used perhaps his most valuable connection in the media, Tucker Carlson, to further this narrative. His show *Tucker Carlson Tonight* was, before he left Fox News, the highest-rated cable news show in the country. Carlson hosted Tate on his show, and later devoted almost three-and-a-half hours to interviewing the two Tate brothers for his newly independent show that would be broadcast on YouTube and Twitter. A clip released by Tate's team showed Carlson arriving at their compound in Bucharest in July 2023 to interview the two brothers and being greeted by Tristan Tate as he walked through the gate, with Tristan telling him: 'I'd come out to greet you but if I step one foot over this line it's straight back to jail'. Tucker was beaming with an almost deranged grin that only grew when Andrew Tate appeared. He broke out into what appeared to be an explosively nervous laugh, exclaiming, 'Wow! What's up man!' Tucker and Tate embraced, and Tucker seemed undeniably star-struck, lost for words, while gazing up at Tate.

With a smile to match Tucker's, Tate told him, 'You're the famous one!' as Tucker protested the claim. The interview that followed is perhaps the most sympathetic interview that any journalist has ever given Tate. When Tucker asked Tate to explain the allegations against him, Tate continued to solidify his narrative, stating, 'I'm charged with being the head of an organised criminal group, which is in charge of recruiting girls to make TikTok videos, to steal the money from the TikTok views'. This interview would, according to Twitter's metrics, go on to be viewed over 110 million times on that platform alone.

It's worth noting that in Andrew Tate's courses, this one on 'OnlyFans Management', he advises his students how to get more paid subscribers for 'their women' on the app. A woman sat to his side tells the camera: 'If you are a new girl, you need to get social media, where you can promote yourself, because that's where all the subscribers come from.' Tate agrees that 'this is the easiest way to get global subscribers', and when men DM the girls on their social media pages, he tells them to respond, 'Yeah, I'm happy to talk to you, but let's talk inside my OnlyFans'.

For Tate, social media sites like TikTok are a means to generate paying subscribers for the women he has working for him on OnlyFans, and this is what the indictment is referring to: that Tate would force these women to make videos for TikTok, apparently for twelve to fourteen hours a day, to drive up their subscribers on OnlyFans. Tucker Carlson, of course, did not bring this up, nor did he bring up any of the content in Tate's publicly available courses. What's more, Tate's deliberately truncated interpretation of the indictment could easily be disproved simply by reading it. But Tate knew that his fans wouldn't read the indictment, or the mainstream press's coverage of it; they would only read his tweets and watch the sympathetic interviews he endorsed. This was all just another bizarre attack from Clown World, which, in its new 'woke' madness, equated making TikTok videos with human trafficking.

But Tate didn't rely solely on this narrative to counter the charges he was facing. He engaged new, expensive lawyers from the US and UK to work alongside his Romanian counsel. The attorney hired to shape the media narrative around his trial was the 'celebrity' lawyer Tina Glandian, whose previous clients included Chris Brown and Mike Tyson. Glandian was brought on board during the brothers' initial detention after arrest and appeared alongside Tate in court in early February to appeal his being held under preventative custody (being held in jail without charge, while evidence was gathered). She then hit the media circuit. She used her TV interviews to declare that the Tates being held was a violation of their international human rights, and that the multiple alleged victims in the case were liars, or not victims at all, but Tate's 'friends'. Glandian described Andrew Tate as a 'free-speech martyr' and, at points, appeared to lean into his Matrix conspiracy, claiming there were 'outside pressures' influencing the case, without elaborating on what these might be. At the same time, Glandian claimed that Tate was playing a character, that what he did was 'entertainment' that was 'not all intended to be taken seriously'.

Another US addition to Tate's legal team was the less glamorous Joseph D. McBride, although he too was no stranger to the media circuit. He had come to the attention of a small section of the US hard-right for his representation of participants in the January 6th Capitol riots, appearing on Fox News, Tucker Carlson's show and Steve Bannon's 'War Room' YouTube series. McBride was – and remains – incredibly public about his representation of the Tates, excitedly announcing the start of their relationship with a video of him and the two brothers smoking cigars in their compound in Bucharest. At the time of writing, 'Tate Brothers' is the second tab, directly next to 'Home', on his website. The nature of what the Tate brothers employed him to do, however, appears to be particularly sinister.

Representing the Tates, on 13 July 2023, McBride launched a defamation lawsuit in Florida against the alleged victim in the Romanian case against the two brothers. The lawsuit sought to claim, in total, up to $5 million dollars from the alleged victim, maintaining that her 'false claims' had led to Tates' arrest and subsequent loss of income. The suit also threatened to sue the woman and her family for $300 million if they did not withdraw their accusations. This was seen by many as an act of intimidation and harassment. A criminal court would already be examining the claims, so why was there a need to sue her? She refused to withdraw her allegations.

The defamation suit seemed to serve two intended purposes: as well as potentially intimidating the alleged victim and her family into withdrawing their charges in Romania, it also allowed her name to be released to the public, including to Tate's baying fans. Her name was withdrawn from public record after a successful court order by the victims' lawyers to have her listed under a pseudonym. With her name redacted from court documents, McBride himself named the woman publicly on the podcast 'Fresh and Fit', which led to her being harassed online. In the podcast, McBride also discussed the woman's 'body count', and implied she had a 'long history' of making false rape allegations to blackmail men. She is, of course, one of multiple women making similar allegations against the Tate brothers. Multiple tweets, still on Joseph D. McBride's account today, have the victim's name in them. Popular Twitter accounts linked with Tate's network, including @TateNews, @ReachMorpheuss and @UncorruptedMen began to dox her as well, bringing up her personal history as apparent evidence that she could not have been trafficked, and posting videos and pictures of her all over Twitter. Despite this harassment, the woman has refused to withdraw her allegations. She remained steadfast in her complaints against Tate, even as her privacy was being violated and her sexual history weaponised by his team.

Twitter grifters who couldn't resist the bait also joined the pile-on. One such was self-proclaimed 'investigative journalist' Sulaiman Ahmed, who became one of Tate's most vehement defenders after his public conversion to Islam. Ahmed used his Twitter profile to spread misleading information about Tate's case, while cosplaying as an independent journalist. In the wake of our first documentary, Ahmed made a Twitter thread that went on to be viewed millions of times, claiming: 'There has been a visceral attack on Andrew Tate by the MSM & alternative media. The attacks have lacked journalistic integrity. Vice, BBC and the allegations have been debunked, but they have brainwashed people.' Then, noticing that his posts on Tate were attracting attention, Ahmed doubled down, and began to tweet incessantly about him, his legal case and Ahmed's belief that Tate was being attacked in an orchestrated way. These tweets also caught the attention of Tate and his team, with 'generals', including Sartorial Shooter, retweeting Ahmed's threads and praising him for his 'journalism'.

Ahmed's 'journalism' took the form of resharing negative articles about Tate, along with words like 'debunked', 'manipulated' and the idea that attacks on Tate were part of an attempt to create an 'extreme feminist world'. As his following and association with Tate grew, he attempted to undertake an 'investigation', seemingly on Tate's behalf.

In June 2023, Ahmed posted a picture of downtown Palm Beach, Florida, to his Twitter account. He claimed that he had 'travelled all the way to Palm Beach for a major story'. Supporters and critics alike quickly realised that he was going there to 'report' on the alleged victim in Tate's case, who lived there. Apparently, Ahmed was in Florida to find people from her past who would be willing to speak, particularly those who could support his theory that she was a 'master of deception'. Ahmed allegedly even turned up outside her parents' house, taking photos from across the street.

Tate's supporters praised Ahmed as a hero on a journey to expose wrongdoing in Tate's case, while his critics took another approach: a number of accounts who devoted themselves to 'exposing' Tate and his criminality, referring to themselves as 'Team Matrix', began tweeting screenshots of their emails reporting Ahmed to the US authorities. They had picked up on the fact that Ahmed did not have a media (I) visa, required by journalists who want to report on stories in the US, and was therefore in the country illegally. (Ahmed has since claimed that he was in Florida on holiday, and happened to be in the area where the alleged victim's family lived.) Others, including more established journalists, pointed out that what Ahmed was currently doing not only violated the alleged victim's right to privacy, but that if there was a direct connection between Ahmed and Tate, it would probably amount to 'witness intimidation' from the perspective of the Romanian authorities. Many suggested that Tate himself had put Ahmed up to this, perhaps even financing the investigation. Legal representatives for the victim stated that 'this effort by Mr Ahmed and the Tates is a conspiracy to silence her [the alleged victim] and amounts to witness tampering', before threatening Ahmed with a civil complaint and the fact that they could report him to US Federal authorities.

Ahmed deleted his Twitter posts about visiting Florida and returned to the UK. He did, however, continue to post about the Tate brothers and the alleged victim in the US, calling her 'the real perpetrator' and describing her 'manipulative exploits'. Tate's further descent into the realm of conspiracies had attracted the support of some of the most consistently misleading people on the internet – among them Sulaiman Ahmed. Despite being constant purveyors of false information, these influencers were incredibly successful at masquerading opinions as facts and exchanging inflammatory lies for followers. Whether at his behest, or not, they became essential to Tate's cause.

As we followed the slow progress in Tate's legal case in Romania, and his continued attempts to discredit his 'enemies', a new obstacle presented itself to him. The British law firm McCue Jury & Partners announced in April 2023 that they were representing three women who would be suing Tate in the civil court, alleging they were physically abused or raped by him. These women were Sally, Helen and Amelia. After years of suffering in silence while Tate became a global celebrity, they would now have the chance to have their stories presented to a judge in Britain's High Court. Matt Jury, one of the firm's partners, was acting for the women, assisted by Jack Beeston, an associate at the firm who was in his late twenties.

Jack was very amiable when we spoke to him, and seemed determined yet aware that the process of bringing these women's claims to court could be lengthy, and would likely involve harassment from some of Tate's supporters. He confirmed that the three women would be meeting for the first time (despite launching this civil case, Sally and Helen had still never met Amelia), before approaching Hertfordshire Police to ask them to reopen the investigation. Jack told us that we couldn't come to or report on the meeting with the police, but that if the women were happy with it, we were more than welcome to be there beforehand when they met.

Jamie – 20 June 2023

Hertfordshire Police station is located in the suburbs of Welwyn Garden City, twenty miles north of London and designed in 1920 to be 'the perfect town', combining the benefits of both the city and the countryside. True to its name, the town has remained a haven of green spaces, but today it's overcast and cold. We're in a church hall we've rented from the local parish council, waiting for Amelia, Helen and Sally to arrive, along with Jack Beeston and Matt Jury. We wanted somewhere private for the occasion, so that the women can meet for the first time without feeling the eyes of the public on them, and so that we could film short interviews with them without attracting attention. We thought about a park, but didn't trust the British weather. Despite it being almost midsummer, rain is likely. The church hall looks like it hasn't been renovated in at least forty years, and can easily seat a hundred people. I begin to worry that the five chairs we've set out in the middle of the hall look bizarre, so repeatedly shuffle them around, in the hope that I'll find some magic placement that makes them look less out of place.

We've decided not to film Amelia meeting Helen and Sally for the first time. Even though as filmmakers it will be a moment we'd love to capture, we know they are already nervous, and that this is huge for them. Particularly so for Amelia, who has been alone in all of this, and has wanted to meet the two women ever since 2015, when she first discovered they existed.

The three women embrace, visibly emotional. I am struck by how close they seem almost immediately.

The cameras then start rolling, and I ask Helen, who is speaking on camera for the first time, to tell us about what the three of them hope to achieve by going to see the police today. She makes it through the first half of her sentence before breaking down in tears, apologising and leaving the room. Sally, who is sat behind the cameras, follows her out, and Amelia takes over. She explains that what happened to them at the hands of Tate has followed them around ever since, hanging over them, a dark cloud, casting a shadow over even their happiest moments. Amelia understands more than anyone why Helen still, seven years later, struggles to speak about what happened to her.

When the interview ends, the three women stand together,
oscillating between tears and words of support, then laughing
and smiling when Sally says something to lift their spirits. We
all eat lunch together, before following them to Hertfordshire
Police station. There will be no tears here. All three of them
still harbour a strong anger towards the authorities who they
feel let them down by failing to charge or prosecute Tate. They
will never truly feel comfort until he faces trial for what they
allege he did to them. As they walk through the doors, into the
police station, we are left standing outside, wondering what
will happen.

We hear later from Jack that despite Hertfordshire Police
reiterating that they felt there was enough evidence to charge
Tate, they refused to reopen the case, and essentially told the
women than it was the CPS's decision that meant Tate was
not charged. The same CPS that the Victims Commissioner
of England and Wales described as having 'betrayed' rape
victims in 2021.* For the time being, these women will only be
able to challenge Tate in a civil court, rather than a criminal
one that could see him end up in prison.

In order to begin the civil proceedings in the UK, McCue Jury
needed to deliver a 'pre-action letter' or a 'letter before claim' to
Tate, giving him the opportunity to either dispute it or accept
liability and offer a financial settlement to the women. Matt Jury
told us that they didn't expect Tate to do either of the above, but
that it was a legal requirement to get the proceedings under way.

* https://www.theguardian.com/law/2021/jul/22/cps-accused-of-betraying-
victims-as-prosecutions-hit-record-low

They knew there was a chance that if the letter was posted to Tate, he and his legal team could deny that they'd ever received it. So, they would need to board a plane to Bucharest and head to the front gates of Andrew Tate's compound to deliver the letter themselves.

Tate's security was far more courteous to Matt Jury and Jack than they were to us, agreeing to tell 'Mr Tate' that they were here to deliver him a letter. Once again, however, Tate did not emerge. Instead, Tate spoke over the phone to one of his security guards, while the rest of the guards murmured in Romanian, forming a circle around him. A Romanian-speaking journalist who was reporting on the events informed Jury that Tate was apparently instructing his security to tell the lawyers to 'fuck off'. In turn, Jury slotted the letter through the gaps in Tate's front gate, secure in the knowledge that the presence of a TV news crew that was following them should cover against any claims from Tate that he had not been issued with a pre-action letter.

When the footage went live that night, Matt Jury and the firm came to the attention of Tate's army of online supporters, joining his ever-growing list of perceived Matrix-hired adversaries, subjected to trolling and harassment by his fans. Tate didn't immediately respond to McCue Jury's letter, but his fans took to social media to yet again dismiss Tate's alleged victims, accusing them of being liars, simply after money or fame. When we spoke to Jack about it all, he was very matter of fact: 'Our clients are quite rightly anonymous, and they're entitled to their anonymity, and they're entitled to not receive abuse for what they went through. So, we kind of have to step into their shoes a bit and be their public representatives. As you guys will be aware, anyone who publicly speaks out about Tate is likely to receive abuse.'

After the continued harassment of the alleged victims, particularly the woman from Florida, McCue Jury, alongside the US-based non-profit NCOSE (National Center on Sexual Exploitation) and a law firm from Philadelphia decided to try and take a stand. On 5 October they held a press conference at the Sheraton Hotel in Bucharest to announce a united position against Tate and his followers' harassment and intimidation. The Tates however, ex-reality TV contestants to their core, wanted a different kind of spectacle. Just as Matt Jury and Jack Beeston were due to leave the UK for Romania, they were forwarded a message that had been sent to a WhatsApp group filled with Romanian journalists. The message was from Tate's PR, Mateea Petrescu, and announced that her team were planning a surprise for these journalists at the coming conference, and the surprise would be 'Tate style'. Petrescu later sent a message saying that the surprise had been cancelled – as Jack theorised, 'perhaps she realised it's not a surprise if you alert everyone'. But whatever the cancelled surprise may have been, Petrescu did indeed find her own way to put a 'Tate-style' spin on the conference.

The conference got under way. Almost every news organisation in Romania was present, in part because of the high-profile nature of Tate's case, but also because Petrescu's message had enticed them, and they were hoping something explosive might happen. As Jury was delivering his initial statement, a small group started murmuring together at the far left of the hall. One woman began to cause a disturbance – supposedly a member of the local press, she had been asking hostile questions, vaping throughout the proceedings, and at one point barged her way to the front of the room. This was, in fact Mateea Petrescu herself, who Matt Jury and Jack didn't recognise at first, perhaps because the majority of her face was bandaged, following an apparent nose job. Petrescu wasn't the only member of Tate's team there who presented themselves as a journalist. Tate's Romanian counsel, Eugen Vidineac, was also present, shouting a question above the noise. Vidineac refused to admit that he was Tate's lawyer, instead claiming to be 'a member of civil society', until a local journalist in the room let the crowd know that this was definitely Vidineac, Tate's lawyer. As Matt Jury said about the whole fiasco, 'the clowns brought the circus'.

Videos of the conference began to circulate on social media, and the episode appeared to be a misstep from Tate's team who, as Jack described, 'try and use a hammer to solve every problem, and it ends up being slightly embarrassing for them'.

On the same day that Jamie was with Tate's alleged British victims, the Romanian court decided to formally indict the brothers. This also meant a judge could decide to hold them in jail until their court date. We were coming to the end of our second documentary, exposing the apparent human trafficking that was being taught and practised inside Tate's War Room. This was potentially our last chance to put these allegations to the brothers, face to face.

Matt had been speaking at a conference in Dublin the evening it was announced the Tates were due to appear in court to hear the judge's verdict. He could only arrive in Bucharest in time by way of three night-flights that carved a wide trapezoid across Europe. Having been in the air all night, he then had to rush straight to the courthouse. His resulting dishevelled appearance was soon weaponised by Tate's fanbase, who began calling him 'Homeless Matt Shea'.

Matt – 21 June 2023

When I arrive, I am one of two journalists here, but a crowd of us soon amasses in front of the courthouse. I scoped out the building on a previous visit and know that Tate will likely drive into the parking lot at the back and then walk down a path on the left-hand side of the court, where he will be confronted by a scrum of reporters. Once he's inside the scrum, there will be little chance for me to ask him a question, so instead, I wait in the parking lot with the local cameraman I have hired. If I am wrong, we can always sprint to the front of the courthouse.

But the arrival of an expensive sportscar tells me I am right. Rather than approach the car and risk the Tate brothers zooming off in fear, I wait behind a large bush for them to exit the vehicle. They step out, flanked by lumbering security guards and a teenage boy filming their walk on his phone. I appear from behind the bush, and Tate immediately notices the camera. He grins confidently. 'You're jumping out from behind a bush. What a nerd.'

'I've spoken to three women now who say that they've been groomed by men who were trained by senior members of the War Room—'

Tate cuts me off. 'Do you have chocolates?' He glances over at Tristan, who is looking down intently at the cigarillo he is lighting.

'Does he have the chocolates?' Tate repeats. 'Does he have fifty grand?'

Tristan offers his brother a reassuring smile. 'I don't think he can afford that.'

I cut off this back and forth with, 'Is the War Room an international grooming cult of some kind?'

Tate avoids eye contact with me, turning again to his brother. 'I don't think he can afford anything.'

Two of Tate's four large security guards, wearing matching black polo shirts and aviator sunglasses, laugh along with Tate's infantile jabs and begin to create a barrier between Tate and me, shoving me backward as our unlikely entourage marches towards the courthouse.

Tristan has gone ahead, breaking out of the circle of security. In about ten steps, the brothers will be swallowed by a crowd of hungry reporters. I jog after Tristan, asking him about Iggy Semmelweis's role in the War Room. Tristan smirks, looking at me briefly before gazing ahead. He never breaks his stride or stops sucking on his cigarillo. My time is almost up. I try a different tack: 'What's your connection to the Doroftei brothers?'

Tristan's smirk drops. For the first time in a long while, he looks visibly nervous. He shoots me a threatening look, before averting his eyes, his cheeks flushing slightly.

'Is this all getting a bit too real now?' I ask, unable to conceal a grin.

In just a few paces, the Tate brothers are engulfed by a sea of microphones, forcing me to step aside. A chorus of voices is shouting, 'Andrew, are you a rapist?'

'Of course I'm not, what a stupid question.' Tate shrugs off the rest of the allegations fired at him by the world's media. Was this masculinity? Walking out of a sports car, muscles bursting through your suit, blowing cigar smoke in the face of reporters who ask you about rape allegations? Many men

have at some point tried to appear more masculine; few have committed this much to the performance. I have often felt insecure about my own masculinity. But watching the Tates flounce into the courthouse to be formally indicted for human trafficking, I found myself thinking for the first time, 'Actually, I'm alright.'

Tate always wanted the limelight, but you have to wonder if, when he first sought the eyes of the cameras on reality TV, at only twenty-one years of age, he imagined that this is where his journey to fame would lead. If there was any shred of fear, insecurity, or introspective thought of any kind, Tate did not show it. Instead, he strolled through the front of the courthouse smiling, with his shoulders back, adjusting the buttons on his skin-tight suit jacket. Later, he would share a Photoshopped image depicting Matt pushing a shopping trolley full of rubbish, created by one of their fans.

Tristan Tate then tweeted:

A wasted life – You know who squandered the biggest opportunity in his life? Matt Shea the DNG of Vice News. If he had fairly and honestly reported on us and The War Rooms wonderful event when we gave him access he'd still be with us now. He would be covering this whole wild roller coaster ride @Cobratate and I have been through, Vice would have the most popular series on the internet and'it wouldn't have gone bankrupt. He would have millions of followers and access to a whole new world of opportunity. Now every door closes in his face. He is a laughing stock in the 'world of 'journalists' and his dishonest and snake like tactic have reduced his entire lifes work to being memed and mocked over boxes of chocolates. He will never recover. Raise a toast ladies and gentlemen to the man Matt Shea could have been tonight, that groundbreaking honest journalist with 1 on 1 exclusive access to the world of what really goes on in the lives of the Tate brothers. It may be over for him. But next time opportunity comes knocking, embrace it. Do not squander it by being a dishonest, dislikable worm. Truth is always the way, it was certainly his ticket to the top. He's missed his flight.

Tate's fans applauded the tweet, calling Matt a liar, a bad reporter and in some posts making homophobic jokes, including one reference to Matt choking on the 'D' when he eats alphabet soup.

At the time of writing, the Tate brothers are still awaiting a trial date. It's unclear what Tristan really believes, but he certainly felt vindicated proclaiming to his followers that our journalism had been debunked.

The Tate brothers had garnered the most loyal following imaginable, an infantilised group of men, and in some cases actual children, who believed Andrew and Tristan Tate were the absolute pinnacle of masculinity, and if they followed their lead, maybe they could be, too. Even if Andrew Tate and his brother are found guilty, will it change the impact they have left behind?

Epilogue

People think Gen Z is progressive, but in many ways, it is the most anti-feminist generation in modern history.

On 26 January 2024, the chief data reporter for the *Financial Times*, John Burn-Murdoch, published a graph that quickly went viral.[*] It showed that an unprecedented ideological divide was emerging in many countries around the world. Young women were becoming more progressive and young men more conservative. 'Gen Z is two generations, not one,' wrote Burn-Murdoch.

Men under thirty are part of the group most likely to feel 'threatened' by advancements in women's rights. Fifty-two per cent of Gen Z think that we've now gone so far in promoting gender equality that we're discriminating against men.[†] Even after the allegations against him were made public, Tate remains hugely popular among young men.

To understand the growing hatred of women, and how it can take hold in the minds of the young men who follow Tate, it would

---

[*] https://www.ft.com/content/29fd9b5c-2f35-41bf-9d4c-994db4e12998
[†] https://www.kcl.ac.uk/giwl/assets/ipsos-giwl-iwd-survey-2023.pdf

be a mistake to see his philosophy as a political viewpoint based in cultural values or arrived at through rational thought. Though these men may find ideologies to justify their misogyny – the traditional gender roles of the American far right, or extremist forms of Islam, for example – they often arrive at their attitudes towards women via the psychological pain of rejection and self-doubt.

Many of these young men are so desperate for a solution to their unhappiness that they blame our modern diets, leading to a growing paranoia around eating vegetables and particularly soy. These foods are thought to cause internal weakness and lower testosterone, leading many – like Eli, who we met in Chapter 7 – to turn to raw meat.

Tate and his cronies have amplified male insecurity to dangerous levels. As Iggy said in the War Room promotional videos, 'If you do not struggle to become an exceptional man, you are nobody, and every female will prove to you: you may as well not exist'.

One member of The Real World told our colleague Tim Hume about the effect it had on his mind. 'You're going to be stuck in your home, thinking you're a victim, thinking people are out there to get everything from you,' he said. 'You're gonna hate women and hold them responsible for everything wrong in your life. You're working all the time because you think it will get you women. And then if it does, you're just going to treat her like property.'

What started as a political and cultural investigation into Tate soon turned into a criminal one and something much bigger, with farther-reaching implications than we had imagined.

Looking at everything we now know: that there are a growing number of women who allege Tate raped and abused them (and the UK police knew about this), that he taught men how to groom women online and that he bragged about many of these things in videos that have been viewed billions of times – one does wonder if Andrew Tate was hiding in plain sight.

We have spoken to women who say that their boyfriends have become physically abusive and threatened to release revenge porn after following Andrew Tate. Consider the supposed 200,000 paying members of his 'Real World' group and his millions of followers on social media. If even a small portion of them follow in the footsteps of their idol, what violent, terrifying future awaits Gen Z women?

And all the while, young men who follow this path are being deprived of meaningful relationships with women. One told us how he discovered Tate when he was twenty years old, in the middle of the Covid pandemic. He had almost graduated law school, and had a training contract lined up, but ended up turning it down to – in his words – 'go all in on this fucking bullshit'. He had always been ambitious, but, after an injury forced him to quit football, he had struggled socially. Then, 'I stumbled upon this guy who was this world champion kick-boxer, had made his own money. Has the network, the lifestyle, the friends, the girls – all this stuff I never really had access to.'

He became hooked on hustle culture and the promise of attractive women that came with it. 'Tristan showed the girls he was sleeping with on Twitter for a year. I realise this was just marketing. The thing that makes a porn addict is the same thing that makes a Tate fan.'

After signing up for the Hustlers University and War Room, he found that 'the more time I spent with these guys, I watched the young, sweet, innocent guy I was completely disappear. I had a girlfriend of five years and completely blew up that relationship because I was listening to these guys. I was going to get engaged. I just became a complete emotionless husk.'

He told us that the men he met on Hustlers University courses hated their lives. In fact, in four of years reporting on Tate fans and encountering them in public, we ourselves have never met a single one who seemed happy. Thankfully, this young man managed to deprogramme himself, and is enjoying life again.

There is cause for hope. Recently, there has been a rise in 'positive masculinity' role models. Ben Hurst is one of the most inspiring. He teaches schoolboys how the patriarchy hurts not just women but them, too, and holds spaces where they are encouraged to talk through some of the negative pressures placed on them as young men. The Labour Party in the UK has unveiled a plan to 'train young male influencers who can counter the negative impact of people like Andrew Tate' in schools.* This is important work, but it's rendered far less effective by the fact that these men are competing against the mind-boggling reach of influencers whose extreme and controversial content is favoured by the algorithms. Hurst has said that he doesn't think he would gain a following of young men if he went online, rather than in person to schools, unless he became 'punchy or controversial or in opposition to something', which he isn't comfortable doing.†

Tate's popularity does not just amplify misogyny, but undermines trust in democracy and the media – in some cases challenging belief in reality itself. Traditional news organisations are failing to catch up to social media, where an increasing number of young

---

* https://www.theguardian.com/education/2024/feb/26/labour-to-help-schools-develop-male-influencers-to-combat-tate-misogyny

† https://www.gq-magazine.co.uk/article/anti-toxic-masculinity-movement

people get their news and views from influencers, rather than from reputable sources.* Social media platforms claim that they, unlike traditional media, do not create content and therefore aren't responsible for what viewers see. But they absolutely are responsible – they control what we as viewers see through algorithms they have designed to feed us the content they have decided we should see. They often claim this feed is merely based on users' preferences and behaviour, but the radicalisation of a large part of a generation doesn't just happen because young men like watching misogynist content. Andrew Tate, by essentially conning millions of young men into misogyny, has shown just how easily manipulated these algorithms are.

Tate's message is potent because it taps into the young male appetite for rebellion, conquest, self-improvement and brotherhood which, whether biological or conditioned, seems to exist in spades. Imagine if these concepts could be channelled differently: rebellion that fights against systems of oppression instead of creating them; conquest that adds value to the world; self-improvement that doesn't eschew intellectual pursuits like studying; and a brotherhood that stands up for all people. Maybe then we would have something that looked like positive masculinity.

Throughout four years of reporting on Tate, it has sometimes felt as though we were looking into two different stories concurrently: the first being the anti-feminist movement that built up around him; the second being the allegations we uncovered against him and certain members of his secret society. But they are two parts of the

---

* https://www.reuters.com/business/media-telecom/fewer-people-trust-traditional-media-more-turn-tiktok-news-report-says-2023-06-13/

same story. The allegations of rape and grooming are the smoking gun that disproves Tate's claim that his misogyny is all 'an act' and exposes the ideology behind his movement for what it really is. The movement around him is what keeps alive the dangerous conspiracy that seeks to discredit our reporting, and that of and others like us. All we can do is continue to restate the facts and hope that time will erode the lies surrounding them, leaving them standing.

In March 2024, Bedfordshire Police force announced that they were investigating the Tate brothers for alleged crimes of sexual aggression between 2012 and 2015 in the UK. The alleged victims in this investigation are new, the alleged crimes previously unheard of. The Romanian authorities have approved the extradition of the Tate brothers, pending the conclusion of their trial there, meaning they will eventually have to face court in the UK.

Acknowledgements

We'd like to thank our editor, Nina Sandelson, and agent, Chris Wellbelove, for believing in the importance of this story. Without your support and guidance it would almost certainly never have been written. Lexi Rose, who, by first alerting us to this story, proved herself to be more soothsayer than development producer. Will Fairman, for his experience and wisdom. Mike Radford, whose sage advice and belief in our reporting led to the first instance in the BBC's 100-year history when an evil wizard was featured on the ten o'clock news. Tashi Hanlon, for her intimidatingly good investigating and producing skills. Our documentary editors Martha Velasquez and Owen Kean for their tireless work. Milene Larsson, Subrata De, Maral Usefi, Joel Shames and Greg Wright, for guiding us through the storm. Joseph Taylor and Charlie Moore, for their steady hands and cool heads on location. To the women who shared their stories: the world is indebted to you. The impact of your bravery will be felt for many years to come.

Jamie:

My family and friends, for pushing me on when I needed it, and distracting me when I needed it even more. My partner, Ellen. Without your support I would have truly lost my mind.

Matt:

My mum, for teaching me about feminism, my dad and brothers, for teaching the right way to be a man, and my girlfriend, Rose, for her unwavering support. And Jamie's girlfriend, Ellen, because without her he truly would have lost his mind.